# DIANA

*Closely Guarded Secret*

# DIANA
## *Closely Guarded Secret*

INSPECTOR KEN WHARFE

*with*

ROBERT JOBSON

MICHAEL O'MARA BOOKS LIMITED

First published in Great Britain in 2002 by
Michael O'Mara Books Limited
9 Lion Yard, Tremadoc Road
London sw4 7NQ

Revised and expanded paperback edition first published in 2003

Copyright © 2002, 2003 Ken Wharfe and Robert Jobson

All rights reserved. No part of this publication may be reproduced, stored in a
retrieval system, or transmitted by any means, without the prior permission in
writing of the publisher, nor be otherwise circulated in any form of binding or cover
other than that in which it is published and without a similar condition including
this condition being imposed on the subsequent purchaser.

The right of Ken Wharfe and Robert Jobson to be identified as the authors
of this work has been asserted by them in accordance with the Copyright,
Designs and Patents Act 1988.

A CIP catalogue record for this book is available
from the British Library

ISBN 1-84317-028-0

1 3 5 7 9 10 8 6 4 2

Designed and typeset by Martin Bristow

All photographs courtesy Robin Nunn and Nunn Syndication Ltd,
except page 15 lower right, which is © Tim Rooke/Rex Features

Printed and bound in England by Clays Ltd, St Ives plc

# Author's Acknowledgements

I thought long and hard about writing this memoir of the late Diana, Princess of Wales. It was not a decision taken lightly but one I now firmly believe is correct if history is to judge her fairly.

But I could not have written this book without the dedication, wholehearted support and friendship of my co-writer, Robert Jobson, who believed, like me, that this story should be told.

Thanks also to my publisher, Michael O'Mara, for his guidance and forbearance but above all for believing in me and the project. I would also like to thank the editorial team at Michael O'Mara Books for their hard work, skill and enthusiasm, particularly my editor Toby Buchan and Karen Dolan, Rhian McKay and Gabrielle Mander.

Thanks too to Robin Nunn at Nunn Syndication for the excellent photographs in the book that brought back so many happy memories.

This book is written with all the men and women of Scotland Yard's Royalty Protection Department in mind. I would like to thank all my friends and colleagues for the friendship and laughter we shared over the years, but above all for their dedication and professionalism which, I believe, cannot be equaled.

INSPECTOR KEN WHARFE, MVO
*August 2002*

# Prelude

N O ONE COULD HAVE FAILED TO APPRECIATE the bitter irony of the day. For years I had been responsible for guarding this woman – with my life, if necessary. Now I was in charge of the police security operation for my department at her funeral. Standing, before the service, at the West Door of Westminster Abbey on Saturday, 6 September 1997, was like being a camera recording a scene in a tragic Hollywood movie. The difference, of course, was that this was painfully real. Everything seemed to be played out in slow motion. The organ resounded to William Harris's *Prelude*; the bells rang out hollowly as the great and the good – from princes and prime ministers to so-called ordinary people – arrived to pay their last respects to an extraordinary person.

Diana, Princess of Wales had made the latter part of the twentieth century her own. In the last two decades of that century, probably only Nelson Mandela approached her in terms of the interest she generated around the world. Now, after thirty-six years, her Camelot was in ruins and the magic, I was sure, would never return. I kept thinking to myself, 'How on earth can this be happening?' As the pallbearers – Welsh Guardsmen, as was fitting – struggled with her lead-lined coffin, it seemed almost inconceivable that the radiant young woman who had once charmed the world was lying silently within it, completely at peace for perhaps the only time in her all too short life. That life had been snuffed out by a combination of high spirits, stupidity and human error. That her death was avoidable made me angry, yet the whole sorry episode had numbed me inside, as it had most of the rest of the world. All I could think was, 'What a waste, what a terrible, utter waste.'

Her sons, whom I had once guarded before I became her own personal protection officer, were nothing if not brave. She would have been supremely proud of the way they stood tall in the face of such terrible adversity. I had often played with them during their childhood. They had always loved to throw themselves into play fights; now they faced the greatest test of their lives. In their dark suits, focused in their grief, they looked like men, not boys, as they walked behind their mother's coffin. On the flag-draped coffin a handwritten card lay among a cloud of lilies. On it, the single word 'Mummy' seemed to say everything.

A great calm fell over Central London that morning as millions took to the streets to pay their respects, lining the route along which the Princess's coffin would be borne, on a gun carriage, from Kensington Palace to the Abbey. As I walked to the Abbey from Buckingham Palace – with the roads closed, there was no other way of getting there – the scent of flowers was heavy on the air. Diana's coffin had been moved from the Chapel Royal, St James's Palace, where she had lain, to Kensington Palace at some time the previous evening. Everywhere her famous face peered out from the thousands of newspaper and magazine special editions being sold on the streets to mark the historic event. The nation had come to a complete halt as television coverage poured into millions of homes; around the world, more than two billion people sat and watched an event that many had believed they would not themselves live to see. At variance with the somber mood, the mourners, many in jeans and T-shirts, were bathed in warm sunshine. Thousands upon thousands packed the funeral procession route as the muffled sound of the bells of Westminster Abbey, which tolled throughout the procession, carried mournfully over the near-silent capital.

Behind the coffin, the procession was led by her two sons, with the Prince of Wales, the Duke of Edinburgh, and her brother, Earl Spencer, heads bowed, walking with them. The tension was electric. As the gun-carriage passed on to the Mall, past Buckingham Palace, the Queen, who had been publicly attacked for her cool response since the death of the Princess, led other members of the royal family who, standing in front of the palace, all bowed as it passed. Above them, from the flagstaff on the Palace roof, the Union Flag fluttered at half-mast. The Queen had finally relented, after yet more criticism in the days before the funeral, and given the order for the flag to be flown thus, the first time in history that it had done so for the death of anyone other than a monarch.

Behind Diana's sons and her ex-husband, father-in-law and brother followed five hundred selected mourners. They were charity workers, nurses, artists, people from all walks of life representing organizations or causes that the Princess had held dear to her heart. Like so many people, I could not help thinking that this deviation from the practice usually followed at such state events was entirely in keeping with the spirit of my ex-boss, who in life had never greatly relished the pomp and circumstance surrounding royalty.

There were 1,900 invited guests within the spectacular Gothic interior of the Abbey. The sun streamed through its great windows. At just after ten o'clock the VIPs began to arrive. Shepherding them to their seats was like a military exercise, and my team had to be alert, not least because some of the world's leading terrorist targets were gathered within this august medieval structure. America's First Lady, Hillary Clinton – whose husband, President Bill Clinton, was one of countless world leaders who, only hours after her death, had publicly praised Diana and her life's work – examined the tributes of flowers near the entrance as she walked past. Two former prime ministers, Baroness Thatcher and John Major, joined Prime Minister Tony Blair and his wife, Cherie, on the long walk from the West Door to their seats in the Abbey.

Mohamed Fayed and his wife entered shortly after the Spencer family. My heart went out to them all, especially Diana's mother, Frances Shand Kydd. Within the next few minutes the royal family arrived. Last, at 10.50 am, came the Queen, the Queen Mother and Prince Edward. In deep silence they took their places near the altar, directly across the aisle from the Spencer family. Then, as the bells of Big Ben tolled eleven, the procession reached the West Door. Eight Welsh Guardsmen, bare-headed, their faces taut with strain, carried the quarter-ton coffin on their shoulders as they slow-marched the length of the nave. A profound hush fell over the Abbey. Prince Harry broke down when the coffin passed. As the tears flowed down his small face, his father pulled him closer and his brother William laid a comforting hand on his shoulder.

As the strains of the National Anthem filled the Abbey, the tension was excruciating, the Queen's embarrassment almost palpable. The bitterness between the Spencers and the Windsors that had come to the fore in the days since the Princess's fatal accident had given the national press something to write about, in a vain bid to try to divert the public's attention away from the media's involvement in the killing of *their* Princess. Yet such accusations were as pointless as they were wrong. The paparazzi may irritate like flies, but they don't kill. Diana's death, I kept thinking, was senseless because it could so easily have been prevented, but it was not photographers and journalists who killed her.

Nor was there any comfort in 'if onlys'. My department had had the care of her for some fifteen years; Mohamed Fayed's team of 'bodyguards' had had charge of her security for eight weeks, and now she was dead. They had failed in their task, and it angered me beyond words.

As I drifted between flashbacks and the awful reality of the moment, I kept saying to myself, 'Come on, Ken, get on with it.' Lord Spencer had invited me to attend the funeral. I had declined, because I had been asked to look after security, although the job had not been easy. Mohamed Fayed had presented one of my first problems in this capacity. He had tried to insist that, in keeping with his bizarre conspiracy theories about the deaths of the Princess and his son Dodi, he was a target – even here. In the light of this, he said, he needed all his cumbersome, supposedly SAS-trained bodyguards by his side within the Abbey. This was a truly ridiculous idea, as though he outranked the Queen or the Prime Minister or the President of France, none of whom had personal bodyguards beside them. Before the funeral, I took some pleasure in reminding his 'protection-liaison official' of what I had said to his security staff when we reviewed security some days earlier, that no heavy protection presence would be permitted inside Westminster Abbey.

The 'Libera Me' from Verdi's *Requiem* shook my resolve; not the soon-to-be-knighted Elton John's specially written adaptation of 'Candle In The Wind', with its tear-jerking first line, 'Goodbye, England's rose', not even Diana's favorite hymn, 'I Vow To Thee, My Country', which had been sung at her wedding. It was Verdi. Contrary to popular opinion, the Princess loved classical music, a passion we both shared. As the 'Libera Me' pierced the air and our souls, I felt the emotion of that piece engulf the Abbey, moving every one of the throng of mourners. Prince Charles looked as though he was being torn apart as the music swelled and dwindled, and finally died away.

Then, just as the congregation was united in grief, Lord Spencer unleashed his entirely unexpected verbal assault, his words thrusting like a rapier into the Prince's heart. No one, other than

Charles Spencer, knew what was coming as he composed himself before delivering a five-minute eulogy that electrified the world. It was a piece of pure theatre, but it was also from the heart.

Spencer lashed out at the royal family for their behavior towards his beloved sister, and savaged the press for hounding her to her death. Throughout the mauling the Queen bowed her head as her godson fired salvo after salvo, talking directly to his dead sister. 'There is a temptation to rush to canonize your memory. There is no need to do so: you stand tall enough as a human being of unique qualities not to need to be seen as a saint.' Nor, he said, was there any need for royal titles – a barbed reference to the Queen's petty decision to remove from the Princess the courtesy title of 'Her Royal Highness' as one of the conditions of her lucrative $25.5 million (£17 million) divorce deal. He said bluntly that his sister had possessed a 'natural nobility', adding, cuttingly, that she transcended class and had proved in the last year of her life that 'she needed no royal title to continue to generate her particular brand of magic.' Never before, in forty-five years on the throne of Britain, had Queen Elizabeth II been publicly and savagely admonished by one of her subjects. Yet, ever the professional, she did not flinch.

What happened next was extraordinary, and something which only those inside the Abbey that day will ever fully appreciate. Lord Spencer's loving yet devastating address was followed by a stunned silence. Then a sound like a distant shower of rain swept into the Abbey, seeping in through the walls, rolling on and on. It poured towards us like a wave, gradually reaching a crescendo. At first I was not sure what it was; indeed, with security on my mind, I was momentarily troubled by it. It took me a couple of seconds to realize that it was the sound of people clapping. The massive crowds outside had heard Spencer's address on loudspeakers and had reacted with applause; as the sound filtered in, the vast majority of the people inside the Abbey joined in. People don't clap at funerals – but Diana was as different in death as she had been in life, and they did at hers. The Earl had spoken the plain truth as he saw it, and the people respected him for his courage as well as for the tribute he had paid his sister. William and Harry joined in the applause; so too, generously, did Prince Charles. The Queen, the Duke of Edinburgh, and the Queen Mother sat unmoving in stony-faced silence.

The service ended with Sir John Tavener's *Alleluia*. I found it uplifting, and at that moment my numbness lifted. The Princess was gone, but I knew that her spirit of compassion would live on, and that her work would not be forgotten.

Outside in the sunshine were millions of people, apparently united in grief. Yet though it may seem harsh or cynical, I felt that there was something spurious about the mass mourning that followed her death and attended her funeral. True, most people had loved her, but they had not known her. They loved the media image; they loved the glamor, the humanity, the sympathetic tears, but they had little idea of the real Diana. Mainly they loved her because of what they had read or seen or heard about her. What they were mourning was an image molded by the media and, it must be said, by the Princess herself from her years in the public eye. Now the press was being vilified. Yet surely, if the newspapers and photographers were to blame, in part, for her death, then the people must also share some of that blame? After all, they had bought the newspapers, pored over the magazines, read the books, sat glued to the television coverage. By another irony, some of them were clutching special Diana editions as they abused photographers who had gathered to record the funeral. As I looked at the hordes of people who had stood for hours to share this day and express their sorrow, I felt vaguely disturbed by it all. Despite her ego, her concern for her image, Diana would not really have wanted this.

Everywhere there were flowers, from single buds picked that morning to enormous bouquets – 'floral tributes', as florists (and undertakers) call them. She liked flowers; she would have liked the people's thoughtful tribute. At Kensington Palace, where I had spent so many happy years, there had been a sea of flowers. They had begun arriving on the morning of the day she died, and now there was a field of them – literally, tons of flowers – outside the gates to Kensington Palace. The smell of them was almost overpowering. Luckily, someone had the sense to have them removed before they began to fade and rot, but still they kept coming.

England's rose may be dead, I thought, as I walked back to my office near Buckingham Palace, but she had certainly made the world sit up and take notice while she was here. To me, she was a magical person, a woman of great character, strength, humor, generosity and determination, but she had needed to be channeled, her qualities guided in the right direction, her self-pity and her sometimes explosive temper checked. Some of those around her played an important part in shaping the person who in death would come to be known as the People's Princess, and who finally became, as she had once publicly hoped, the 'queen of people's hearts'.

It is a truism to say that someone's death tends to make us view that person through rose-tinted glasses. Certainly I remembered Diana like that for a while, and so, I'm sure, did almost everybody. But she was certainly no saint, as her brother had publicly insisted. She would have laughed her infectious laugh out loud at the very thought of it.

Lord Spencer had said in his eulogy that Diana was every inch a real woman, not some iconized image. True, she loved her image, and hated it when she was not in the newspapers, or when a picture showed what she thought of as her bad side. In fact, she was as vain as are most of us, someone who really cared about what she looked like, and how she appeared to other people. She could laugh at herself, though, something that perhaps showed that, at heart, she had as much humility as vanity. Which is why, in the end, she would not have wanted millions of people – especially the 'ordinary people' with whom she empathized so much – to mourn for her.

Before the day of the funeral I had stolen a solitary moment with the Princess, saying my own silent farewell to her as she lay in the Chapel Royal. It was cold. She lay at one end of the chapel in her coffin, her standard – the standard of the Princess of Wales – draped over it. I murmured a prayer, and talked out loud about some of the things we had done, some of the amazing places we had visited and extraordinary people we had spent time with. I remembered our last meeting. For once she did not answer me in that somewhat high-pitched, slightly affected voice of hers, so often with laughter bubbling near the surface. I shed no tears, nor do I think she would have expected me to. But like millions around the world I was moved by the loss of someone who had, as she had so earnestly wished, 'made a difference'. Someone who had flown in the face of convention; someone whose very presence could light up a room filled with people close to death; someone who by just touching a man dying of AIDS could completely change our attitude to that terrible disease. Now she was silent, her life ended needlessly, her ready giggle stilled for ever. I had shared much with her during the years when I had served her. Life, I thought, goes on, but I was convinced it would never sparkle in quite the same way again.

In a final irony, as I walked across the park that day, I met a journalist I knew from my days with the Princess, and who had known her well. He was crying his heart out.

# Chapter 1

'THIS IS THE THIRTY-SECOND WARNING.' Giving Diana's police security code I spoke quietly and without inflexion into the radio, then returned it to the side of my seat in the Jaguar. We never signaled the arrival of the principal any earlier, as to have done so would have been poor security. Radio calls are easily monitored.

'Oh Ken, anyone would think the world was about to end.' The woman in the back of the car always found our procedure amusing. 'For goodness' sake, it's only little old me coming home,' she added with a girlish tickle in her voice.

Seconds later the dark green Jaguar XJ6 approached the police security barrier and, after being waved through by the constable on duty, swept into Kensington Palace. In the back of the car sat the most famous woman in the world, Diana, Princess of Wales. I always sat in the front, next to her trusted chauffeur – and my friend – Simon Solari. We were the only people in the car.

Only half an hour earlier, the Princess and I had stepped from Concorde at Heathrow after a flight from Dulles International airport, Washington, DC. Exhilarated, she had hardly been able to sit still in her designated seat, and had talked non-stop about her charity mission to America, during which she had made a friend of the First Lady, Barbara Bush. Indeed, the President himself had delayed a meeting to chat with Diana, and his decision to join them had impressed her. On that trip we had traveled under the names Mr and Mrs Hargreaves, although none of Concorde's crew had been remotely fooled. At the time she was already beginning to revel in her success as a royal personage – in fact, an international celebrity – in her own right.

Now we were back at Numbers 8 and 9 Kensington Palace, her official London residence. The Prince of Wales, her husband, was not waiting for her inside.

'Home sweet home,' Diana sighed, with more than a hint of irony, although without bitterness.

It was just after 10.35 pm on a dark autumn night in 1991, and I had been doing this job for nearly three years. The Princess, however, had been doing hers for nearly ten.

There are not many days when I do not think of Diana, Princess of Wales. Her illuminating smile, her sheer presence, and above all her yearning to live life to the full, have never left me. I am sure I am not the only person to be haunted in this way, although, with each year that passes since her death, fashionable opinion seems increasingly to insist that our memory of the once vivid woman has become not only more distant, but more uncertain. There is no shortage of commentators who want us to believe that the Diana legend is fading, or even that the substance behind that legend was of little worth.

The Diana I knew was full of fun; almost always in search of laughter, not wallowing in self-pity and tears as she is now so often portrayed. There were, of course, dark clouds in her life, but they would soon pass to allow her nature to shine brightly once again. Yet since her death on 31 August 1997 history has all too often presented a very different – not to say distorted – image of this extraordinary woman. Worse, since 1997, a PR offensive has been waged in some quarters against a dead woman's memory. Her name has been dragged through the mud, her principles derided, her motives corrupted, and even her sanity questioned. It has been, in my view at least, a vicious and one-sided war, and as in any war, the truth has been the first casualty.

For nearly six years, from 1988 to 1993, I shadowed the late Princess in my capacity as her Scotland Yard personal protection officer (PPO, or, in layman's terms, her police bodyguard), during the most traumatic period of her life. For most of that time she was a joy to work with. As her senior protection officer it fell to me to deal with her more sensitive private engagements and public appearances, and my relationship with her was, by the very nature of the job, an extremely close one. Due to the unique position in which I found myself, however, it was inevitable that my duties could not always be clearly defined. Naturally she and I freely discussed all matters affecting her security, but we also talked openly about her life, including the most intimate aspects of it. Consequently, during my time with her, I was not only her police officer but also a trusted aide and confidant.

While this may seem a conceited view, it has its roots in the nature of my profession: if I had not liked and trusted her, I could not have done my job efficiently, while she would hardly have tolerated a protection officer whom she did not trust. There was an open-door policy between us; my independence, given that I worked not directly for her but for Scotland Yard, meant I could and would always speak freely and truthfully, unlike the army of courtiers employed by her husband, the Prince of Wales, and by the Queen. The uniqueness of my role gave me, I believe, an unrivalled appreciation of the true Diana, the woman behind the public mask.

I am the first officer from Scotland Yard's elite Royalty and Diplomatic Protection Department to publish an insider's account of service with that department. This may seem an empty claim, but I believe it is a unique story because it was shared with Diana. Most of our experiences were known only to the two of us. I would never have put pen to paper had the Princess been alive today. Since her death, however, I have become increasingly concerned at the way she has been portrayed by the media, by journalists and writers, even those who claim to have known her well. I have come to feel that unless I tell of my years with her as I saw them through my policeman's eyes, then people now and in the future will receive a corrupt impression of her.

My intention in writing this book is simple – to set the record straight about the woman who herself once claimed that I knew her better than anyone, and in doing so, to tell the simple truth about one of the most remarkable, complex and alluring public figures of the latter part of the twentieth century.

When I joined the Metropolitan Police service as a special cadet in 1964 at the tender age of sixteen, I never dreamed that I would one day shadow one of the world's most famous women. A chance meeting with an old friend sent me on a journey that changed my life for ever.

At the age of thirty-four I was already a police inspector, more or less assured of a rapid rise through the hierarchy at Scotland Yard.

One evening in the summer of 1986 I arranged to have a quiet drink with Jim Beaton, a clever and experienced officer, who had been honored with the George Cross for saving Princess Anne, and who had been a chief inspector at Kensington police station when I was a 'skipper' (sergeant) there in the late 1960s. I had always trusted him as a colleague, and, I suppose, regarded him as my mentor. He had had a varied and successful career since our days at Kensington together, and had been promoted to the rank of superintendent. He was also the Queen's personal protection officer. As we sipped glasses of his favored single-malt whisky, Jim came to the point. In confidence, he told me that his department, Royalty Protection, was looking for a police inspector to take charge of guarding the Queen's grandchildren, Princes William and Harry, the sons of the Prince and Princess of Wales, and thus heirs to the throne after Prince Charles.

'It's time for a change, Ken. You go for it – you have nothing to lose,' he urged, before adding, 'I'll put a word in for you.'

Next morning, with Jim's endorsement ringing in my ears (and a head that was slightly the worse for wear after the night before), I applied for the job, and a few months later, in November 1986, was appointed to the department.

Until then I had enjoyed a full and varied police career; I had walked the beat, served undercover in both the Vice and Drug Squads as a long-haired, bearded detective, and had even arrested a serial killer. Surely looking after two small children, even if they did have royal blood running through their veins, could not be that difficult? Thinking about it, I found that I was not worried by the prospect of protecting members of the British royal family; after all, it was just a job.

Even so, and although I had had a few brushes with the famous and the infamous during my career, I had the sense to recognize that royalty promised to be very different. Being a police officer in London from the late 1960s to the late 1980s was never dull. As a naive probationer I had been sent to investigate a disturbance in the West End after answering a flashing blue-light signal in the heart of Piccadilly Circus (in those days, the streets were still dotted with black 'police boxes', to which every officer had a key, and in which there was a telephone; when an officer was needed to attend a scene a blue light flashed on top of the box nearest the incident). On the other end of the phone was a crusty sergeant of early 1950s vintage, who sent me in search of what he described as 'an awful noise'. It turned out to be a wonderful, indeed, historic, commotion; The Beatles – John Lennon, Paul McCartney, George Harrison and Ringo Starr – the greatest pop group of their day, were jamming their hearts out on the roof of the Apple headquarters at 3, Savile Row in London's Mayfair. Well, I had been asked to look into the disturbance, so I made my way through the building to the roof where, courtesy of my job, I had a front-row seat among a few of the group's colleagues and a handful of invited guests. When I approached drummer Ringo Starr, who was the nearest member of the band to me, and asked what was going on, he smiled, handed me a beer – which I handed back – and said in his thick Liverpool accent, 'Are you all right, mate? Don't look so worried.'

He then gestured with a drumstick for one of the fixers once again to offer me a drink while he got on with the job in hand of playing the beat for 'Get Back!', which eventually reached such a deafening crescendo that it stopped the traffic in the busy street below us. Obviously, I could not accept the drink as I was on duty, but the music was intoxicating enough. The song finished to rousing applause from the fortunate people present. By now I had been joined on the roof by about six or so other police officers; like me, none of them asked The Beatles to desist.

'Are we free to go now, officer? I promise I'll come quietly,' John Lennon said with a wry smile and a wink as he returned to the studio below.

Perhaps the most high-profile arrest I was involved in was that of the British serial killer Dennis Nilsen in February 1983. His was a story that genuinely shocked people and it remained headline news in Britain (where, thankfully, serial killers were and are a rarity) for weeks. He was clinical to the point of coldness in everything he did, and especially in the killing, dismemberment and disposal of the young homosexuals he invited back to his flat in North London. As is the case in so many crimes, his undoing came by chance. The police were called in after a workman clearing a blockage in his drains made the grisly discovery that the obstruction was caused by human remains. As an inspector at Hornsey police station at the time, I was sent as one of the arresting officers to bring Nilsen in. He was an iceman, unmoved by what he had done and entirely fatalistic about what was happening to him. Then, as we were driving back to the station, with Nilsen handcuffed in the back, silenced but unperturbed by his arrest, still contemplating the magnitude of his crime, he suggested we go back. Persuaded, we turned round. There was more horror to come. Back at his very ordinary house, a huge pot stood on the stove in his very ordinary kitchen. Lifting the lid, I, by now a hardened police officer, was not fully prepared for the sight that greeted me. In the pot was a partly boiled head, half skull, half cooked flesh. Nilsen was eventually given six life sentences, one for each of the murders of which he was convicted, and will live out his life locked behind bars; locked, too, inside his own macabre world.

Neither of these two incidents could be said to have particularly prepared me for the new service I was about to join, however. If I had to try to pinpoint a reason why I joined the roller-coaster business of guarding the British royal family, it would be that, by the early 1980s, I had become thoroughly disillusioned with what was happening on the front line in the Metropolitan Police Service. Having left the Complaints Investigation Bureau, the department that investigates internal police corruption, I was posted to North London in 1982 as a newly promoted inspector. Then, after just a couple of weeks at Hornsey police station, I was asked to write the divisional action plans for the district, spelling out how we could tackle the key areas of crime. Surprised, and, I must admit, a little flattered, I believed that here was my chance to make a real difference. Frustration soon set in, however, when it became clear that despite being praised for my work, my recommendations were not acted upon. Within two years I joined the District Support Unit, a new 'people-friendly' term for the controversial task force, originally known as the SPG (Special Patrol Group), and which later became the Territorial Support Group. I made a number of influential friends, some of them senior officers, and in 1983 I was recommended for promotion to chief inspector, seemingly destined, at least in terms of rank, for higher and greater achievement with the service. My promotion was blocked, however, and after a while I began to get the feeling that someone higher up the so-called 'police food chain' did not like my face. Or me.

A few days after I was passed over for promotion, the area I was policing was mobilized to deal with the Broadwater Farm riots, a series of violent and bloody disturbances that brought turmoil to race relations in Britain and changed the face of front-line policing for ever. Broadwater Farm was a run-down housing estate Tottenham, North London, which was also a hotbed of crime, drugs, and violence. The majority of its inhabitants were black working-class people; most were law-abiding, but the estate had virtually become a 'no-go' zone, dominated by gangs and drug dealers. In 1985, when the police raided the estate in an attempt to reinstate order, violence erupted among the lawless factions there, and the officers withdrew. Senior officers then decided that we had to go in behind helmets and riot shields to restore order. During the ensuing battles one of the men on my relief, Police Constable Keith Blakelock, an honest and distinguished officer, was brutally murdered and his body mutilated after he was cut off from other officers by a mob. I was sickened, and grieved both for him and his family. Matters grew worse in the days that followed, and were made worse still by the widespread, lurid and often exaggerated reporting of the media. Infuriated by the way the service pandered to the self-styled 'community leaders' who, in the wake of the murder, continued to peddle anti-police propaganda, I resolved to leave the service. What was the point of good, decent human beings putting their lives on the line for others if nothing was going to change? I felt that Keith had died for nothing. If he was not to be defended after death then I did not want to serve any more. The community leaders used Keith's death as a political platform; his presence on the estate and the fact that he was a police officer as a political football. It was as though it had been his fault that he had been brutally murdered just for being in the wrong place at the wrong time, and just for doing his job.

A few days after his death, exhausted and emotionally strung out after the frenzied atmosphere of the riots, I resolved there and then to hang up my blue inspector's uniform, placing it in my police locker. I have not worn it since; not even on the day when I was formally invested with an honor by the Queen.

As it happened, I didn't need to. Not long afterwards I took that fateful drink with Jim Beaton, and some little while later I transferred to the Royalty and Diplomatic Protection Department. From there on in my uniform was usually to be a Turnbull & Asser suit (paid for, I might add, from a special clothing allowance from the department) which covered my 9mm Glock self-loading pistol, supplied by the Firearms Department at Scotland Yard. The nature of the job meant my wardrobe had to be upgraded and had to include tailored suits and morning dress for accompanying members of the royal family to Ascot, weddings or funerals, and both types of evening dress, black tie for official or formal dinners, and white tie for the most formal of banquets. I was now a member of the elite Royalty Protection Department charged with guarding the 'heir and the spare' to the British throne.

In November 1986, a few days after joining the department, I was introduced to the Prince and Princess of Wales in person at Sandringham, the Queen's estate near Kings Lynn, Norfolk, in the east of England. I first met Prince Charles while he was out shooting. He was charming; the epitome of the perfect English landed gentleman, although he struck me even then as perhaps a little eccentric. He was relaxed – after all, he had had policemen around him ever since he was a little boy – and he wished me well. As I walked back towards the main house with Superintendent Colin Trimming, the Prince's protection officer, Charles and his fellow guns continued to knock a small proportion of the pheasant population from the crisp autumn sky.

On reflection, it seemed a trifle odd that our introduction should have been effected in a Norfolk field during a break in the Prince's sport. My first encounter with the Princess, however, was an altogether different experience. It took place in the entrance hall of the red-bricked main house, where Colin and I found the tall, elegant blonde waiting for us. She approached us to greet me. As Colin was about to make a formal introduction, the Princess giggled coquettishly:

'You must be Ken. I have heard so much about you. I am Diana,' she said, as though I had no idea who she was. There was no formality – she was completely natural.

'Ma'am, I know who you are, I've heard so much about you, and it really is a pleasure to meet you,' I fumbled in response, trying to sound bright.

She appeared to be in excellent humor, if perhaps a little over-excited, and, compared with Charles, seemed so fresh and young in outlook. I had no idea that our lives would become so closely entwined, believing then that my appointment as senior protection officer to Princes William and Harry would last a year, after which, if I continued in the force, I would be reassigned back to front-line policing.

'I don't envy your job, Ken,' she said after Colin had told her that I had been appointed to head up security for her two sons. 'They can be quite a handful – but remember, I am always around if you need me,' she added reassuringly.

# Chapter 2

FEW JOBS REQUIRE MORE EXPERTISE, or more discretion, than that of a protection officer. I am not talking about the ample-bellied bouncers often seen guarding pixie-sized pop stars, or the phalanx of heavily armed US Secret Service agents sporting designer sunglasses and – at least as depicted in Hollywood movies – whispering into hidden microphones in their lapels. I am talking about the professionals in tailored suits who are as at ease mingling at a diplomatic reception as undergoing the training exercises at the Special Air Service (SAS) base in Hereford. There will be no bulges in his or her well-cut suit as the weapon will be neatly concealed in a holster in the small of the back. Yet even though professional protection officers may be armed, they know that their ultimate tools are information, and the skill and experience that allows them to use it.

For security reasons, how the officers for the elite Royalty and Diplomatic Protection Department are trained has to remain secret. What I can say, however, is that once an officer is selected, having demonstrated the right characteristics for the job, he or she then undergoes an extensive system of specialist courses. I know that, to be accepted on the course, an officer has to be of a very high standard because I have been an instructor on a number of courses, and was one of the instigators of the new Metropolitan Police protection course which, I am proud to say, has now been adopted nationally.

Once potential officers, men and women, have passed all these courses, and have mastered the specialist skills, including advanced driving, first aid, physical fitness and firearms proficiency, they are ready for the next stage. Only then, having attained an exceptionally high standard, are they invited to attend the national bodyguard course. It is there that the importance of interpersonal skills and communication is stressed.

To ensure the personal security of the two princes it was essential for them to trust me, which meant that I had to get close to them. Much has been made in the press about the relationship between the princes and their protection officers, often with exaggerated claims that they regarded 'their' policeman as some form of surrogate father. This of course was nonsense. To William and Harry the Prince of Wales was always 'Papa', and nobody could or would ever take his place. It is fair to say, however, that I had an avuncular relationship with the boys, which Diana actively encouraged.

In the months that followed my appointment I did not have many dealings with the Prince and Princess – certainly not to the extent that I had at first anticipated – as I set about the task of drawing up an action plan for the young princes' security. Even then, aged five and three years, they knew they were special, different from others, despite their mother's determination that they should, as far as possible, be raised as 'normal' children. But they were also boisterous children, full of energy and surprises. In terms of security, developing a good rapport with the boys was essential because they had to trust me completely if I was to protect their young lives – with my own, if necessary. I impressed on them from the outset the need to tell me exactly what they were doing at all times. In time we came not only to like but to respect each other, and as a result they responded positively.

In the early days I had a fairly regular routine. On weekdays I would accompany William to Wetherby prep school in Notting Hill, a short distance from Kensington Palace, where I would spend the day until it was time for him to go home, and at weekends would look after both princes' security, usually at one of the royal residences on a rota basis. I handed over to a static officer (one who guards a specific location rather than a person) once they were inside the secure Kensington Palace compound, where several other members of the royal family, as well as a number of senior courtiers, had grace-and-favor apartments. These accommodations are in the gift of the Queen and are usually rent-free or carry only a nominal fee. They are often given to more distantly related members of the family or loyal courtiers.

Weekends would usually be spent at Highgrove, the Gloucester-shire estate Charles bought in August 1980, not quite a year before his marriage, for over $1,125,000 (£750,000). Set in 348 well-wooded acres on the edge of the picturesque Cotswolds, about two hours' drive west of London, it was here that Charles, in particular, felt most at home and able to forget for a time the pressures of public life; moreover, and despite claims to the contrary, the Princess too grew to like the place. Highgrove's sweeping parkland lies within the country of the Beaufort Hunt, something that helped sway the Prince, a keen foxhunter, to buy it. Most significantly, perhaps, it was also just seventeen miles from the home of Camilla Parker Bowles, at Allington, near Chippenham.

Security at Highgrove was second to none, at least as private houses go in England. Equally impregnable was Paddy Whiteland, an inscrutable individual who to all intents and purposes was the heartbeat of Highgrove. Paddy, who sadly died a few years ago, knew exactly how the place ticked, and how to keep it ticking. I first met this blunt Irishman, a significant figure in Prince Charles's life, in January 1987 when Charles and Diana were away skiing in the exclusive Swiss resort of Klosters. Since the Prince and Princess were accompanied by a team of expert police skiers, I remained in Britain with William and Harry, who continued their routine of weekends at Highgrove. As Paddy shuffled into the staff kitchen, his thick, unkempt white hair almost standing on end, he brought with him an overwhelming aroma of horses. Flashing a roguish grin, he stuck out his hand and introduced himself. I liked him immediately, but instinctively knew that he was someone who needed to be handled with care. His rustic simplicity belied his ruthless guile, for his rugged exterior was simply the outer casing of probably the most cunning – and powerful – individual on Charles's staff, the color sergeant, if you like, of the Prince's Praetorian Guard. If someone wanted gossip to reach Charles all they had to do was to tell Paddy and within hours the Prince would hear. Nobody was safe, and especially not Diana and her inner circle.

With Charles and Diana away there was a relaxed air about Highgrove. When they were there, the Highgrove staff lived and breathed the tension of their employers' failing marriage, which they knew was doomed even if the press and the general public didn't. The dressers, butlers, chef, and other indoor and outdoor servants had to live with the daily pressure and the endless rows when Charles and Diana were in residence, so when they were away they tended to treat the interlude like a national holiday.

The fun rubbed off on the young princes too, who from the first were quite relaxed about their parents' absences, and seemed to accept me as much as I enjoyed being with them. At the weekends we really bonded. Even so they both missed their mother, William especially.

Diana had a very clear idea of how she wanted her sons raised. She had already axed their first nanny, Barbara Barnes, a traditionalist whose protestations that 'the princes need to be treated differently, because they are different' fell on deaf ears where their mother was concerned. Although I liked Barbara, and believed that she had William and Harry's best interests at heart, I felt Diana was right to try to raise her sons as normally as possible. Moreover, despite their birthright, and largely thanks to their mother, they have developed into remarkably balanced young men.

Barbara left after a series of disputes with the Princess and increasingly Diana's personal staff came to realize that the nanny was on collision course with her employer, and was therefore a dangerous person to be allied with. Her power battle with Diana over the children could have only one victor, and it became just a matter a time before she was sent packing.

Diana felt that the way the royal family raised children was, at the very least, odd. Convinced that the reason Charles was cold and distant was due to a lack of physical and emotional love during his childhood, she determined that the same would not happen to her beloved boys. So when Olga Powell was brought in as a replacement, she was under no illusions about who was boss. Her nanny style had to comply with Diana's style of mothering or she too would be out.

As far as the children were concerned Olga was a breath of fresh air. She very quickly saw the lie of the land. Privately, she explained to me that the Princess was a jealous mother, and as such had to be handled with care. As their protection officer it was essential that I did not fall into the same trap as Barbara. On numerous occasions when the princes and I were messing around together Olga would advise caution. It was imperative, she said, not to come between the Princess and her children, for if Diana felt she was losing control of her boys, she would step in and assert herself. Olga, who had not even taken on the job full-time, was happy to play it Diana's way.

The deep, loving bond between Diana and her two sons, so

often remarked upon, was truly wonderful to witness. When she was away in Klosters she missed them terribly, and was ecstatic when they were reunited. Her face lit up with love when I returned with William and Harry from a lunch with Lord Vestey's children, whose parents lived near by. It was as though she had not seen them for years. I let an excited William toot the car's horn as Diana, tanned from her skiing break, stood on the steps of Highgrove with her arms outstretched, ready to embrace her boys. That evening the family enjoyed a relaxed meal together, during which Charles and Diana appeared more comfortable with each other than they had for months. Although she had raised countless protests against going skiing, the break appeared to have done them both good.

Olga's appointment coincided with William's first day at Wetherby. From the start, however, Diana made it clear that wherever possible she would drive William to and from school each day, her official engagements permitting, so that they would, at the very least, start their day with a loving kiss. Perhaps the fact that she came from a broken home left a void in her that was never properly filled; she knew that this was so important in their development. Only illness or official duties would prevent her from doing what she saw as her parental duty.

Diana's love for her sons was absolute and wholly consistent. Nevertheless, it brought with it some problems. Seeing her as *the* celebrity mother on parade, the well-to-do – and extremely competitive – mothers with sons at the school knew they had to try hard if they were to match up to the world's most famous and glamorous woman. So the morning school run was like nothing so much as a catwalk show for thirty-somethings, and stunning mothers dressed to kill in designer clothes became a standard feature. I remember one afternoon when I was standing on the steps of the school, waiting for the Princess to arrive to collect William, when one of the mothers, a tall, statuesque, aristocratic woman who was the sister-in-law of a famous billionaire, pounced. Just as she was in the process of planting a kiss of greeting on my ruddy cheek the Princess walked up the steps.

'Having fun, Ken?' Diana said, pointedly. I knew I would be teased about the incident later.

Prince Charles was, and no doubt still is, an extremely busy man. His hectic public schedule inevitably meant that I spent more time with his children than he did. As a result, when they wanted somebody to have a playful fight with, they turned to me. They were always great fun, and often their peculiar antics made me roar with laughter. On one occasion, however, a joke I made to William about his pronunciation led to a potentially embarrassing confrontation with Charles. William speaks with that slightly clipped upper-class English accent which, to many people, can sound a little odd. One day he persisted with pronouncing 'out' like 'ite', and when I teasingly corrected him he insisted he was right because his father always said the word like that. As I was walking through Highgrove's sculpted grounds a few hours later, Prince Charles approached me.

'Ken, I understand you have been giving William elocution lessons,' he said, his tone suggesting a reprimand without actually saying so. I had clearly overstepped the mark, and this was the Prince's gentlemanly way of telling me to keep my nose out of family business. I took the lesson to heart, although when Diana found out about my telling-off she thought it was hilarious.

William and Harry loved to rough and tumble, and they always fought dirty. I had my own bedroom at Kensington Palace, so that I could sleep there when duty required. As regular as clockwork they would knock at the door, and a small voice would say, 'Ken, do you want to fight?'

It was not really a request or even a question; it was a statement of what was going to happen. The two princes made the perfect royal tag team. One would go for my head and the other attack my more sensitive parts, landing punches towards my groin, which, if they connected, would make me keel over in agony. For just a few minutes of mayhem these two boys, who were to become the focus of so much sadness and sympathy after their mother's death, were just that, two boisterous little boys. So much now rests on their shoulders, not least the future existence of the monarchy as a viable and creditable institution, but at the time I was pleased to share and enjoy their moments of play. Certainly, both their parents seemed to appreciate it. Charles would pop his head around the door of whichever room we were in and, with a slightly quizzical look on his furrowed face, would ask; 'They're not being too much bother are they, Ken?'

'No, sir, not at all,' I would gasp as I recovered from another fierce royal punch. In fact the poor man looked a little relieved. It was not that he was not a good father, despite the black propaganda being circulated about him at that time, it was just that he found the kind of horseplay that his boys sometimes needed at that stage in their lives somewhat confusing. The Prince loved his sons, of that there was no doubt, but he always seemed a little wrapped up in his work and the cares of his position actually to join in. William and Harry adored their father in return, while they regarded me as a jovial uncle who was always on hand to fight with.

They knew, however, that I was also there to protect them and their mother. Boys, whether they are princes destined to be kings or not, are invariably enthralled by the whole business of security. Harry, in particular, was fascinated by all the equipment police use in carrying out protection duties. He longed to join in, and plagued me daily to let him do so. On one occasion after I had become the Princess's protection officer he arrived unannounced in my room.

'Ken, can I use the radio? I just want to see how it works,' he said. Harry was and still is an endearing character, and I relented, handing him a police radio and showing him how to use it. Then I gave him specific instructions to go to several designated points and check in, using the radio. He was ecstatic. Here was his chance to be a real police officer, using real police equipment. For the next few minutes I received regular check calls from Harry as he followed my instructions to the letter. We agreed that he could visit Lady Jane (Diana's sister) in the stable block, a short distance from the entrance to Kensington Palace, but with CCTV coverage. I spoke with Lady Jane who confirmed that he had arrived. Soon after, Lady Jane rang me to say that Harry was on the way back. I informed the police at the barrier. Harry didn't show. Growing anxious, I contacted the police box, but the officer on duty told me he had not seen Harry. Faced with a potential security disaster – of my own making – I was about to send out a search party when Harry radioed in.

'Harry, can you hear me? Where the hell are you?' I said as calmly as possible, desperately trying to appear untroubled by his disappearing act.

'Ken, I am by Tower Records in the high street,' he explained. Oh God – he'd left the palace grounds altogether and had walked east along Kensington High Street. Thank heavens the radio had the range to transmit over the extra distance.

'What on earth are you doing there? Harry, come back to the Palace immediately,' I barked. I ran to meet him.

[28]

Within minutes he was safely back, although what shoppers in the busy high street thought when they saw the Queen's grandson walking along the pavement clutching a police radio I have no idea. Harry apologized and promised he would not do it again. In truth, some of the blame was mine – and I certainly would have been blamed if something had happened. The Metropolitan Police would have taken a very dim view indeed – although that would have been nothing compared with the Princess's likely reaction. (Luckily, she never found out.)

As I have said, despite their birth and position, William and Harry at heart were just brothers in search of adventure. Like their parents they are both thrill seekers who love speed. Here I was in luck, for through a friend of mine I was able to satisfy their craving. Martin Howells ran Playscape, an excellent go-kart-racing track in Clapham, a place that allowed men the chance to be boys again, and boys the chance to dream of being Formula 1 drivers. Both the princes loved visiting the track and constantly pestered their mother to take them. One weekend at Highgrove when Diana could take no more, she begged me to call Martin and ask him to bring down two of the go-karts, which were capable of speeds of up to 40mph. He agreed and in due course arrived with the machines, then helped me to set up a course around Prince Charles's beloved grounds. The go-karts tore up the garden, with William and Harry imitating their racing heroes as the Princess howled with laughter and cheered them on. I think she privately enjoyed the fact that Charles's grounds were being used as a track, his secret garden transformed into a chicane as his sons battled for supremacy. The Prince, of course, knew nothing about it.

There was another incident at Highgrove of which he remained blissfully unaware. The Princess might easily have remained in her ivory tower, but that was not her style. Instead, she would wander into the staff kitchen where she would pick at the latest creation of her chef, Mervyn Wycherley, and the three of us would often chat for hours over a bottle of wine from her husband's cellar. She would kick off her shoes, sometimes putting her feet up on the large wooden table, and talk about her day or catch up on gossip, often roaring with laughter at one of the irrepressible Mervyn's mordant remarks.

The kitchen was no place for the faint-hearted, however, and certainly not for animals, particularly Charles's beloved Jack Russell terriers. On one occasion his favourite, Tigger, dared to venture into Mervyn's kitchen when I was there talking to him. Mervyn, a stickler for hygiene, had just finished cooking, and took exception to this canine intrusion. He scooped up the unfortunate animal and placed it in the oven which, although switched off, was still warm. Just at that moment Charles poked his head round the door and asked, 'Has anyone seen Tigger?'

As the dog scratched furiously at the oven door, Mervyn told the Prince that he had seen the dog heading for the garden. Charles set off in search of his 'best friend', whereupon Mervyn quickly opened the oven and sent the dazed – and rather hot – terrier on its way.

# Chapter 3

FOR SOME INEXPLICABLE REASON I was feeling apprehensive as I approached Kensington Palace. I had been summoned there for what was termed a 'cozy fireside chat' with the Princess. It was not, of course, the first time that we had talked; in fact we knew each other reasonably well by then, not only because I had been in charge of protection for her sons, but also because I had acted as her protection officer on a number of occasions throughout 1987 as a back-up to her team, and we had worked well together.

That morning, however, my composure had deserted me. Still, no good would come of delaying, so I pressed the polished brass bell push next to the imposing black door and waited. Seconds later I was greeted by the uniformed butler, the imperturbable Harold Brown, who politely asked me to wait while he informed the Princess of my arrival. The hall was surprisingly gloomy for a palace, although comfortable, with a deep lime-green carpet throughout. After telling the Princess that I had arrived Harold ushered me into her sitting room, where she stood waiting to greet me, her bright eyes matching her smile of welcome. This room was her sanctuary, a very feminine space with elegant antique furniture on which stood ornaments and countless framed photographs of her sons. Tall windows opened out on to a delightful walled garden which I would later come to know as one of her favorite places to hide on summer evenings, when she wanted to escape the almost constant attention that went with her position. She politely suggested I sit on one of the two sofas upholstered in plain pink fabric that flanked the fireplace, and asked her butler to fetch some tea. With a soft, 'Very good, ma'am,' he left and we were alone.

Sitting on the other sofa, she looked every inch a princess. Her blonde hair was immaculately dressed, and she wore a smart navy Catherine Walker dress in cream and blue with white high-heeled Jimmy Choo two-toned shoes. She had just returned from an official engagement in London and was, as she called it, 'chilling out', with Mozart's Mass in C playing on her stereo. Then she suddenly giggled, which led me to laugh too. It was her way of setting someone at their ease in such enforced intimacy. After seven years in her royal job, the Princess had learned how to break the ice with easy grace.

'Ken, I am so glad you have decided to take me on,' she said, then added, 'I'm sure I am seen as a poisoned chalice by you boys,' referring to the protection team. I laughed, slightly uncomfortably, but assured her with a commendably straight face that this was not the case. I insisted that I really was looking forward to my new position; nobody had put a gun to my head to force me to take up the post, I said.

'You're clearly not a very good liar, Ken,' she joked, 'You're going to have to improve on that technique if you're going to survive in this madhouse.'

I was saved from having to reply to this rather loaded remark by Harold, who just at that moment knocked on the door and entered bearing a tray. He set it down and began pouring tea from a silver teapot into two delicate china cups.

'How do you like yours, Ken?'

'Builder's please, ma'am,' I replied. She looked quizzically at me. 'Very strong, ma'am – you know, as builders take it.'

Harold quietly departed, and for the next half hour the Princess and I chatted like old friends. Inevitably the subject kept returning to her sons and how quickly they were growing up.

'You see them nearly as much as me, Ken – certainly more than their father,' she said. But I was not going to take the bait. Under no circumstances was I going to be drawn into the Waleses' private battle, and I said nothing. She pulled back. It was, after all, too early in our relationship for her to launch into a full-scale assault on her husband, and she knew it. Changing tack, she told me how very proud she was of her sons, and how much she wanted them to grow up with a genuine sense of normality, even though she knew that their status made them different from other young boys.

'I know it is going to be tough, Ken, given who they are, but it is so, *so* important to me that they grow up not only knowing who they are, but what the world is really like.'

Even then, I knew that she meant what she said. In my time with them I had already accompanied her on the London underground, and she had even taken them to visit down-and-outs living rough on the streets of the capital. She was a woman of action, not idle talk, and she was as good as her word.

We did not really discuss my approach to security, and in particular her personal protection. I think we both took it as read that we were experienced professionals and knew what our respective roles would be, and that what we did not know we would have to learn as we went along.

On paper, my job was simple – to keep her safe at all costs. This meant that either I or one of my team would be on duty with her from the moment she got up to the moment she went to bed – without fail. (At night, she was guarded by static protection officers inside the palace, or other royal residences in which she might be staying.) I would travel with her wherever she went, at home or abroad, in public or in private. I would be her shadow, walking a pace away, constantly searching the faces in the crowd for the one that might be a potential threat. Both the Princess and I knew the form, but, typically, when she did raise the subject of her security, she joked about it.

'So, Ken – basically, you are my last line of defense?' She looked me up and down critically as she said it, but there was a hint of laughter in her eyes. 'So does that mean you will take a bullet for me?' she went on. This was typical Diana, testing, half joking but still serious. I was ready for her, however. Looking straight back at her I replied, 'Only one bullet, ma'am. I find more than one a little uncomfortable.'

For a moment she was silent, then she laughed – I had responded, as it turned out, in exactly the right way. Naturally, I then assured her that I would do everything in my power to avoid any such drastic action, adding that, with her assistance, I hoped to be around for a very long time.

I had met the Princess before, of course, many times, but never for such an intimate conversation. I found her immensely engaging. She was compassionate, interested, funny and street-wise, with a keen intelligence that belied her lack of academic qualifications. I knew my new job was going to have its ups and downs, but I found that I was looking forward to riding this royal roller-coaster at her side.

'I am sure we are going to get along just fine, Ken,' she said, as I stood to leave, before adding, 'We'll make a good team.'

With that vote of confidence I turned and left, making my way through the palace complex and back across Kensington Gardens before catching a taxi back to the department's headquarters close to Buckingham Palace. The meeting had gone well, I felt, and I was delighted. A few days later I was formally confirmed as Personal Protection Officer to Her Royal Highness the Princess of Wales.

If you are not born to it like 'blood' royals, having a bodyguard around you twenty-four hours a day can be tough to take. I suppose my being there must have been an ever-present reminder to Diana that she was different; that she had become a potential target for faceless terrorists or deranged stalkers, or any one of the thousands of cranks out there (and any policeman can tell you just how many there are). Before I joined, she had already attended an anti-terrorist course at Stirling Lines, then the headquarters of the Special Air Service Regiment at Hereford; we would return there periodically for refresher courses, which included her taking a driving course on how to handle possible terrorist attacks, during which she drove through smoke bombs tossed in front of her car. I also took her to the police range at Lippitts Hill in Loughton, Essex, where officers licensed to carry firearms, myself included, have to complete regular proficiency tests on the range to ensure we qualify for the job. If a personal protection officer failed to meet the necessary standard he or she would be immediately switched to other duties. On one occasion she brought William and Harry with her, who reveled in firing a .38 Smith & Wesson revolver, under the close supervision of a police instructor.

For all her mood swings, her unpredictability and occasional outbursts of frustration or rage – and I have to emphasize that this was an exceptionally difficult time for her both in terms of her marriage and her place within the royal family – the Princess recognized that we had to be with her, and while at times she must have found our presence claustrophobic, we knew that she appreciated our diligence. Although she had joked about me being her last line of defense, she knew that it was in fact true. We both recognized that if I was to keep her safe, then there could be no secrets between us.

For members of the British royal family, life can never be completely private. Rank and title bring with them great privilege, wealth and prestige, but rank and title also mean that their secrets are never truly their own. There have always been – and always will be – over-attentive servants eavesdropping on conversations, or maids who survey personal correspondence too closely while tidying a desk, or even housekeepers paying rather too much attention to clothes or bed linen. That is not to say that such people are not honorable or discreet, but they still *know*. Then there are people who have to know, in order that the whole business of royalty can be run smoothly and without scandals, as well as others, often senior courtiers, who make it their business to know. So for royalty, even the most cherished private moment must, by the very nature of the job, be shared, or at the least be on somebody else's 'need-to-know' list.

In addition, the more senior the royal, the greater the need for their every movement and action to be – discreetly – known, since otherwise it becomes almost impossible to protect them. Being both the wife of the Prince of Wales and a very high-profile figure in her own right, Diana was no exception and, as her protection officer, I was perhaps the one person with whom she needed to share those secrets without constraint. If she was planning to visit the theatre with friends, or to dine privately with a male admirer, it was imperative that I should know in advance who these people were, and where she intended meeting them, in order to protect her effectively.

Within days of joining the Metropolitan Police Royalty Protection Department in 1986 I had become party to many of Diana's most intimate secrets, passed to me semi-officially. A handover was arranged in the kitchen at Highgrove; nobody else was present as Chief Inspector Graham Smith, Diana's senior police protection officer, and I sat down and chatted over a cup of coffee. What he told me was of no real surprise; indeed, gossip being what it is, I had already heard much of it at second or third hand. The principal subject of our conversation was the Princess's love affair with Captain James Hewitt. Graham spelt out the situation calmly and clearly. The wife of the heir to the throne was having an affair with an officer of the Household Cavalry, and it was not for us, as her police protection officers, or for me in particular, to moralize, or even to have an opinion about it. Our job was simply to ensure above all that she remained safe, which in turn meant that the affair had to remain secret. Graham told me that in his professional view Hewitt would never compromise the Princess's security. He was co-operative, sensible and happy to be guided by the police; moreover, he fully accepted that the safe houses in which he met his lover had all to be checked for security and rated as being safe, before an assignation could take place.

The Princess first met James Hewitt in London in the summer of 1986, a few months before I joined the department, at a party thrown by her lady-in-waiting, Hazel West. For Hewitt, it clashed with a dinner engagement and he almost did not go – in which case, one of the most celebrated love affairs of the latter part of the twentieth century might never have started. Diana later told me of this first meeting, and although the sadness that followed their eventual parting tainted the telling of it, it was clear that she always adored Hewitt. She said that their first conversation was completely natural, and it was this that first attracted her to him – he helped to make the whole experience of meeting and talking more enjoyable, and they got on famously from the start.

At some point during the conversation Hewitt told her that he was a riding instructor; when she in turn spoke of her long-held fear of riding, he offered to help her overcome it. As a result, another meeting was arranged, and before long what has become one of the most notorious affairs in recent royal history had started. At this time, although nobody ever confirmed it to her, Diana knew in her heart that Prince Charles was still seeing Camilla Parker Bowles. Shattered by her husband's betrayal, the Princess was ready for an affair. Hewitt, a natural womanizer, appreciated her emotional and physical needs. From the first, he gave her the attention and affection she relished, and would later provide the passion she yearned for.

The private friendships of both Charles and Diana were common knowledge to those on the inside, but not to the public. Of course, there had been murmurings in the press, but no one had come close to exposing either of them. At this stage I did not have to cope with the added tension of covering Diana's tracks; that responsibility fell to Graham Smith (or 'Smudger', as I called him), who headed up her security until he fell ill with the cancer that eventually killed him.

But throughout 1987, while I was overseeing security for Princes William and Harry, 'Smudger' called on me to assist her protection team, and I stood in for him as senior officer on a number of occasions. I suppose it was a natural transition, as my duties with the young princes meant that I was in daily contact with Diana, and we had already established an easy rapport. When acting as her protection officer, my duties varied from carrying out reconnaissance for her police team ahead of her official visits, to accompanying her on engagements. These ranged from film galas in London's West End (occasionally with Prince Charles) to the more mundane opening of a civic center in Harrow or accompanying her to the wedding of a friend. It was all good experience and, in retrospect, it is clear that I was unknowingly being groomed for the next stage in my Scotland Yard protection career.

To survive in the surreal world of Charles and Diana one had to adapt quickly or face eviction. I watched many innocents axed for no greater crime than upsetting the frail sensibilities of either the Prince or Princess. Diana, to her credit, was often the first to admit her capriciousness, and frequently regretted hasty judgments. In fairness to her, as well, her mercurial behavior should be seen in the context of the tension of her failing marriage. In such circumstances her mood swings were perhaps forgivable, if not excusable.

It must have been terribly embarrassing, if not humiliating, for her to have to hold up her head among her personal staff, most of whom knew that her husband was seeing Mrs Parker Bowles, and had been doing so for a considerable time. The staff were caught in the crossfire of marital disharmony, and had to show discretion about Charles's involvement with Camilla Parker Bowles or face retribution. Equally, they were aware that, if crossed, Diana was capable of exacting ruthless punishment, and never more so than if she learned of, or even suspected disloyalty. Conscious of the predicament in which his friendship placed his staff, Charles did at least try to avoid putting them in such an invidious situation. By and large he kept his arrangements private, their trysts only really known to trusted policemen and his most loyal servants. Yet all his careful plans and calculated evasions fooled no one. Everybody on his staff knew exactly what was going on, but kept it private for fear of being ousted, a certain fate if they were ever caught gossiping. Nevertheless, some regarded the behavior of their royal employers as an opportunity for personal advancement. History tells of countless devious royal aides and courtiers, prepared to tell tales of a rival's disloyalty and the indiscretion of others in order to curry royal favor, and the court of Charles and Diana was no different.

While the Prince and Princess conducted their romances in private, their country home, Highgrove, once Charles's private sanctuary, had now become a marital battleground. As a newcomer, even before Graham's kitchen-table briefing, I soon appreciated that the marriage was in deep trouble. Charles was at best cold towards his young wife, while she was sometimes hysterical, and at her worst could be simply vile. Privately, she would later repent, but faced with her husband's coolly distant behavior towards her, this was her only means of provoking a reaction. The Prince was not prepared to give an inch to his demanding wife; as heir to the British throne, he genuinely believed that his birthright decreed that he did not have to. If that meant upsetting his beautiful princess, then so be it.

I lost count of the number of times the Prince arranged to meet his friends after promising a special dinner with Diana. Her reaction was understandable and often volatile. 'Stuff your rotten friends, stuff them! – they are not *my* friends,' she would scream after he revealed that their private plans had been scrapped because he was entertaining some of his circle. Unmoved, the Prince would rejoin his party, explain that the Princess had retired with a headache, and continue as if nothing had happened.

Such scenes were, however, a symptom, rather than the cause, of the cancer within their marriage. Charles and Diana spent weekends at Highgrove, but it was very rare for them to have an entire weekend there alone together. Visits by Charles's ex-girlfriends, staff told me, were common. In any event, the house was full of guests; if it was not Sarah Keswick, wife of 'Chips' Keswick, it would be the Duchess of York or any number of other acquaintances. Charles appeared to relish the arrival of friends at Highgrove, perhaps because their presence meant that he did not have to spend too long with his wife, whose manner and behavior he found both irritating and frustrating.

Summer weekends were also dominated by the Prince's love of polo. Inevitably, his passion for the sport would lead to rows between the royal couple, since Diana found polo both recklessly dangerous and mind-numbingly dull. Matters were made worse by the press. Even when the Princess did bow to pressure and take her sons to the polo field to watch their father play, the photographers inevitably focused on her. Indeed, the only time the press would show any interest in the Prince and polo was either when Diana was present, or when he made a mistake, fell from his pony and injured himself. Nor did his own attitude help. If Diana did attend a polo match and, through no fault of her own, found herself on the front pages the next day, the Prince would complain that she had been playing up to the cameras. 'Quite the glamor girl,' he would say disdainfully. The poor woman simply could not win – she was damned if she attended a match, and damned if she didn't. When Charles adopted this stance Diana would fly into a rage, whereupon he, desperate to avoid confrontation, would usually wander off to tend to his beloved garden. 'If only I was as important as your garden. Go on, talk to your flowers!' was one of her favorite taunts as the discomfited Prince left the room.

Charles's passion for polo had taken its toll on him over the years, leaving him with serious lower-back problems. He was forced to carry out a series of demanding exercises to free the muscles and ease the pain, which at times left him hardly able to move. Colin Trimming, his protection officer, always carried a special cushion in the car to support the Prince's back. For myself, I could not understand why he was putting himself through so much pain; it was as if he was trying to prove something to himself. Quick to capitalize on a weakness, Diana persisted with her point-scoring. One of her favorite ways to goad him was to urge him to abandon the sport he loved. 'For heaven's sake, Charles, why don't you give up polo? You're just too old now.' Given her involvement with James Hewitt, an accomplished polo player, this was probably a little too much for the proud Prince to take. Even so, her barbed comments always silenced him, as he diplomatically chose to ignore her petulance.

By the autumn of 1987, relations between the Prince and Princess had reached an all-time low. By now, they were hardly speaking to each other. Diana, perhaps in a vain attempt to force her husband to take notice of her, seemed to revel in antagonizing him. He, in return, would barely acknowledge her existence. Inevitably, the Princess turned to James Hewitt for solace and support, and I have little doubt that without him she would have been unable to cope.

Yet while she may have been infatuated, she still had a job to do, with the result that she would sometimes go weeks without seeing her lover. I think she preferred it; it kept the relationship fresh, interesting and alive. Most of this I saw at first hand, for although technically I was still William and Harry's protection officer, I was increasingly chosen to stand in for Graham, as his illness began to take its toll.

Fate is often at its kindest when someone else is suffering its cruelty. As I pondered the possibility of switching to other duties within the Metropolitan Police, once my assignment heading up police protection for Princes William and Harry was completed, it intervened again. Tragic circumstances beyond my control changed the course of my life, and in doing so thrust me into the full glare of the royal spotlight. My friend and colleague, Chief Inspector Graham Smith, the Princess's senior personal protection officer, was suddenly taken ill. For weeks he had been complaining of a sore throat and bad cough. I had repeatedly urged him to see his doctor but he insisted that it would pass, adding that he did not want to make a fuss. To my horror, and that of many others, when he did eventually seek medical advice, he was diagnosed as suffering from throat cancer. At first, nobody realized quite how serious his condition was, and, typically, he stoically tried to soldier on, vowing that he would beat the disease. Yet although it was to be many agonizing months before Graham was to succumb finally to the cancer, it was soon obvious to everyone, including him, that he was incapable of continuing the active side of his duties full-time, and that he would have to drive a desk at the headquarters instead.

I was now in overall charge of all aspects of Diana's life. Among many other things, this meant that, whether she liked it or not, I would now have to know about all the extraneous aspects of her life, including the most private.

I first met James Hewitt at Knightsbridge Barracks in Central London in 1988 soon after my appointment as the Princess's personal protection officer. I had driven Diana to the barracks, accompanied by Hazel West, her lady-in-waiting, who was there in the role of respectable chaperone. A few minutes after arriving, James came strolling over to greet us, accompanied by another officer, a lieutenant. After some small talk about their riding lesson, Diana gestured to me and said, 'This is Ken. He has taken over from Graham and will be with me for some time.' James then proceeded to treat me to that slightly affected, slightly over-enthusiastic welcome which is one of the specialities of the British Army officer. It seemed a little absurd to me and confirmed my preconceived ideas about the so-called 'officer class'. Of course, they were not all public-school-educated buffoons, but many of them seemed to be excellent impersonations of that stereotype, although James's manners were always perfect.

For some reason, Hazel always brought a plastic container of cold sausages with her on such days, and would offer them to the men present, including me. Dutifully, Hewitt's fellow officer took one of the disgusting-looking sausages and munched on it. Hewitt did the same. I declined. As the lieutenant finished eating, swallowing it practically whole to avoid the horrible thing staying too long in his mouth, he said to the Princess, almost choking, 'May I say, my lady, that that was possibly the finest sausage I have ever tasted?' I rather wished I'd taken one of the beastly things, as it would have helped stifle my laughter.

Over the next few months I watched with interest as the romance began to unfold. James was used to the ever-present royal protection officers and was therefore relaxed in our company; I think he somehow believed that our being there meant that his relationship with Diana had been officially sanctioned. It may be that this gave him some comfort; at the very least, official sanction would mean that he no longer had to worry about committing treason. (It is said that a person who attempts sexual relations with a senior member of the royal family may, under certain circumstances, be charged with high treason.)

For all his cavalry-officer's mannerisms, James was a charming and very likeable man, and we hit it off straight away because we both knew our parameters. As soon as he realized that I was only concerned about the Princess's safety and not there to judge him, any concern he might have felt evaporated. For her part, Diana hoped that she had at last found a man whom she could trust. He injected excitement and youthful vitality into her life at a time when she really needed to be loved. This was something her husband found it impossible to do, even if he had been inclined to. Yet Charles was no fool. He knew what was going on between Hewitt and his wife, and it seems clear now that, after years of difficult marriage, he was very happy for it to continue. It suited him. In purely selfish terms I could see his reasoning. If another man was keeping his wife happy it meant less trouble for him. Diana craved attention, and, lacking it, was often spoiling for a fight. With James on the scene, however, she became mellow, more contented, and, most importantly for the Prince, less obsessed about his own friendship with Camilla Parker Bowles. Later, he claimed he only took up that liaison again after his marriage had irretrievably broken down. In reality I believe he had never stopped loving Camilla.

At first, Diana preferred not to talk openly to me about her affair. This was understandable, if a little disingenuous. Our journeys back to London from the West Country, where James's mother had a cottage that became the secret scene of most of their trysts, were often a little tense, and I could almost feel her embarrassment.

'Nothing is going on, Ken,' she would say, her face flushed red.

'Of course not, ma'am,' I would answer. 'Whatever you say. You know my only concern is for your safety.'

She must have thought that I was blind, or stupid, or both. After all, creaking floorboards in an old English cottage can speak louder than the most frank confession.

Despite the secrecy, however, her passion nearly brought disaster. On our journeys back to London, she would often take the wheel and, buoyed by the exhilaration of her secret love, had a tendency to drive too fast, frequently exceeding the legal speed limit. I repeatedly told her to slow down, but she would comply reluctantly. One incident, however, did make her more cautious in her driving, at least temporarily. As she raced back from one of her illicit meetings with Hewitt at around 100 mph, I spotted a patrol car following us at speed. The flashing blue light and the blare of the siren followed. Diana flushed scarlet with guilt as she began to pull over.

'Ken, you'll have to sort this out,' she said defiantly as we braked to a stop. The police car pulled up behind us, and I watched in the wing mirror as its driver climbed out, put on his cap, and walked towards us.

'Sorry, ma'am,' I said quietly, 'you're on your own. I have warned you about your speed, and I am not here to cover up this offense.'

The unfortunate traffic officer got the surprise of his life when he realized that he had stopped the Princess of Wales. I got out of the car, identified myself and had a quiet word with him, telling him that it was not my job to intervene in any way. He then asked me if I wanted to deal with it but, making sure we were out of the Princess's hearing, I told him that it was outside my jurisdiction and that it was entirely up to him as to how he chose to deal with the situation. Diana, with her eyes at their most doe-like and her head tilted sheepishly to one side, stepped out of the car and was then given a polite reprimand by the officer, who would have been entirely within his rights to report her. Being the Princess of Wales had its advantages, however. She escaped with a verbal caution and was told to slow down in future. I drove the rest of the way home and Diana, aware that explaining to her husband why she was in the West Country would have taken some doing, was certainly very relieved. For the next few weeks, at least, I noticed a distinct change in her driving style, although it was not long before she was back to her old speed-obsessed ways.

In those heady days the press did not really know the extent of the Princess's friendship with Hewitt; between us, we did a pretty good job of keeping it quiet. As a result, Diana gradually came to realize that it was easier to work with me than against me. Without any formal discussion of the subject she became more relaxed about the extent of my knowledge of her relationship. In short, she came to trust me.

The dishes were clattering away in the kitchen as the garlicky aroma of the Tuscan feast I was preparing oozed through the snug cottage. That evening I was chef as well as protection officer, in what the press would undoubtedly have called the 'love nest' of the Princess of Wales and her riding instructor – Sheiling Cottage, the Devon home of Shirley Hewitt, James's mother. The Princess and her lover sat together on the sofa, sipping home-made orange vodka purloined from Prince Charles's cellar at Highgrove. This was the safest of their safe houses. The evening was a riot of singing and risqué joke-telling, fuelled by the meal I had prepared. Even the Princess devoured every morsel. She was blissfully happy, and this contentment seemed to eradicate, if only temporarily, the bulimia that had plagued her throughout her adult life, especially since her marriage.

At around midnight I dealt the final hand in my poker game with James as the Princess went into the kitchen, rolled up her sleeves, and set to work on the mountain of washing up I had created. When she finished, she emerged from the kitchen and declared that it was time to retire. Within seconds she and James had disappeared up the creaky staircase to the master bedroom, leaving me to share a nightcap with Shirley. My berth was far less comfortable than the beds occupied by the rest of the house party, usually a camp bed or the couch. As I curled up with a blanket to cover me I could not help thinking how surreal my existence had become.

Diana was always the last to rise in the morning. By 8.30 Shirley would be in the kitchen preparing breakfast, helped by James, who would tactfully leave the Princess asleep in his bed. Eventually, Diana would emerge, her hair ruffled, and usually wearing a baggy jumper and tight-fitting jeans. A couple of mouthfuls of toast and a sip of piping hot tea would suffice for her breakfast, but she was always keen to be alone with James, and would hastily arrange for him to take her riding or for a walk. Their favorite haunts were the pebbled beach at Budleigh Salterton and an area of moorland known as Woodbury Common, where there was no real danger of her being recognized.

I am sure that James would have been quite happy to have stayed at home, but the Princess would insist on their going out. It was part of her way of feeling 'normal'. She knew that when she was in London she could not just go for a stroll whenever the mood took her, but this was rural Devon, and just doing ordinary things like going for a walk with her lover without me following behind made her feel good about herself. Of course, when they went off together either I, Allan Peters or Peter Brown, the other protection officers, would be in close contact. Even so, I could sympathize with Diana's craving for privacy, and I did my best to accommodate her without compromising her security. I insisted, however, that if we were not following them (rather bizarrely, like the chaperones to beautiful Italian maidens of old) they would keep in touch by taking with them a police radio tuned in to my frequency. This was pretty much the limit of our intrusion. For the rest of the time, Diana would disguise herself by wearing a headscarf, and since nobody expected to see her strolling along a windswept beach or across a piece of moorland she was never recognized.

As the affair progressed, the Princess and Hewitt inevitably became more brazen about their relationship. After a time I warned Diana that if she wanted to avoid detection they would both have to be careful. Unable to conceal my concern for her, I assured her that I would do my best to cover her tracks, but added that she had to be consistent. If she was forced to lie, she should make the lie as close to the truth as she could. She took my advice, using a form of code when telephoning ahead to James's mother to talk to him, or to let her know that she was coming, and sometimes even adopting a spurious cockney accent. On the whole, however, the more complex a deception plan, the less its chances of succeeding. The first time Diana used her false name it completely baffled Shirley Hewitt, who picked up the telephone to be greeted by a whispering, rather odd voice on the end of the line, obviously a woman's, asking to speak to James. When Shirley asked who it was, the woman said, 'Julia.' The name stuck. From that moment Diana became 'Julia', while among other codenames Highgrove became 'Low Wood'.

In terms of secrecy and security, the subterfuge was a total success. Although the media were aware of the rumors, no photographic or other concrete evidence of the affair ever materialized (until Hewitt himself decided to tell all), thanks largely to a concerted effort to be careful by all concerned. Diana, however, was always terrified about being found out, especially by the media, even warning me that if it came to it I would have to cover up for her. Once again, I gave her my word that I would do all I could. I could not help reflecting, however, that she was displaying a rather curious double standard, inveighing against her husband in private for conducting an adulterous affair, while desperately concealing the fact that she was herself guilty of the same behavior. Perhaps this was simply because she did not want to award the moral high ground to Charles.

Moreover, her impetuosity and passion could cause her to lose her common sense and walk a dangerous path.

It may never have been possible for the Princess of Wales and James Hewitt to enjoy an equal relationship, but both her chances of personal happiness and of maintaining the discretion of their liaison were compromised, in my view, by Diana's decision to fund, at least in part, her lover's lifestyle. I was appalled when she told me that Hewitt, who always seemed short of money – not altogether surprising in a 'smart' regiment where officers are still expected to maintain a high standard of living – had told her that he needed to buy a new car and that his army pay would not stretch to the TVR he wanted.

Diana had a hugely generous heart and decided to give him the cash. I bluntly told her that giving her lover the money would be a terrible mistake. I did not risk pointing out that it would perhaps border on conduct unbecoming an officer and a gentleman first to hint that he needed, and then to accept, such a sum from the Princess. However, I felt I had to remind her that the transaction could have dreadful consequences. If she was found out, the press would go into a feeding frenzy, and the Palace would have all the ammunition it needed in its support of Prince Charles. Some might even have misconstrued it as a payment to buy her lover's silence. With a willfulness when thwarted that I came to know well, Diana's response was to tell me that I was being paranoid. According to her, without a care in the world she withdrew $24,000 (£16,000) in cash, which was duly delivered by a bank official, and she said she put it in a briefcase to hand over to James Hewitt.

The affair brought other problems, not all of them of Diana's making. The constant malicious rumors, which still persist even now, long after her death, about the paternity of Prince Harry used to anger Diana greatly. After her separation from Prince Charles she freely, and even publicly, admitted to having had an affair with Hewitt; but those apparent 'friends' of the Prince of Wales who continue to whisper that Harry may be Hewitt's son should be ashamed of themselves, both for their allegations against a woman and her son, who cannot defend themselves, and for their mathematics. Only once did I ever discuss it with her, and Diana was in tears about it. On the whole she did not care what such people said about her, but if anybody turned on her sons it wounded her deeply. The nonsense should be scotched here and now. For one thing, the dates do not add up. Harry was born on 15 September 1984 – that is a matter of record. Diana did not meet James until the summer of 1986. And the red hair that gossips so love to cite as 'proof' is, of course, a Spencer trait, as anyone who has ever seen a photograph of, say, Diana's sister Jane as a young woman knows perfectly well.

At some point in our conversation, Diana admitted that, 'I don't know how my husband and I did have Harry because by then he had already gone back to his lady, but one thing that is absolutely certain is that we did.'

And I believe her absolutely.

For a time, at least, the affair not only exhilarated Diana, but lifted the spirits of everyone close to her. Her friends and supporters and most loyal assistants saw again something of the old Princess, still dutiful, but now with an air of purpose and gaiety about her. At last Diana was beginning to face her demons.

The unspoken 'understanding' between Charles and Diana meant that during the week the Prince rarely came to Kensington Palace, and they effectively used Highgrove at weekends on a rota basis, neither being there when the other was. James became a frequent visitor to both residences, and of course would stay the night, although all of us took care that his arrivals and departures were screened from prying eyes and, even more important, prying cameras. He would even join in the play fights I would have with William and Harry around the garden pool at Highgrove. Such was her state of domestic happiness that Diana simply roared with laughter when we once threw her into the pool fully clothed, making an almighty splash. There were, of course, times when her work commitments meant that she and James could not see each other. Her workload was heavy. She would have engagements at least three days a week, sometimes four. This kept me and her back-up office team busy, because for every visit there had to be a security reconnaissance, after which I had to write a report and briefing notes for the Princess. If I have given the impression that most of my work consisted of shepherding Diana to and from secret assignations, then I must add that it is a false one; the bread-and-butter of my job was the assessing of security and the protection of the Princess twenty-four hours a day.

In its elegant surroundings, the Royal Ballet School exudes an air of history and excellence. Children who join the prestigious $30,000-a-year (£20,000) boarding school dream of becoming stars on the international stage, just as Diana had as a girl. She had grown too tall to achieve her dream, but now that she was a princess she wanted to see exactly what went on there. As a result, she dispatched me and her then equerry, Patrick Jephson, to carry out a reconnaissance ahead of the visit, planned for two weeks later. The recce (as we called it) – the chance to survey a venue and assess the security implications ahead of a royal visit – was an essential part of the job. The fact that you were not accompanied by your royal principal made it much simpler, too.

As we were admitted to the school's inner hall we were greeted by a tiny, yet extremely elegant, woman who said, rather theatrically, 'Gentlemen, I have been expecting you. Do come in.'

This was the legendary prima ballerina Dame Merle Park, director of the school at White Lodge in the beautiful surroundings of Richmond Park, West London, but in her day one of the Royal Ballet's brightest stars. Her Autumn Fairy in Frederick Ashton's *Cinderella*, which she danced until the mid-1970s, has, according to the experts, never been surpassed. Other dancers envied her natural facility and innate musical sense, although she apparently saw nothing remarkable about her talents; 'I know it sounds trite, but I would have been just as happy dancing through a field of poppies,' she once famously remarked. Looking at this indomitable woman, whose slight frame belied an equally famous inner steeliness, I had no difficulty in believing that she had said that.

'I am so delighted that Her Royal Highness is paying us the honor of visiting the school. Everyone here is so thrilled – absolutely thrilled,' she enthused. Then, with the niceties out of the way, we got on with the job in hand, walking the route the Princess would take, to ensure that she would encounter no surprises, or be placed in any sort of risky situation.

'I propose to introduce the Princess first to Dame Ninette de Valois, our founder and Governor,' she began. This was another of the great names in ballet: Ninette de Valois made her stage début in 1914, and toured with Diaghilev in the 1920s, becoming one of the pioneers of British ballet, and a choreographer and teacher of enormous distinction. At once, Patrick started taking meticulous notes so that he could draft a full factsheet to brief the Princess.

'Then we will proceed through the Salon, where our Director of Music, Mr Blackford, will be holding a practical music class with the First Form,' she said, flinging the door open to make a dramatic entrance.

'Then, gentlemen, we will go through the Library, where the Princess will see children working with Mr John. Next into the Pavlova Studio and then on to Forms Four and Five, where the fifth-year students being taught by Monsieur Anatole Grigoriev are engaged in some French oral.'

At this point, I'm ashamed to say, Patrick and I were overtaken by an attack of the giggles. Dame Merle, realizing that her words might have been misconstrued by her two inane male guests, icily remarked,

'I see, gentlemen. Perhaps I ought to rephrase that?'

Two weeks later when we returned with the Princess Dame

Merle made no such slip of the tongue, although, knowing the Princess's sense of humor, I am sure that she too would have been unable to resist laughing. None the less, the visit was a triumphant success, and I could glimpse in Diana's excitement and enthusiasm something of the girl who had once longed to dance.

For some reason, at about this time Diana seemed to have to perform an unusual number of engagements out of town in Devon and Cornwall (the Prince of Wales is, of course, also Duke of Cornwall, with considerable land holding in the West Country). She was, however, far too professional to mix royal business with personal pleasure, despite the fact that James Hewitt's country home, in the shape of his mother's cottage, was also in the West Country. There was, though, one pleasure in which she freely indulged. Perhaps oddly, for a woman who, it would later be claimed, was a martyr to bulimia she usually had a healthy appetite. As a consequence, whenever we went to official engagements in the West Country the Princess was always keen to get hold of some clotted cream and Cornish pasties – proper ones, not the pale imitations sold in London. Pasties were among her favorite snacks, and she also liked to bring some back for her sons. So invariably my first job on arrival for our visit was to instruct my counterpart from the local Special Branch, Detective Inspector Peter Rudd, who justifiably believed that he was there to counter a possible terrorist threat or worse, with his first mission of the day – to ensure that the Princess had a box of Cornish pasties and some clotted cream to take back with her.

On one occasion, however, DI Rudd took this assignment rather too seriously. Instead of returning with the customary half-dozen pasties and a pot of cream, he sent a local distributor into a frenzy when he turned up brandishing his badge and telling the manager that the Princess loved Cornish pasties and clotted cream. He returned from his mission with several boxes, each containing two dozen pasties, and two giant vats of clotted cream. As we flew back to London on a BAe146 of the Queen's Flight, the aircrew looked a little surprised by our cargo – it looked as though we had just made a royal visit to the local supermarket. There were so many pasties that when we got back to Kensington Palace Diana decided to hand them out to the policemen on the gate, and thereafter we were rather more cautious about instructing police officers to gather local delicacies.

Most trips out of London took a day or less, but often enough we would travel farther afield, necessitating a stay away from Kensington Palace. When accompanying the Princess on an 'awayday' as she called regional visits, we would often use the Royal Train, which, after HMY *Britannia*, is the grandest form of royal transport, its old Pullman carriages and opulent long dining room easily putting the Orient Express to shame. For long journeys the train would leave late in the evening and, at a suitably secure place en route, pull into a siding so the royal personage on board could eat and, more importantly, sleep in comfort before carrying out a day-long visit in whichever region of the country was being visited. I was stood down on those occasions as the British Transport Police would surround the carriages and provide night security, while a static corridor man from our department kept watch inside the train.

We had just such a journey to Cheshire in July 1988, the train stopping short of our destination to allow the Princess a decent night's sleep. Next morning, however, she came to breakfast looking haggard and somewhat disheveled. She clearly had not slept well.

'Are you all right, ma'am? You look a little out of sorts,' I said, as I tucked into an enormous English breakfast in the elegant surroundings of the long dining car.

'Well, not really, Ken, I didn't sleep a wink.'

'Why not, ma'am?'

'Well . . . there was a man outside my window marching up and down all night,' she replied. There was an edge to her voice that boded ill for the nocturnal marcher.

Listening, I found I could indeed hear the sound of regular footsteps crunching past the window on the gravel bed of the permanent way. Curious, I went to find out what was going on. Outside, to my surprise, I spotted a uniformed constable of the British Transport Police pacing his way alongside the train.

'Excuse me!' I yelled. 'What on earth do you think you're doing?'

The startled officer came to an abrupt halt mid-step and said; 'Well . . . I'm engaged in security, sir.'

'Fine, but why do you have to march on the bloody gravel? If you must march up and down, would you do it on the bloody grass – there's a thousand acres of it out there to march about on,' I replied sternly.

At this point the Princess, who had followed me to the carriage door, began to giggle as I continued to give the unfortunate chap a dressing down. Then, in typical Diana fashion, she decided to defend the man she had dispatched me to admonish.

'Ken, don't be too harsh – he's got a job to do.'

# Chapter 4

ONLY A FEW WEEKS AFTER MY APPOINTMENT I had my first taste of life working alongside the Princess abroad. It proved to be a crucial, perhaps even a defining moment in our relationship. Fourteen summers and seemingly a lifetime ago on a cliff-top with breathtaking views of Palma, the principal city of Majorca, she and I sat talking beside a swimming pool in the heat of the mid-afternoon sun. The pool was in a courtyard within a magnificent palace complex and the Prince and Princess were there as the guests of King Juan Carlos of Spain. To an onlooker, our conversation must have appeared to be intense. Occasionally, I would try to lighten the mood, and our discussion would then be broken by her laughter. Within seconds, however, she would turn serious again.

'After Harry was born our marriage just died,' Diana said in hushed, conspiratorial tones. There was genuine sadness in her brilliant blue eyes, but, although my heart went out to her, I simply nodded and said nothing.

'What could I do?' she continued. 'I tried, I honestly tried, but he just did not want me. He just wanted her, always her. Do you know, I don't think I *ever* stood a chance.' It did not take a detective to understand that the 'he' referred to the Prince of Wales, and the 'her' to his mistress, Camilla Parker Bowles.

Now and again, Diana, wearing a bright orange bikini, would lean back on her sunbed and run her fingers though her blonde hair as she soaked up the sun. Still new to this job, I was surprised at the informmality. That hypothetical onlooker might easily have mistaken us for man and wife, or perhaps even people who had once been lovers. As fanciful as this may seem, it was not that far from the truth, for our burgeoning relationship was certainly destined to become very close. Indeed, together we would share more experiences than many people do in a lifetime.

She sighed, her eyes closed against the harsh light. 'Do you know,' she declared. 'I really think it is time I spread my wings.'

Had this statement been made by any other woman struggling to come to terms with her failing marriage it would have been cause enough for concern, but that it was made by the Princess of Wales meant that it had far greater resonance, promising repercussions that would go to the core of the British Establishment.

This was perhaps the most crucial moment in my relationship with Diana. As that relationship evolved over the coming years such intimacy would become commonplace, but our poolside conversation at the King of Spain's summer home, the Marivent Palace in Majorca, proved to be a milestone. Its importance lay in the fact that this was the first time that the Princess had confided in me, revealing the dark clouds looming in her life. I admit that, at the time, I felt a little uncomfortable as she poured out her troubles, although such familiarity was soon to become part of my daily life. I realized, however, that this was no chance encounter. The Princess had contrived the meeting earlier that day, after Prince Charles had left the palace for an engagement. Once alone, she had picked up the phone in her private suite and called the hotel where I was staying, a few miles away in Palma.

'Ken, can you come and see me, please? It is rather important,' she said when I answered. There was an air of urgency to her voice, which immediately led me to ask if she was worried about her personal security, that being, after all, the reason for my presence on the island. She assured me that she was safe, but added that she would prefer to speak to me face to face, as what she wanted to discuss was a sensitive matter. Telling her that I would be there as soon as possible, I left the hotel and, a few minutes later, arrived at the gates of the palace where the Spanish sentry on guard, who had been told to expect me, gestured for me to proceed. A second or two later an immaculately attired royal official, clad in a dark uniform of heavy cloth clearly unsuited to the warm climate, escorted me to the pool area, where the Princess was waiting. She got up from the sunbed where she had been relaxing to greet me.

'Hallo, Ken, it is so good of you to come,' she said, adding, 'I am so sorry I dragged you away.' I said 'Good afternoon, ma'am,' and told her that I had not been busy, and so had not minded being 'dragged away'.

I had not been her senior protection officer for long, and so I was a little uneasy about her reasons for asking me there; she was, after all, perfectly safe within the confines of the palace, with its numerous military and police guards. I sensed almost at once that she needed someone to talk to, and she did not feel that there was anyone in her entourage, or the Prince's, in whom she could confide. Although her surroundings were luxurious, she felt trapped and friendless. I suppose that, under the circumstances, she felt that I was her best option.

'It's awful, Ken. Juan Carlos is frightfully charming but – you know – a little too attentive. He is very tactile. I told my husband, and he says I am just being silly.' She paused for a moment, then added, 'Do you know Ken, I think the King quite fancies me. I know it sounds absurd, but I'm sure it's true,' she declared, a mischievous smile dancing across her face.

For once, I was lost for words. Utterly confused as to how to respond, I made a pathetic attempt to appear unfazed by what the Princess had said. Was she really suggesting that I should have a quiet word with the King of Spain about being over-friendly? I was not sure then, or even now, whether she was joking, for her sense of humor could be wicked. Almost immediately, however, the conversation switched to matters that clearly troubled her more, and I began to realize the full extent of her personal unhappiness. Her tone was calm, and there was no malice in what she said, just a kind of weary acceptance. She explained that she had only agreed to accompany her husband to Majorca in an attempt to put on a 'good show' – she wanted, she said, to show the world that she was happy to be on holiday with her husband, whom she still loved. Above all, she wanted happiness and security for her sons, and she knew that, to achieve them, the boys needed a stable life that included both their parents.

It struck me that she was speaking with complete honesty when she ruefully admitted, 'You know, I don't go out of my way to be awkward, Ken, but my husband just makes things impossible.

'I used to blame myself, to hate myself. I used to think it was my fault, that I was not good enough. Nobody [I believe she meant no one in the royal family] ever praised me, can you believe that? After all I've done for that family.'

As she spoke, Diana began to paint an unsettling picture of isolation and rejection. I knew that the marriage was in a terrible state – no one in her ambit, or the Prince's, could fail to know that – but I found it disturbing that she was prepared to talk so openly about it. I was not even employed by her, or the royal family, but by Scotland Yard; either she was desperately short of sympathetic listeners, or she felt that she simply had to confide in someone she trusted, however new to her circle. In the same quiet, almost emotionless voice, she went on to explain that the gulf between her and Prince Charles was now so wide that nothing could bridge it. For her, she told me, loving a man who did not love her in return – and worse, loved someone else – was tearing her apart. I sympathized, but felt helpless to advise or guide her. It would, in any case, have been presumptuous for me to do so, and besides, instinct told me that all she really wanted was someone to listen to her. I had heard her dismissed in royal circles as a silly girl, but this was not the immature rambling of someone in love with the idea of being in love. I had only to hear her talking in this way to appreciate that this was a woman experiencing pain to her very core. Yet as she recounted her fears for the future – her own and her sons' – the feeling of worthlessness that Charles's unrepentant infidelity engendered in her, and her overwhelming sense of marital claustrophobia, I could sense the weight lifting from her. I realized that, just by letting me hear her wretched confession, she was finding a kind of solace.

I am not, I hope, a callous man, and I was genuinely shocked by her confidences, just as I was flattered by the trust she seemed to have placed in me. What she had told me was explosive, the kind of secret that could not be shared with even the closest of friends. Diana's misery could not be said to affect her security, but if it were ever to become common knowledge the lid would be blown off the Prince of Wales's marriage, with who knew what consequences for his wife, his children, the Queen and her family, even for the monarchy itself.

Then, for the first time in my hearing, she spoke what I would come to think of as one of her trademark expressions. 'Nobody understands me, Ken,' she said, although I felt I was beginning to. And, however self-pitying the remark, I was beginning to think she was right.

It is important to view our conversation in perspective. It

preceded the publication of Andrew Morton's ground-breaking book, *Diana: Her True Story*, by four years, and although, even then, in 1988, the national press was beginning to question the state of the Prince and Princess's marriage nobody had come close to exposing the dark reality. That would come only when Morton's exposé of the Waleses' relationship, and of the less than creditable parts played in it by some members of the royal family and by the Palace apparatchiks, appeared in 1992.

Diana had not finished with me yet. 'Do you know we have not slept in the same bed for years, Ken?' she admitted, not without a touch of embarrassment. As she said this, I could not escape the feeling that, deep down, she believed that the estrangement was her fault. Then, long before the rest of the world was to learn how her depression had driven her to try to commit suicide (no matter how half-heartedly), she listed the occasions when she had tried to take her own life, and the reasons why: 'It was a cry for help, Ken, but nobody ever wanted to listen,' she whispered.

As she talked, I had become increasingly aware that this was a very unhappy young woman indeed. Yet I remained unsure as to her reasons for confiding in me. Was it a test, a way to see if she could trust me? Was it simply, as I had at first thought, that she needed to tell somebody or otherwise go mad under the emotional and psychological strain? Or did she so desperately need an ally, faced as she was with an indifferent husband, an inimical Palace hierarchy, and the hostile coterie that made up Prince Charles's 'Highgrove set'? Throughout the hour or so we sat and talked she repeatedly returned to the core problem – her husband's relationship with Camilla. She believed that his flagrant, even brutal, disregard for her feelings was a betrayal, the greatest of her young life; and, I have come to believe, that it was one from which she never recovered. She was unable to contain her tears as she recounted her story. There was no vindictiveness in what she said, just a pervading sense of misery. I felt terribly awkward, sitting next to a woman who should have had so much to live for, but who instead was quietly describing her personal despair. Despite her beauty, position and wealth it was clear that life had dealt her a cruel hand. I knew, of course, that there are always at least two sides to every story, but even so my heart went out to her and, perhaps against my better judgment, I told her so. I also gently reminded her that she had much to be thankful for, not least two sons of whom she could be immensely proud. At the very mention of their names her sadness seemed to lift and the smile returned, lighting up her face.

'You are so right, Ken. I am so lucky. William and Harry are so precious, so very precious.'

Aware that, because of her confidences, I was on dangerous ground, I gently tried to move off the subject of her marriage, with all its problems. Perhaps selfishly, I felt that at this early stage in our professional relationship what the Princess was telling me was simply too hot to handle. I defy anyone, however – even those critics who now so clinically blame her difficulties on the state of her mental health, insisting that she was suffering from 'Borderline Personality Disorder' – to feel anything but sympathy for her. Even so, I had to tell her that I felt uneasy about being embroiled in her unraveling marriage. She was not used to people speaking to her with such frankness, and it may be that she appreciated my candor; in any event I managed to conveniently switch the topic to our mutual love of classical music. Clearly she understood perfectly what I was trying to do, as sensitive as she could be to other people, and responded accordingly.

Diana's problems and her personal sadness were subjects the two of us would discuss time and again over the next few years. There would be moments of great happiness, too, for she was not given to wallowing in self-pity, or at least not for long. On that afternoon in Majorca I had answered her call for help (that I had little choice in the matter would not have occurred to her). From then on, she felt she could trust me; in time I hoped she would respect my advice. Our working relationship, as well as the friendship that developed subsequently, was rooted in the sense of mutual trust that brought us together in the Marivent Palace and I knew that, as a result, I would have a better chance of effectively protecting her from danger, and perhaps even from herself. For if the Princess knew that she could confide in me, no matter how great or how sensitive the secret, then there was no reason for her not to tell me exactly what she was doing or planned to do at all times.

Our private tête-à-tête came to an abrupt end when the Princess suddenly spotted the Queen of Spain's sister walking towards us across the courtyard. I thought this the perfect opportunity to make my excuses and return to the safety and solitude of my hotel room. It proved a vain hope. In an instant Diana's mood was transformed. Her despondency vanished (or at least, being the consummate actress she was, she was able to mask it) and she began making polite conversation as though she had no cares, no secrets, no sadness of her own. Moments later, without allowing me the hint of a warning, she repaid me for my attempts to switch our earlier conversation away from her troubles to my passion for music. Before I knew what was happening she suggested that I give an impromptu singing performance for Queen Sophia's sister, an elegant and refined woman who, I am sure, would have preferred not to have to endure what was to follow. I was flabbergasted when the giggling Princess suddenly leapt to her feet, turned to the unfortunate woman and announced, 'Ken has a wonderful singing voice. He wants to sing us a song.' Then to me, 'Go on, Ken – it would be wonderful if you'd sing for us,' she gushed.

Pushed reluctantly into the limelight, there was nothing I could do except take a deep breath and sing one of my personal favorites ('Myself When Young' from *The Rubáiyát of Omar Khayyám*, arranged by Lisa Lehmann). To add to my embarrassment, however, Queen Sophia arrived at the pool midway through my rendition, my first, (although as it turned out, not my only) Royal Command performance. My considerable efforts – by now I was scarlet from the heat, the exertion and the embarrassment – earned polite applause from my audience, followed by an equally polite call for an encore which I tactfully declined. Hot and breathless, I said my goodbyes and left the royal presences, the Princess by now chatting amiably with her hostess. As I walked away, however, I caught Diana's eye, at which she mouthed the words 'Thank you' to me, and smiled. Making my way back to my hotel room to the sound of cicadas and the rustle of bougainvillea in the warm breeze, I could not help laughing about my mercurial new principal. So this is what it is really like to be protection officer to the most famous woman in the world, I thought.

If nothing else, my solo effort that afternoon brought a result that I could never normally have hoped for. The Princess had seemed captivated by my interest in music. She said that she was fascinated by opera, which she said stirred her emotionally, but admitted that she did not fully understand it. Enthused, I spoke of my own passion for the art and, that evening, gave her a copy of *Understanding Opera*, which she devoured. Moreover, my performance had led her and Queen Sophia into discussing their mutual love of music, and their admiration for the great opera singers. As a result, the Queen invited us to go to see José Carreras perform on the following day, the first time the singer had appeared in public since his recovery from leukemia. The Princess joked that, after listening to my effort, it would be a real privilege to hear another great tenor. Horrified by this comparison, I pointed out rather woodenly that I was actually a baritone.

Next day, 15 August, the Princess and I, with Queen Sophia, her sister, and the queen's aide, flew in the King's private jet to Barcelona, leaving Prince Charles behind. After landing, our car formed part of a huge convoy, mainly of police, which first took us to a village on the outskirts of the city, where we visited a friend of the Queen in a very small house overlooking a beautiful square, in which a colorful and elaborately decorated dais had been built. On that makeshift stage, once the niceties were over, the magnificent Montserrat Caballé (whose work became more widely known to the general public after her brilliant rendition of 'Barcelona' with the late Freddie Mercury, lead singer of Queen) performed a series of Puccini arias. It was an exquisite performance. Diana was inspired not only by the singing, but by the spontaneity of the moment; alive with anticipation, she was as enlivened I had ever seen her. At the end the diva joined us at a reception, during which she and the Princess chatted like old friends.

This, as it turned out, was only the beginning. We returned to the cars and the royal convoy then headed for a castle in Barcelona, where Diana attended another reception (with me, as usual, never more than a pace or two away). It was here that Diana first met the soccer player and England international Gary Lineker. At the time he was the top striker for Barcelona, although he was by no means a typical soccer star. He had considerable natural charm, and the Princess enjoyed flirting with him.

Once the reception was over we walked with Gary to our seats in the auditorium within the castle precincts, where José Carreras was about to start the concert. I have never seen a performance so faultless, nor so professional. If the great tenor had any nerves he did not show them – and this, remember, was his first appearance in public after a long lay-off resulting from his gallant struggle against a terrifying disease. His performance was absolutely astounding and the finale left the audience in a frenzy of appreciation. Eventually, he encored 'Granada' five times, with the ecstatic crowd showering him with flowers, so that by the end he was knee deep in rose petals.

After the performance we were escorted to yet another reception, this one held in honor of Carreras. Even without her trademark high heels, Diana towered over him, as she did many of the famous people she met in the course of her royal duties, but his sheer presence commanded the entire room. He exuded a charisma to which she seemed drawn like iron to a magnet. She had obviously studied the book I had given her the night before, determined not to appear ignorant in front of the great man. She asked him several very astute questions about opera and the art of singing it, and told him that she had been thrilled by his performance of 'Granada'.

On the return flight back to Palma Diana was elated, bubbling over with the day's excitements. The gloom of the previous day had dissolved, so that she seemed a completely different person. For someone whose private world was in turmoil and whose life was full of confusion she was, for a few brief hours, wholly inspired.

It may be that our conversation in the Marivent Palace, and the long hours she must have spent turning her problems over in her mind, had determined the Princess on the course she would take, failing marriage or not. Certainly, that autumn, while she and the Prince were at Balmoral, the Queen's Highland estate in Aberdeenshire, she resolved to make a fresh start. She decided she had let herself down, made too many 'cock-ups', as she bluntly called them, and announced privately to me that she was going to take her royal responsibilities much more seriously.

'I've got a job and I'm bloody well going to get on with it,' she said as I accompanied her on a walk along the River Dee, the great salmon river that runs through the Balmoral estate.

'It makes me sick, ' she went on. 'Everybody says I loathe this place' – looking around at the rolling Scottish countryside, the trees bathed in the browns and rusty orange of autumn – 'But it's not the place. I love Scotland. It's just the pervading atmosphere generated by those Germans [her in-laws] that drains me,' she said, pointing towards the vast mock castle that her husband's great-great-great grandfather, Prince Albert of Saxe-Coburg-Gotha, the Consort of Queen Victoria, had designed and built. I knew by then that she invariably went to Balmoral determined to be strong, and returned running on empty, emotionally exhausted by her troubled marriage and the claustrophobia of living with the royal family at close quarters.

I felt there was no doubt that James Hewitt's role in Diana's life had Prince Charles's unspoken agreement. So when the Life Guards officer received an invitation to the Prince's fortieth birthday party in November 1988, all his fears of being beheaded for the treasonable act of sleeping with the wife of the heir to the British throne seemed to evaporate. Less flippantly, he seemed to feel that his affair was looked on, if not with favor, then at least with acceptance, by those in the royal family who knew about it. He began to relax more, while everyone close to Diana, perhaps even the Prince himself, seemed gratified, if not relieved, by the fact that she appeared to be much more content. Deep down, however, as she told me, she felt that there was something tawdry in the reality that both she and her husband had secret relationships, and for the sake of the country – or at least of the monarchy – they had to continue to live this lie.

For myself, I became quite fond of James. I thought he was a typically nice cavalry officer. After a while, however, he seemed to become troubled by the emotional demands Diana placed upon him. I remember once, during a particularly quiet afternoon at Sheiling Cottage, at least for me, he tried to escape from her.

'Ken, I need some time off,' he said. 'The Princess can be so demanding.' I smiled but said nothing, wondering just how many men would have given anything to change places with him.

In truth, however, the Princess of Wales's romance with Captain James Hewitt was already beginning to wane. For despite her lover's considerable attentions, Diana still craved more in her life. She began to see him less and less, and when he called would blame her work commitments for the long gaps between their meetings. As I have said, she seemed to ignore her own infidelity, but would explode with rage at Charles's relationship, and once again became obsessed with her husband's friendship with Camilla Parker Bowles, no matter how discreetly he behaved. I have to say that hypocrisy of this nature was her métier. In Diana's mind, perversely, there was no contradiction in her behavior, which gives an insight into her complex character. It was not my place, however, to highlight such sanctimony, although I was perfectly placed to do so, since I, perhaps more than anyone else, knew exactly the nature of her relationships with the handsome young men whose attentions she – naturally – encouraged.

# Chapter 5

THERE CAN BE NO QUESTION that when they worked together, Charles and Diana generated a prodigious energy. It seemed to those who operated in their slipstream – the Palace hierarchy, their respective staffs, and professional 'royal watchers' like writers and journalists – that as the public face of the royal family they were unsurpassable. Sadly, by the late 1980s their joint appearances had become increasingly rare, and I and others close to them could only watch as their personal relationship deteriorated still further. They even instructed their aides to compile their respective diaries in such a way as to restrict their joint engagements to the occasional film première at Leicester Square or such setpiece royal events as the Queen's Birthday Parade ('Trooping the Colour'), Royal Ascot, the Garter Ceremony at Windsor, Remembrance Sunday and the annual staff lunch at Christmas. Joint trips abroad also began to dwindle at around this time as the Princess, honoring the commitment she had made at Balmoral in the autumn of 1988, decided it was time to spread her wings and go solo.

By the beginning of 1989 the battle lines had been clearly drawn up between the two camps, and the Waleses' household was not a place for the fainthearted. To the outside world everything in the royal garden was rosy. In reality, the flowers had died and the petals long since fallen – all that was left were sharp, uncompromising thorns. The more astute commentators outside royal circles already sensed that something was very wrong with Charles and Diana's relationship.

Without naming the couples' respective lovers, even broadsheet newspapers like the *Sunday Times* had already printed articles surmising that Diana, like royal wives throughout history, had accepted the time-honored royal option of a cool and arranged marriage in which the husband, at least, could largely behave as he wished, provided he were discreet and attended to his royal duties. In effect they were saying that she had settled for a business relationship; in actual fact, however, they were wrong. For Diana, partly schooled as she was in the romantic novels of her step-grandmother, Barbara Cartland, had never stopped believing in the Holy Grail of true love. To her, there was no reason why her husband should behave so coolly and, arguably, even cruelly towards her. Perhaps the romantic Diana was right; but the realists among her inner circle led her to think that to strive for that ideal must inevitably lead to disappointment and pain.

By now the media's love affair with Diana was also beginning to wane, just as the spice was beginning to go out of her liaison with her lover, James Hewitt. For some – to me – inexplicable reason Sarah, Duchess of York, had become the new darling of the media. It proved to be a brief interlude, for the honeymoon period could not and did not last, and it was not long before 'the Redhead', as Diana called her sister-in-law (Sarah, in return, referred to Diana disparagingly as 'the Blonde'), fell out of favor too. Her arrival on the scene some three years earlier had been a mixed blessing for the Princess. At first she had regarded the extravert Duchess as an ally and a friend, but their initial closeness dissolved when Diana began to view Sarah as a potential threat to her own popularity. Each woman disliked competition, especially in terms of press coverage, from the other, and both were capable of becoming almost hysterical with rage and frustration if one was thought to have received more, or more favorable, notice in the media than the other. Diana would even purposely arrange extra engagements to clash with the Duchess's so that she could upstage her rival. As a result, the bad press, mostly about her relationship with Prince Charles, that started to come her way early in 1989 baffled and infuriated the Princess. She could not understand why reporters, many of whom she had come to know on first-name terms, had taken to writing such damning things.

Sometimes she would vent her feelings to me when we were alone together. 'It's their job – it's what they get paid for,' I would explain, holding back from saying that what the journalists were writing was actually a slightly under-spun version of the truth. If they had printed the real story – affairs, estrangement and all – then all hell would have broken loose. To the public, and to many journalists and commentators, she was still the glamorous wife of the heir to the throne, the mother of two fine boys, and the most popular member of the royal family, with the possible exception of the Queen Mother. The world did not want to learn that there were feet of clay at the end of those famously elegant legs.

Soon, I knew, it would be impossible to keep the lid on the truth. For the time being, however, as Diana traveled the country, or smiled her way through several overseas tours, the crowds were content to believe in the myth of a princess as happy and fulfilled as she was beautiful. For her part, Diana's own deepening unhappiness led her to seek solace from those worse off than herself. Despite living in comfort, she empathized with the sick, the poor and the desperate, seeming to draw strength from their pain, and genuinely anxious to share their misfortune. Yet as the more cynical newspaper columnists began to turn on her, the great Diana road-show, dependent as it was on the media, was in danger of becoming unstuck, with its star turn coming to be regarded as a disaffected woman unable or unwilling to support her hard-working husband.

Diana instinctively knew that she had to transform her public image from fashion clothes-horse to charity workhorse if she were to have any chance of winning the publicity war, either against the royal family as a whole, or against individual members, especially Prince Charles and the Duchess of York. More importantly, she knew that reaching out to society's untouchables was the right thing for her to do, not because it would win her points with the press and public, but because she knew that she could help them – she could, as she herself put it, 'make a difference'. The change in her was immediately apparent during the visit she and the Prince made to Indonesia in 1989. Even before the pre-visit security review she had insisted that the official program should include a visit to a leprosy hospital in Sitanala, on the outskirts of the capital, Jakarta.

The scene that greeted her inside the hospital was hellish, like an Old Testament vision rendered by one of the grimmer Flemish painters of the fifteenth century. It was a place where she found it difficult not to weep, where sufferers lived in the patient acceptance of a terrible, wasting disease, made the more terrible because it is so obvious and so visible.

As others in her entourage reeled away, almost too horrified to look, Diana, a woman born to a life of privilege, seemed to be truly inspired. She instinctively knew that she could help, could focus the world's attention on a disease that to most people in the West owed more to biblical times than to the twentieth century. She was driven by the photo call, although not in any self-serving way. She knew what the images of her with these tragic victims would achieve.

She was right. The impact was astonishing. Leprosy, until she embraced its cause, was hardly a fashionable concern. Once Diana took up the fight, money poured in to the leprosy charities, such was the impact of her patronage.

The Princess's success with causes was not reflected in her marriage. As Charles's behavior towards her cooled to the point of freezing, so her passion for charity work reached new heights. Journalists, who until then had focused on what she looked like or what she was wearing, began to use the phrase 'Caring Di' in their reports.

In March 1989, the Prince and Princess made an official visit to Dubai, one of the small sheikhdoms that together comprise the United Arab Emirates. Tension was already beginning to grow in the Gulf region as Saddam Hussein, President of Iraq, rattled his saber with threats to 'reclaim' Iraq's southern neighbor, Kuwait. Before we left, Prime Minister Margaret Thatcher had personally advised Prince Charles against playing in a polo match in the desert, which he had originally agreed to do, because MI6 had warned of assassination threats by fanatical Iranians. (The eight-year war between Iran and Iraq had ended the previous year, but many Iranians were angered by the support given to Iraq during that conflict by Western nations, notably America and Britain.) With this backdrop the mood among the royal party was somber, and Colin Trimming, the Prince's protection officer and my immediate superior, and I knew that we would have to be especially vigilant. Eventually the Prince pulled out of the match, spending the afternoon kicking his heels in the Sheikh's heavily guarded palace in the capital, while people who had paid $300 (£200) a head to watch him play voiced their disappointment. The Prince's decision annoyed his hosts, who accused the British government of overreacting, Dubai's Minister of Protocol, Humaid Bin Drai, remarking angrily, 'Your Prince was perfectly safe with us. We discovered no threat to his security. I do not know where the British Government get their information from.'

Whatever their feelings about the polo match, our hosts could not have been more hospitable. When Dubai's ruler, Sheikh Rashid al-Maktoum, heard that the Princess's scheduled British Airways return flight was delayed by two hours, he told her that he could not bear to think of her being put to such inconvenience and placed his personal jumbo jet at her disposal to take her home. Within a short time the vast Boeing 747, painted in the red-and-white livery of the Dubai flag, was ready for take-off with, besides the crew, only the Princess, myself, her hairdresser and her press spokesman on board. Thanks to the Sheikh, we arrived back at Heathrow at dawn the following morning. To have hired a jumbo would have cost tens of thousands of pounds, compared to a first-class return ticket which, then, cost $1,482 (£988) (and for which the British taxpayer footed the bill).

Although, privately, the Prince and Princess remained at logger-heads, publicly the outward show of togetherness continued. None the less, the situation within their marriage had gone from bad to worse by the time the couple set out on an official tour of Hungary. As it would turn out, Hungary was to be one of their last great acts of togetherness. Amazingly, the press swallowed the Palace spin and focused on how well Charles and Diana appeared to be getting on. That was in public; behind closed doors, however, nothing could have been further from the truth. Perhaps Fleet Street's finest cynics had been overcome by the history and romance of the setting, and by the tour's timing. After all, the communist system was collapsing in Russia and all over Eastern Europe, and the beautiful city of Budapest and its artistic people were once again free from authoritarianism. It is even possible that the wonderful romance of the place and the moment had an effect on the Prince and Princess, although I doubt it.

Diana the consummate actress could put on a show; but Diana the private person could not and would not live a lie. She felt that she was now ready to take center stage in her own right, to star in her own solo show. It was of no concern to her if this meant that the old stagers, the other senior members of the royal family, suffered by comparison with her glittering star. Indeed, to her, this upstaging of the *ancien régime* made her solo performance all the more rewarding. Such trivialities aside, however, she knew that her public persona carried with it tremendous power, a power that she could harness to help to change the world and the plight of its people for the better.

In any evaluation of the Princess's achievements, the part she played in focusing the public's attention on the terrible disease AIDS, promoting awareness, understanding and even compassion, must be among her greatest. With one handshake, she did more to dispel, almost overnight, the myth that the disease can be caught through simply touching a victim than a thousand press conferences given by the most eminent and convincing doctors. Diana knew her power and reveled in it, and, as with leprosy, the struggle to help AIDS sufferers the world over became almost a religion to her. She felt driven to help these people, but it was a risky crusade, for it brought criticism from within 'the Firm', as insiders referred to the royal family, and especially its senior members.

I once had to console the Princess as she broke down in tears as we were driving back to Kensington Palace after a meeting with the Queen at Buckingham Palace. She was always very nervous of the Queen. At first, she told me, she had been welcomed into the family, and believed that Her Majesty was a great supporter of hers. For her part, the Queen knew that, if handled with care, the young Princess was a great asset to the royal family, if not the jewel in its crown, then certainly the sparkle on its diadem. By the time I joined her team, however, Diana had come to be viewed by the Palace as a serious and escalating problem, moving Prince Philip to state his belief that she needed to be handled with care. In truth, she had become a thorn in the side of the monarchy. To put it simply, she outshone or overshadowed the rest of the Firm, including her husband, something that irritated Prince Charles considerably.

So when she embarked on her mission to rid the world of ignorance and prejudice about AIDS, at a time when little was known about the disease by the general public, it seriously worried the Queen and her advisers, according to Diana. Members of the royal family, especially beautiful princesses married to the heir to the throne, should, the Palace felt, steer clear of controversy. Perhaps, in their eyes, becoming the champion of AIDS sufferers was one step too far from the accepted royal duties of smiling at babies or patients in hospitals, visiting old people and schools, opening factories or launching ships, or making royal tours of foreign countries to boost British business interests. AIDS was dangerous territory, and the Palace believed that Diana's involvement could backfire on the House of Windsor.

It was not unusual for me to have to console a tearful Princess, for she could be highly emotional. This time, however, she said that she had good reason to weep. During their interview, the Queen had told apparently told Diana, in no uncertain terms, that although she admired her courage and conviction in confronting and publicizing the AIDS issue, she thought her daughter-in-law was misguided. Drawing on her own years of experience, it would seem that she had warned Diana that she was in danger of letting the cause envelop her, so that she would come to be seen only as the champion of what many people still regarded as a 'gay plague'.

After her tense meeting with the Queen Diana had emerged, distraught, into the palace forecourt, where I was waiting with the car. Sobbing, she blurted out to me, 'The Queen does not approve of what I am doing on AIDS, Ken.' Then – a familiar litany – she added furiously, 'That *bloody* family, after all I have done for them. I just cannot win. Everything I do is wrong.'

I tried to reason with her. It was undoubtedly true, however, that her stance on the issue had led one acid-penned critic to label her the patron saint of sodomy. As she began to calm down I told the Princess that I, and many others, thought she was doing a fantastic job for the homosexual community, as also for AIDS sufferers who had contracted the illness through being born to an HIV-positive parent, or from blood transfusions, but that perhaps there was a danger that she was losing her perspective on the issue. She was not in the mood to listen, however. In her anger and frustration she was determined to play the victim, a role she really enjoyed, albeit rather masochistically.

Yet despite the Palace's attitude, Diana continued her AIDS crusade with the zeal of a missionary. She could not be swayed from her course. She deserves every credit for her work, but it reached a point at which nobody, not even the monarch, could soften her approach, even when there were good reasons for doing so. I remember on one occasion her passionate devotion to the cause threatened to backfire in just the way the Queen had perhaps foreseen. This was during a visit to a hospital in London's East End, which had been transformed into a hospice for dying AIDS patients.

Unfortunately, the Princess's visit came at a time when the local National Health Service resources in the area, Shoreditch, were being cut back drastically. The local people were outraged because while waiting lists for treatment for 'ordinary' ailments were growing ever longer, the Princess was using her official time to comfort AIDS victims. An angry crowd gathered at the Mildmay Mission Hospital in readiness for Diana's arrival.

As we drove to the hospital, I learned over the radio from officers already there that the atmosphere among the crowd was in danger of turning ugly. From a security viewpoint I did not envisage it getting out of control, but in considering ways of avoiding trouble I came up with an idea which, I thought, was an ideal way to placate the hostility of the crowd that had gathered with their banners. Turning in my seat, I suggested to the Princess that we might pay a brief visit to the local old people's home too. Anne Beckwith-Smith, her lady-in-waiting, who was traveling with us, agreed, but Diana was by now obsessed with only one thing.

'Ken,' she said, looking at me intently, 'what is happening to these poor souls in this hospice is simply horrendous. Horrendous. We have to do something to stop this disease spreading, and we have to find a cure for them.' I agreed with her wholeheartedly, but still urged her, in the interest of good public relations, to spend a few minutes among the elderly as well. The Princess, clearly somewhat irritated by my impertinence, was having none of it, however, and the protesters, having made their point, soon left.

The Princess had a remarkable gift with AIDS patients. She never tired of visiting them; never grimaced at the sight of their ravaged bodies and sunken features; never did anything but empathize with their terrible plight. In return, the patients felt special. For them, a visit from the beautiful and sympathetic Princess of Wales was something to stay alive for, and I am convinced that this actually happened in several cases, no matter how far-fetched it might seem.

Regardless of one's personal view on this subject – and I have to admit that in those unenlightened days I too regarded AIDS with horror as well as pity, and wanted as little to do with it as possible – no one could be anything but admiring of Diana's courage and tenacity. She believed in what she did with all her heart and soul, but, more importantly, she genuinely did make a difference. She showed the bigots and the homophobes up for what they were, silencing the ignorant. I did not always agree with her stance on AIDS, not least because I felt that there were many equally deserving cases, from the old and lonely to sick or abandoned children. Yet to be fair, Diana did her best to ensure that her time and influence were spread across as many needy causes as possible, although none captured her interest as much as AIDS.

Tragically, more than a decade later, AIDS is still a killer. Nevertheless, the way in which ordinary people now understand the disease and all the pain and suffering it involves is in no small measure due to Diana. Despite my reservations at the time, I too have to accept that in her short life she undoubtedly made a tremendous contribution towards a more positive perception of the disease, while also showing many of those suffering from AIDS that they were not forgotten. She gave people hope, and in a world of cynics demonstrated that kindness and compassion are neither futile nor forgotten. Ignorance is bliss to some; by confronting the disease and, literally, embracing those stricken with it the Princess was able to change the attitudes of many, perhaps even millions.

There are still bigots, of course, and they are always among the first to criticize. Some of these have said that the Princess needed to champion the cause of victims not because she wished to help, but because she was a victim herself. Certainly there is truth in the statement, though it is far from being the whole truth. One thing that her decriers cannot steal from her, however, is what she achieved in opening the world's eyes to the human disaster, and in making people think about, or rethink, their attitudes towards it. She was not alone in her work, nor would she have claimed that she was – there have been, and still are, many selfless people, famous or unknown, who have labored tirelessly in the cause of AIDS awareness. But she was the first truly world-famous person to embrace that cause publicly, and to put all her considerable publicity 'clout' at its disposal.

Yet the Queen may have had a point if she had indeed urged the Princess to balance her public duties. At the time I could see exactly what she had been trying to make Diana understand – namely, that her association with a disease then often held to be a kind of self-inflicted plague visited upon promiscuous male homosexuals, and prostitutes, would inevitably weaken the royal family's standing in the public eye. But I believe that the Palace failed to appreciate what Diana actually stood for, or to appreciate the impact she was capable of making. Diana was the homosexuals' champion precisely because homosexuality was no longer safe – she wanted to help. Nor, as was becoming increasingly apparent, was any unprotected sex unless both parties were certain that neither was infected. Diana knew that the power of her personality could at least make a large slice of the population not only stop and reassess their often crass and misconceived judgments about AIDS sufferers, but also understand the nature of the dangers that sexually active people now faced.

In her own much used expression, Diana could not win. She was damned if she tried to do something, and criticized if she did not. To make matters worse, at about the same time as her meeting with the Queen she had also received a broadside from her maternal grandmother, Ruth, Lady Fermoy, about the way she was dressing. The Princess was wearing a pair of figure-hugging trousers she had recently bought, and thought, quite rightly, that she looked good in them. Seeing her as she walked into the Palace, Lady Fermoy, a lifelong serving courtier and a close friend of the Queen Mother, was appalled, to the extent that she cornered her granddaughter and called her a strumpet. Understandably, Diana felt she could no longer even trust her own family. In the car on the way back to Kensington Palace, as she wept about what she termed the 'double attack' upon her, I felt desperately sorry for her, although I was powerless to do anything other than offer such comforting words as I could muster. It is not given to policemen, even those on royalty-protection duties, to confront senior courtiers, far less the monarch herself.

Leprosy and AIDS would not be the end of Diana's involvement with controversial issues. Towards the end of her life she was accused of political interference, and of dragging the royal family into dangerous political waters, by the stance she took against land mines. For Diana, the cause was another AIDS. Land mines were (and are) a scourge of humanity, and the cause of countless deaths and maimings among the innocent. If she took a highly public stance against them, then the world would come to its senses and they would be banned for ever. Never mind that mines are a cheap and effective defense for armies in the field, especially ill-trained or ill-equipped armies. Never mind the views of those with vested interests – they must be cleared and then banned. She simply could not understand those who challenged her childlike logic. For her, if a single child lost a leg to a land mine, the solution was simple; ban the mines. While this may have been naive – there was a predictable outcry among the armed forces, weapons manufacturers, arms dealers, and others, for instance – it focused attention on the issue. In her mind, billion-dollar arms deals were not relevant. Clearly bemused by the chorus of disapproval that surrounded her widely publicized trips to the minefields of Bosnia and Angola, she declared, 'I am not a politician, I am a humanitarian.' It is exactly how she wanted to be remembered.

The word 'humanitarian' embodies the very essence of Diana. She believed that she could change humankind for the better. She tried; she raised our awareness, and our spirits, for a while, and then was cruelly snatched from us. But that, emphatically, does not mean that she failed. For me, Diana made us examine ourselves for a moment. That alone, no matter how fleeting that moment, makes her life worthwhile.

# Chapter 6

G IVEN THEIR ITINERANT LIFESTYLES – not to mention their illicit love affairs – the mobile telephone became an essential tool for both Charles and Diana. The Princess in particular was almost addicted to hers, as she was to the landline telephone until the small, reliable mobiles became available, and constantly updated to the very latest model. Knowing that calls made on a mobile are not secure, I advised her to be cautious, urging her to use some sort of secret code (obviously the person on the other end would have to know the code as well) when speaking on the mobile in case others were listening in, accidentally or deliberately. Unfortunately, she dismissed my warnings as the first stages of paranoia which, coming from her, was a little rich, given that she quite often displayed an 'Everyone's-out-to-get-me' mentality herself. I personally found the mobile revolution easy to resist (until quite recently, anyway), preferring instead to use my dependable Scotland Yard pager. In an age of rapidly changing communications it at least gave me some semblance of being in control; in addition, it was secure and, when I wanted it to be, silent.

Diana's addiction to her 'talking brick' also rubbed off on some of her staff. Dickie Arbiter, her talkative press officer, a former reporter for Independent Radio News who reveled in his poacher-turned-gamekeeper role, seemed to have his mobile permanently attached to his ear. Its ring tone, permanently set on 'loud', was particularly irritating. I had frequently suggested that he turn the thing off, but Dickie always thought he knew best. Dickie's come-uppance came one day in April 1989, at the Britannia Royal Naval College, Dartmouth (the navy's officer-training establishment). The Princess, in a spectacular bright red tricorn hat and a matching suit with large brass buttons, emerged from the main building and walked on to the raised dais from where she had been asked to take the salute at the Lord High Admiral's Divisions, the Royal Navy's version of a ceremonial passing-out parade. On the saluting platform she was flanked by the Commodore of the College and other senior officers, while I and other members of her entourage stood a little to the rear. As the mass of uniformed officer cadets marched in time to the beat of the Royal Marines band, the Princess, who was in a gaily flirtatious mood, was doing her utmost to retain her composure.

'Look at all those uniforms,' she remarked wickedly to the Commodore standing beside her, her eyes wandering up and down the massed ranks of cadets, who by now had come to a crashing halt and were standing rigidly at attention.

'Hmm . . . and royal weather for you too, ma'am,' added the Commodore, not quite sure how to react to this royal personage's flirtatious manner.

'But of course, Captain,' she replied, 'the sun always shines on the righteous.'

As I have said, Diana was an inveterate giggler, and when in that mood the tiniest incident could send her into paroxysms of barely suppressed laughter. Dickie, who had been standing just behind the Princess provided it. For just as the band finished playing and came to attention directly in front of the Princess, his mobile rang out. In the sudden silence after the music, it sounded as loud as a trumpet. The Princess could hardly contain herself as Dickie, flushed scarlet with embarrassment, fumbled desperately in his pockets for the offending instrument, which for once was not welded to his ear. From that day on I understand he switched off his phone when attending official functions.

Dickie Arbiter may have learned his lesson, but unfortunately the consequences of the royal couple's dependency on mobile phones were to be far more wide-reaching, and more damaging. Mobile-telecommunications technology was in its infancy at the beginning of 1990, and transmissions were very far from being secure. At the same time, a portable directional scanner could be purchased for a few hundred pounds which, when connected to a receiver like those used by amateur radio hams, would allow an unscrupulous operator to eavesdrop on the most intimate mobile-phone conversation. True, bugging other people's conversations is illegal, but the offense is almost impossible to police effectively. By the end of 1989 two unprincipled people had already secretly captured and recorded two indelicate royal conversations that must have surpassed every illegal eavesdropper's greatest expectations.

In January 1990 an amateur radio ham named Cyril Reenan approached the *Sun* newspaper, offering to sell tapes of a conversation between Diana and an unidentified man she referred to as 'James'. It was extremely recent, having been recorded on New Year's Eve. Stuart Higgins, a senior executive of the newspaper and an erstwhile confidant of Camilla Parker Bowles, agreed to meet Reenan. Having heard the tapes Higgins, who had met the Princess before, was convinced that the woman to whom the mystery 'James' kept referring as 'darling', 'honey' and 'Squidgy' was indeed the Princess of Wales. During the conversation, 'James' spoke of looking forward to wrapping his 'warm, protective arms around her in a couple of days'. The nature of the conversation confirmed beyond doubt that the two were close; she even talked of not wanting to get pregnant. This was simply sensational material, particularly for a tabloid newspaper.

Higgins, like many newspapermen at the time, was in tune with the Diana story and so was aware of the rumors circulating about the Princess and an army officer named James Hewitt. He correctly deduced, however, that the man on the tapes must be a different James because at one point in the conversation Diana complained that she had dressed Hewitt 'from head to foot'; in addition, the other 'James' said that he had been obsessed with her for three months and Higgins knew that Diana had been involved with Hewitt for much longer. He therefore set his Fleet Street bloodhounds to work on finding the identity of this second James.

Although *Sun* reporters tracked down the Princess's besotted beau, James Gilbey, within days, in the event the story of the intimate phone conversation did not surface until 25 August 1992. The management of Rupert Murdoch's News International (which owns the *Sun*, among other papers including *The Times*) were not as convinced as Higgins that the woman on the tapes was indeed the Princess of Wales. Murdoch's man-in-charge in London, Chairman Andrew Knight, therefore decided to sit on the tapes, banking them in the *Sun*'s safe where they were to remain – a ticking time bomb under the royal family, had they but known it – to resurface with dramatic effect more than two years later.

I will address the impact of what came to be called 'Squidygate' upon the Princess and others, including me, later because at the time Diana, the royal family and others close to them were all blissfully unaware of the tapes' existence. This is, however, a good point at which to examine the influence of Diana's coterie of male friends who played so important a part in her life. For although James Hewitt was her most significant admirer, he was by no means the only one.

As we have seen, by the time I became her protection officer Diana, tired of being spurned by her husband in favor of an older woman he had never stopped loving, had already been driven into an affair with another man. According to her, Charles had returned to Camilla as early as 1984, before the birth of his second son, Harry, on 15 September that year. Later, in a secretly taped interview for Andrew Morton's book, Diana repeated what she had confided to me by the pool in Majorca: 'As Harry was born it just went bang, our marriage, the whole thing went down the drain . . . By then I knew he had gone back to his lady but somehow we'd managed to have Harry.' The Prince's rejection of her was, for Diana, the final irreparable crack in an already fatally flawed marriage.

Prince Charles may have turned his back on his beautiful young wife, but other men – young, well-bred, rich, powerful or good-looking men, and sometimes all of those – were fascinated by this naturally provocative woman, and more than willing to try to take his place in her affections. She in turn clearly enjoyed the power she seemed to exert over many men. Infidelity and the title 'Princess of Wales' do not mix, however, and I have never believed that Diana was naturally given to unfaithfulness; besides, she was terrified of discovery, and knew just how dangerous it might be to carry on an illicit affair in the enclosed world of Palace circles. Yet as the marriage deteriorated, Camilla's hold over Charles seemed to tighten, until, inevitably, something had to give. It has become almost a cliché to say that Diana craved love. She had every intention of finding fulfillment, and since her husband had made it obvious that he did not want her, her adultery became inevitable.

In the event, it was not to the rich or famous that she turned for male companionship. In fact, the men whose company she sought or welcomed tended to be all of a type. To a man, they had to have one thing in common – patience, and bundles of it. They were invariably good-looking, public-school educated, and from landed families, although by no means always rich themselves. They played bridge tolerably and enjoyed going with her to the cinema or to dine, discreetly, at the trendiest restaurants, but small talk, the ability to chat endlessly for hours about almost nothing at all, seemed to be their specialty. They also had to know how to please the Princess, which meant sharing her liking for risqué jokes and playing adult games like Twister. Invariably, they all had pet names for her. James Gilbey famously called her 'Squidgy', but her childhood nickname 'Duch', short for Duchess, was the favorite.

Before her marriage, her early suitors, she told me, had usually been disappointed cast-offs of her married elder sister, Lady Sarah McCorquodale. Diana had loved to mother them; indeed, a part of dating the young Lady Diana Spencer was the advantage of having your shirts washed and ironed – a huge plus for feckless young bachelors. She used to joke about it to me, confiding that all she had ever really wanted in life was to be a loving wife, caring for her man and her family. Perhaps it was true, at least in part, but I knew Diana by now, and knew too that she was addicted to the buzz that her extraordinary life gave her.

She did love to care for her men, though. Any new man in her life received the benefit of her clothes sense – and her purse. One or two of them, like Hewitt, whom she had adored according to her own very public admission, had the good fortune to be 'dressed from head to foot' by her. She always picked up the bill too, which for someone like Hewitt, who seemed to be permanently short of money, was an added advantage.

There was one rather curious effect of all this. Even if they did not look like a 'Dianaman' at first, within a few weeks the cloning process was complete. I often thought that if the men whom she admired, such as Hewitt, Gilbey, Philip Dunne, David Waterhouse, and Rory Scott, were lined up in an identity parade, then one would hardly be able to tell them apart. All were tall, of similar physique, dressed and spoke in the same manner, shared the same tastes and the same circle of friends, and often the same mannerisms. They may have differed slightly, but all had one thing in common: they were nothing like her serious-minded husband, twelve years her senior, and by his own admission a man who acted older than his years.

Diana's flirtatious remark at the Royal Naval College had not been entirely frivolous. She once joked with me, 'I do so like men in uniform.' I lightly replied that it was a good job therefore that I had to work as a plain-clothes police officer.

'Oh no, Ken, not you. I couldn't fancy you,' she said. Deadpan, I told her the feeling was mutual. Used to male admirers falling over themselves for her she was not sure how to take that. It was an interesting exchange, however, in the light of one of the more persistent rumors about her.

Scotland Yard advises any would-be protection officer that strict protocol must be followed, and emphasizes that it is important that the officer should not get too close to his or her principal. They stress detachment, so that the officer can focus entirely on the job of security. Sometimes this is easier said than done, and especially with someone of the Princess's warmly sympathetic, confiding, and often vulnerable nature. In 1986 a rumor surfaced, and was widely circulated in both Palace and Scotland Yard circles, that the Princess had become 'too close' to her then protection officer, Sergeant Barry Mannakee. He was summarily discharged for overstepping the invisible mark of propriety between himself and Diana. Nothing was ever proved, but the rumor was strong enough, allegedly, for the Palace, fearing another royal scandal, to instruct Scotland Yard to act to prevent a recurrence. The Queen had been aware of the relationship between her daughter, Princess Anne, and her protection officer, Sergeant Peter Cross, and he too had been moved from his job. The last thing the Palace wanted was for another serious transgression of this nature to become public.

Years later, James Hewitt would claim that Mannakee was killed by rogue British intelligence officers. Without a shred of credible evidence, he suggested that these had somehow 'arranged' a fatal accident when, in the spring of 1987, Mannakee was the passenger on a motorcycle that collided with a car in the East End of London (the bike's rider survived).* Hewitt alleged that Barry's death had been no accident, and added that secret agents acting for the British intelligence agencies planned to dispose of him just as they had Mannakee. He also claimed that Diana had told him that she and Mannakee had enjoyed a passionate affair. As 'proof', he said that the policeman had given the Princess a cuddly toy, a brown teddy bear, which she kept on her bed. According to Hewitt, when he saw

* British intelligence, for so long pilloried for inefficiency, not to mention treason, appears to be terrifically skilled at arranging fatal road accidents, if some of the conspiracy theories surrounding Diana's own death are to be believed.

it and observed that he thought it a rather intimate present for a policeman to give her, she said, nonplussed, 'But we were lovers.'

It is undoubtedly true that Diana and Mannakee were very close; perhaps, in the eyes of the Palace and of Scotland Yard, too close. Because of the long hours spent in each other's company it was almost inevitable that a close friendship would grow between them. Having myself been the Princess's protection officer, I too became close to her – as I have tried to show, that was the nature of the job. To suggest, however, as Hewitt did, that Mannakee was murdered because of their intimacy is the stuff of romantic thrillers. Their alleged affair is said to have started in 1985 when Prince Harry was less than a year old, at a time when the Princess was suffering from postnatal depression. I was not with the Royalty Protection Department then, so I do not know whether this is true or not, but, like anyone else on the inside, I heard the rumors when I transferred to the department. Certainly, whenever speculation about the relationship was raised in the press it was categorically denied by the Palace that anything inappropriate had happened between Diana and her protection officer. That, of course, does not necessarily make it untrue.

What is true is that by 1985 the rumors among the Waleses's staff that she and Mannakee were having an affair grew stronger. Senior members of staff complained to the Prince that he was showing signs of over-familiarity with her during public engagements; moreover, Diana, a natural flirt, was said to have encouraged her protection officer in his attentions. Finally, an unsubstantiated rumor began to circulate, alleging that the two of them had been discovered in a compromising position by a senior member of Charles's staff on the eve of the wedding of the Duke and Duchess of York in July 1986. This proved to be the last straw. Just days after the alleged incident, Mannakee was moved to other duties in the Diplomatic Protection branch and out of Diana's life for good. A year later he was dead.

Whenever Barry's name came up in our conversations, the Princess told me with complete straightforwardness that the speculation about a relationship between her and the policeman was untrue. Having by then had some years in which to reflect on the rumors, she claimed that the allegations were part of a smear campaign against her by Prince Charles's camp. Diana was not averse to embellishing the truth, but I believed her then and I do still. Undoubtedly Mannakee, who was much older than her, became more than a policeman to her. He became a very close friend, a good listener whom she saw as a father figure, someone who would support her when she was down and say 'You can cope, Diana.' Having been in much the same position myself, this has always struck me as the most convincing answer to the rumors.

When, in 1987, Prince Charles broke the news of Mannakee's accidental death to Diana as they were traveling to RAF Northolt, from where they would fly to Cannes for an official visit to the film festival, she burst into tears. But why would she not? It was after all a natural reaction, especially in such a highly emotional woman who had just learned of the sudden death of a close friend. To suggest, however, that she went beyond simply crying on Mannakee's shoulder and began an affair with him is at best speculation, but it is speculation of a particularly cruel kind, not least because both parties are dead, and cannot therefore defend themselves.

James Gilbey, the man on the infamous 'Squidgygate' tapes, re-established himself in Diana's life in the autumn of 1989, and came to be an innate part of it; indeed, even when she was seeing James Hewitt up to three times a week, Gilbey was always around. He became completely obsessed with her, and although she was never as close to him as she was to Hewitt, she found him an enjoyable distraction, not least for his urbanity. Although Gilbey was by no means her only or most significant admirer, the Princess – so long starved of love – found that she enjoyed beguiling more than one man at a time. As she grew in confidence – partly as a result of her affair with Hewitt, and partly because of the decisions she had taken about her life and work – Diana was not afraid to play one admirer off against another, so that there were times when she was enjoying the attentions of more than one man at the same time. In order to do this, she increasingly came to rely on trusted friends to provide 'safe houses', places where she could spend hours with a male admirer, confident of absolute privacy away from the prying eyes of servants (though with her faithful protection officer somewhere close at hand).

She often used the elegant London home of Mara Berni, owner of her favorite restaurant, San Lorenzo in Beauchamp Place, as a meeting place. (She would later use the London home of her close friend Lucia Flecha de Lima, wife of the Brazilian Ambassador, as a sanctuary.) I told Diana of my concerns about the extent of the Italian restaurateur's knowledge about her private life, but she insisted that Mara was completely trustworthy. It was also in Mara's house in Knightsbridge, just a few minutes' walk from Harrods, that she would meet some of the mystics and fortune-tellers with whom she became involved. She would spend hours locked away with these people, whom she grew to depend on. For myself, I regarded them with suspicious cynicism and told her so, to which she replied that although she doubted their veracity, she found them to be of increasing importance in her life. Each one told her a different story, and she seemed perfectly happy to accept that, something that highlighted her increasing insecurity, as well as the desperation of her quest to find solutions – any solutions – to the problems in her life.

As it happened, my first serious brush with the paparazzi who would dog Diana until her death came when she was tracked down to one of her so-called safe houses, the mews house in South Kensington belonging to her friend Kate Menzies. She had enjoyed an evening with her close friend David Waterhouse, a former Guards officer, whom she had met some years earlier through the Duchess of York during a skiing holiday in Klosters. As they talked into the night, I continued to keep a close watch outside, and when I went out to get the car I became aware that we were not alone. Somehow, one of the most skilful and tenacious freelance photographers of the time had traced the Princess. Now he was moving in for the kill.

Charming and clever, and very good at his job, Jason Fraser knew that a photograph of the Princess leaving a friend's house where she had spent time with a handsome man in the dead of night, would make him a small fortune. The red-top tabloid newspapers would have a field day, while the opportunities for syndicating the shots worldwide meant that Jason must have been seeing dollar signs flashing up before his eyes as he prepared to catch the Princess when she left.

What he did not know, however, was that even as he was preparing to pounce I had him in my sights. At around 1.30 am Diana was ready to leave, and I had come back inside to escort her to the car. As we walked through the door into the street there was Fraser waiting for his prey. The sudden, savage glare of his flashgun and the whir of the camera's motor drive stunned the Princess, and she rocked backwards, shocked and surprised.

At once, Diana became hysterical, bursting into tears at this gross intrusion. I grabbed Jason, pushed him against the wall and demanded the film. He refused, mumbling something about his photos being in the public interest and that I had no right to touch his camera. After a short, meaningful dialogue, however, he opened the back of the camera, pulled out the film cartridge and handed it to me. Thereafter, the mood calmed down considerably. Diana walked to the car, while Jason and I had a little chat. We agreed to meet the next day, when I said I would return his film to him.

Next day we met for a coffee. I remember commenting on Jason's jacket then reached over and opened it at the button in mock admiration. What I was actually doing was checking for a microphone or bug. Satisfied that he wasn't wired, I handed him back the negatives, obviously minus any shots of Diana's early-morning departure. The young photographer laughed as he took the film, and we parted on good terms with a handshake. I told him that I knew he had a job to do, and he respected that I had one, too.

Perhaps, I was wrong, and Diana's clandestine meeting with a handsome young man at her girlfriend's house in the dead of night was indeed a matter of public interest. With hindsight, I think that it probably was, but not back then, or at least not as far as the Establishment – still desperately promoting the marriage of the Prince and Princess of Wales as happy and stable – was concerned. On the following Sunday a version of the story appeared on the front page of the *News of the World* which was remarkably accurate. There was no accompanying photo of Diana leaving the flat, however, and the story soon died.

Years later, by which time I was protection officer to the Queen's cousin, HRH the Duke of Kent, I ran into Jason by chance. He had never been anything but charming to me, and when I approached him outside Kensington Palace, where he was loitering in the hopes of obtaining a saleable photo, he thrust out his hand in greeting.

'What are you doing here, Jason?' I asked. 'Oh, don't worry, Ken,' he replied. 'I'm not interested in minor royals.'

'Jason, it's not a bloody bird sanctuary,' I retorted, which got a laugh from the photographer, who has a first-class reputation for catching royals and celebrities on film off-guard and when they least expect it. He himself recently briefly flirted with the role of senior, designer-suited executive with a national newspaper before returning to his more natural habitat as a highly rewarded pursuer of celebrity. And, as I say, he is very, very good at it.

Her interest in Hewitt may have been declining, but Diana was not about to let a little thing like the tailing off (or even the temporary cessation) of an affair stop her in her course. In fact, I believe it made her stronger and more determined. She had, after all, bigger fish to fry. Not only was she beginning to carve out a niche in the public arena all for herself, but she was now seriously considering the idea of actually leaving her husband and establishing a rival court. If that seems incredible now, it is worth remembering that back then, with the intense support she generated, Diana believed that she was capable of anything. In December 1989 *Vanity Fair* reported her transformation into 'dedicated Di', adding that 'Some people are beginning to talk about her as a saint'. Once again I urged caution when she privately described her plans to me, citing the *Vanity Fair* piece, but although she dismissed the article as 'silly', it certainly had longevity, adorning the coffee table in her sitting room Kensington Palace for longer than most of her magazines.

As a result of her new-found determination, by early 1990 Diana talked of nothing but escape, although I sensed that her eagerness to flee the Palace, as well as a loveless marriage, had more to do with her rekindled friendship with Sarah, Duchess of York. The royal wives met for lunch once a week, as they had used to do before Diana's marriage. In one sense, this showed the Princess at her most scheming and manipulative. She was canny enough to realize that if she was to bolt the royal family, then she needed a partner in crime, and in Sarah she found the perfect assistant. Gullible, malleable, rarely careful of consequences and always willing to please, Sarah to Diana was the perfect guinea pig, to be used to test the water if she herself feared that it was too hot. For a time, the two women bonded, not only because it had been Diana who engineered Sarah's entry into the wealth and fame of the royal family by encouraging her romance with Prince Andrew, but also because both were outsiders, and both were locked in unsatisfying but seemingly unbreakable marriages.

Despite being among the most senior ranking royals, both women felt that they were never truly part of that family. True, Diana felt this more deeply than Sarah, who at least initially believed the false promises and enthusiastic response she received from 'the Firm', particularly from the Duke of Edinburgh. Diana, however, unlike her husband and brother-in-law, Prince Andrew, was not scared of Prince Philip, or 'Stavros'* as she privately referred to him, and his strictures against her left her largely unmoved.

By now the two sisters-in-law were as thick as thieves, despite my repeated warnings to the Princess against listening to Sarah. I had many times advised her against making such an alliance, but my doubts had fallen on deaf ears. I hasten to add that this was not because I did not like Sarah – I did – but because I knew that she was a bad influence on the Princess. Nor was I alone in believing this. Senior members of the Queen's Household were equally concerned. They believed that the Duchess, whose indiscreet affairs were well-known in Palace circles, and whose extravagant behavior was so often an embarrassment to the royal family, was in danger of self-destructing and might therefore bring the wife of the heir to the throne down with her. The matter was so serious that one high-ranking courtier went to the Queen to air his concerns. Stony-faced, the Queen dismissed his fears by saying that she believed there was nothing to worry about, but later confided in Prince Philip, who in turn tackled his two elder sons about the behavior and attitudes of their respective wives. As the wife of Prince Andrew, the Queen's favorite, Sarah had until then lived a charmed life, enjoying a much warmer relationship with the Queen and other members of the royal family than Diana. Prince Charles's famous comment to the Princess – 'Why can't you be more like Fergie?' – was wounding precisely because it was so in tune with his and his family's view of her.

For her part, Diana knew that the Yorks' marriage was close to collapse. Andrew's adolescent pursuit of golf, fast cars and not always very high-class parties, as well as his long absences in the Royal Navy, demonstrated his failure to face up to the harsh realities of marriage and fatherhood. Sarah had sought comfort elsewhere, and had confided her infidelity to Diana, who was shrewd enough to appreciate that it could only be a matter of time before the volcano erupted. Even given the precedent of the

* *Private Eye* first referred to the Duke of Edinburgh as 'Phil the Greek', because he was the son of Prince Andrew of Greece. In fact, the Greek royal family is of German descent, via the throne of Denmark, as the Prince's original surname – Schleswig-Holstein-Sonderburg-Gluckstein – shows.

divorces of Princess Margaret and Princess Anne, she knew that if she was to escape the gilded royal cage, then she would need Sarah to open the door and fly free first.

The Duchess was close to a breakdown when, in 1992, she fell for John Bryan, an affair that would, in the end, secure her exit from the royal family. Bryan, a man whose name would later become synonymous with the notorious toe-sucking incident in the South of France, was a close friend of Sarah's Texan lover, Steve Wyatt. Given the hovering media, who sensed blood, it was only a matter of time before she would fall victim to her own indiscreet behavior, and Diana knew it.

# Chapter 7

'GRAN-GRAN' WAS THE PET NAME William and Harry used for their great-grandmother, the Queen Mother, while the Queen was always 'Granny'; but to the police, there was only one 'Supergran' – Diana's mother, the Honourable Mrs Frances Shand Kydd. To Diana she was simply 'Mummy', the one person in the world to whom she could always turn. A great deal of nonsense has been written about the allegedly unsympathetic relationship between the two women, much of it based upon the improperly understood notion that Frances 'bolted' while Diana was a child, abandoning her four children to run off with another man after her unhappy marriage to Diana's father had failed. It is certainly true that Frances abandoned the marriage, but what is less often remarked is that she fought hard to keep custody of her two youngest children, Diana and Charles, only to be betrayed in a celebrated – indeed, sensational – court case by her own mother, Ruth, Lady Fermoy, who testified against Frances in favor of her aristocratic son-in-law Johnny, the eighth Earl Spencer. Even after the divorce and custody hearings were over, Frances did everything possible to spend as much time as she could with her impressionable daughter and young son, Charles.

What I witnessed in private told a very different story from the widely held one of mother and daughter at odds with one another, for Diana and 'Granny Frances' (the boys' pet name for her) enjoyed a close and loving relationship. When Diana was at her most troubled, and really needed the most private of counsel, it was to her mother that she would always turn.

Whenever Frances came to Highgrove, or when we went to her home near Oban in the west of Scotland, William and Harry were ecstatic. Diana's mother was an excellent mediator, and at High-grove was one of the few people capable of breaking the bitingly cold silences that reigned between Charles and Diana. Journalists tended to assume that because the Princess and her mother lived so far apart geographically, contact between them must be limited. In reality they kept very much in touch, and whenever Diana wanted to escape with her sons, we would decamp *en masse* for Scotland to her mother's remote hideaway for a healthy dose of normality. The young princes loved these visits, and they were always a tonic to Diana.

At the time Frances lived in a whitewashed farmhouse on the remote island of Seil, a few miles south of Oban. As with any proposed visit by the Princess, private or otherwise, I would be sent in advance to ensure the place was secure. Although such an investigation would be very discreet, it was essential to liaise with the local police at Oban, who enjoyed a good relationship with Frances, and to ensure there were enough rooms in the nearby Willowburn Hotel at Balricar for back-up protection officers. It is not too much to say that Seil was the setting for one of the best holidays the Princess and her sons ever took together, far outshining the more glamorous and exotic foreign trips she made that the press highlighted.

In August 1989 the three of them spent a week-long holiday with Frances. It could not have come at a better time, for the Princess was close to breaking point. Seil and the surrounding area had everything that two active and adventurous small boys could hope for. With the sea on its doorstep, open countryside, river inlets and rowing boats, it was better than any adventure playground.

Good forward planning meant that we arrived there undetected by the media. It delighted her that here her boys were able to play as normal children away from snoopers, and away from the restraints of royal life. Diana, too, had complete freedom. She was able to go off on long solitary walks without me or the back-up officers. I knew that she was relatively safe on the island, but as a precaution I insisted that she always took with her a police radio tuned to my waveband, in case she encountered difficulties. This was, I think, a measure of the level of trust that had developed between us since I had taken over as her senior personal protection officer. True, I was not acting by the book, and doubtless my superiors would have been horrified, but it worked. The Princess appreciated our working relationship and the freedom it brought her, and for weeks afterwards her feelings of being trapped would seem to evaporate.

One of Diana's many qualities was that she really was, at heart, a natural girl who liked taking care of others. She took no domestic staff with her when she went to visit her mother. It meant she could really be herself. Perhaps curiously for a woman of immense privilege, she relished the domestic chores which the absence of her sometimes over-attentive staff allowed her. She delighted in doing the dishes after dinner and in washing everybody's clothes; she even offered to iron my shirts, though I initially declined. Eventually, however, I relented and handed one of them over, joking with her that I could not imagine the Queen ironing one of my colleague's shirts. The image of Her Majesty standing at an ironing board with one of her shirtless bodyguards before her sent the Princess into fits of giggles. As she stood in the kitchen with just a towel wrapped around her, ironing my shirt, William joined us. He had developed the idea that his mother had a crush on me and, being full of mischief, put this to her. The Princess told him not to be so silly, at which he suddenly tugged at her towel so that it dropped to the floor, leaving the wife of the heir to the throne naked before me. Diana slowly picked up the towel, covered herself again, and promptly burst out laughing.

There was a relaxed family atmosphere to her holidays on Seil that was especially welcome because it was so rare in a life filled with official functions and all the other trappings of royalty. I helped prepare the meals that the family and I would enjoy at Frances's old table. We would sit there eating, drinking and regaling each other with stories far into the night. Such times were truly golden, and I am glad to have been able to share them. Much of this was owed to Frances, a decent, down-to-earth woman, humorous, intelligent and kind, who has been, and sometimes still is, much maligned. During the days, as I kept the two princes occupied, the Princess was able to discuss with her mother the full implications of her increasingly desperate situation. Frances was the perfect sounding board. Not only was she a sympathetic ear, but she had a wealth of experience in marital disharmony, having been through one of the most celebrated divorces of the sixties.

She knew of the private relationships of both her daughter and her son-in-law, but still gently urged Diana to fight to save her marriage, knowing that she still loved Charles, if only for the sake of her sons. Frances, more than most people, knew the agony of being separated from her children.

Just over a year later, Frances came to stay at Highgrove for the weekend at the invitation of the Prince who, curiously, for he liked her, timed it so that he was away and Diana had the run of the house. It was wonderful for the princes to have Granny Frances around, and they could barely contain their excitement when she arrived. As always, Frances revived her daughter's flagging spirits. It was one of those beautiful September weekends when the summer seems to have forgotten that autumn is already here. The weather was perfect for lounging beside the pool, and there the two women, so similar in character and looks, sat and talked for hours. It was not difficult to guess what they were discussing. Both were genuinely sad to be parting when Monday morning came. They promised not to leave it so long before they met again. Then Diana embraced her mother on the steps before waving her off.

I had, and have, a great deal of time for Frances Shand Kydd. She did everything she could to support her daughter, but also to save Diana's marriage, if only for the sake of William and Harry. Her wisdom, her experience, her kindness, were always at Diana's disposal, and the Princess knew it, and was glad of it. Sadly, however, by the autumn of 1990 matters had reached a point beyond any person's repair.

Throughout her life within 'the Firm', senior members of the royal family privately disapproved of Diana's headline-grabbing acts of public caring. In reality, however, they all, Prince Charles included, coveted the positive media attention she attracted. It is undoubtedly true that since her death the royal family has embraced much of the style and many of the ideas she pioneered.

To accuse the Princess of cynically using the sick and dispossessed to bolster her image, as some commentators have done, is as unjust as it is untrue. As I know only too well, there were many occasions when she would have preferred to have stayed at home playing with her sons. That she did not was because she felt a clear sense of her duty, as well as a profound sense of responsibility to the ordinary men and women who often waited for hours to see her. She never willingly let anyone down.

From an early age, Diana wanted to help those less fortunate than herself. She was by nature a giving person, but during the first few years of her marriage, when she was in her early twenties, she lacked the confidence to put her wishes into practice. By the late 1980s, however, she was beginning to realize her power and potential. She was also genuinely interested in how other people coped with their given lot.

The late Cardinal Basil Hume and the Princess were kindred spirits. They forged a close friendship and Diana even flirted for a time with the idea of converting to Catholicism.* She once asked me what I thought of the idea but, perhaps too glibly, I told her that she would make an interesting subject for the priest who heard her confession. None the less, I am sure that the only reason she did not join the Catholic Church (as her mother had done) was because she was worried about the backlash from the royal family if she had done so. Ironically, the removal of the bar on the heir to the throne marrying a Catholic is likely to be one of the reforms that will be introduced before Prince Charles becomes King.

Diana's first experience of the harsh reality of homelessness came in September 1989 after Cardinal Hume (Archbishop of Westminster, and thus the Roman Catholic Primate of England and Wales) invited her to make a private visit to the Passage Day Centre in Carlisle Place, near Victoria in Central London. The center, run by the Catholic Church, was located in a large basement, where there were kitchens, tables and, above all, heaters. On the day of the visit I placed two police officers, dressed in shabby clothing, down there to monitor security, since we could hardly adopt a stop-and-search policy for a sympathetic visit. They were already in place when the Princess and I arrived at around 10.30 am on 11 September. Most of those using the center were sad cases, people simply cast aside or forgotten by society; many were hooked on drugs or alcohol, or tormented by mental illness. Since no member of the royal family had ever done anything like this before, the Princess was naturally apprehensive as she stepped from the car to be greeted by Cardinal Hume and Sister Barbara Smith, who were waiting on the pavement outside the center.

That day, Diana had discarded her designer clothes and was dressed in jeans and a sweatshirt. Once inside and with the

* The Queen's cousin by marriage, the Duchess of Kent, converted to Catholicism; the Duchess's sister-in-law, Princess Michael of Kent, is a Catholic by upbringing.

formalities over, I decided to give her a free hand. For about an hour she chatted easily to these desperate people, discussing the conditions they lived in and the food available to them, and a hundred other things besides. I should stress that, in 1989, I doubt whether any member of the royal family would even have contemplated making such a visit. Prince Charles, to his credit, has since followed Diana's lead, as have William and Harry (although they made some of these visits with their mother), but the royal family's involvement with these and similar less glamorous causes would never, in my opinion, have come about but for her example. She was without doubt a pioneer, and a brave one at that. Her life would have been a great deal easier – and a great deal less beset by criticism – if she had simply sat back, dressed extravagantly and looked good at royal engagements, and deferred to her husband. But Diana was different; more importantly, she wanted to have a positive effect on the world around her. What she lacked in formal education she more than made up for with an inquiring mind and a desire to learn from first-hand experience and face-to-face meetings.

At the center, she simply sat down among these unfortunates and talked to them. For obvious reasons, a policeman's experience of the homeless, of alcoholics and drug addicts, and of the mentally disturbed, is not always a happy one, but as I watched Diana at work my fears lifted. This woman, who herself came from a privileged background and had married into one of the most famous and richest families in the world, did everything she could to appreciate her conversants' situation and understand what had led them to such despair. Within minutes the skeptical ogling and transfixed stares had disappeared, and for a brief while these down-and-outs seemed to forget who she was. Despite my decision to let her mix freely, I remained close to the Princess just in case of trouble. It was a prudent decision because at one point a florid-faced man, whom I would have guessed to be in his mid-forties, unkempt and wearing filthy clothes, suddenly decided to confront her. Breathing alcohol fumes all over her, he launched into a tirade.

'It's all right for the likes of you to come down here just for half an hour. You want to try living on the streets . . .'

As I prepared to move him away, Diana turned to me, indicating that she did not want me to intervene. As he reeled off his complaints, peppered with expletives throughout, she remained calm and relaxed.

'It's okay, Ken,' she whispered, 'I'm fine.'

She then looked the red-faced man in the eye and, without flinching, replied:

'Well, the reason I am here is to see exactly what it is like, so that I can help in any way I can.'

That serene, unflustered and above all, sympathetic response won over those around the man, and he was shouted down. He had made a point that worried the Princess, however. In the car on the way back to Kensington Palace it was clear that his comments still preyed on her mind.

'Perhaps he's right, Ken,' she said, as she mulled over the criticism. Trying to reassure her, I told her that what she was doing was right.

'Ma'am, you must be true to yourself. Follow your instincts and you won't go wrong.'

For a few seconds she sat in quiet contemplation. Then, speaking with complete and uncomplicated honesty, she said, 'This is the work I want to get involved in from now on, Ken. If I can make something positive happen for these unfortunate people, and people like them, then there is a place for me.'

It was a theme to which the Princess would continually return as, in the years that followed, she strove to stamp her humanitarian mark upon the world. She was always conscious that she was open to the criticism that she was only doing it for self-publicity. Nothing could have been further from the truth. Many of her visits were carried out in private, and she put just as much into an engagement, if not more, when the cameras were not there as when the media turned up *en masse*. She would return many times to the Passage Day Centre, sometimes accompanied by her two young sons. Yet again she was determined that although the princes had been were born to privilege and wealth, they should understand the difficulties faced by others less fortunate than themselves. It is a lesson that William and Harry have never forgotten, and for which Diana should be for ever credited.

In the autumn of 1989 James Hewitt, the man whom Diana would later tell the world that she had 'adored', was sent to Germany on a two-year posting. He had originally agreed to accept ceremonial duties* at headquarters – which had given him the freedom to conduct his affair with Diana – on the understanding that he would be transferred to active duty if he was given command of his own tank squadron. For the sake of his career he had no choice, having been promoted to squadron commander with the rank of temporary major, but to take the posting, especially as tension was growing in the Gulf and the British Army was on high alert. Perhaps realizing the effect that news of his posting would have on the sometimes volatile Princess, he did not tell her until the last possible moment.

At first Diana tried everything in her power to prevent Hewitt from accepting the posting. She even suggested that she would raise the issue with his commanding officer. James, horrified, since such a move would almost certainly have wrecked his army career (to say that the Household Cavalry would have frowned on one of its officers conducting an affair with the wife of the heir to the throne would be a massive understatement), insisted that she would do no such thing. He was, in any case, by now beginning to suspect that her passion for him was starting to fade, for it was now that Diana, who always craved attention and who felt that the one man on whom she thought she could depend had betrayed her by accepting his move to Germany, began seriously to question the sense, as well as the safety, of pursuing the relationship. Their conversations on the telephone became less frequent until, without telling Hewitt, she resolved to end the affair. By this time she had already invited or encouraged the attentions of James Gilbey.

I am convinced that Diana believed that by allowing her affair to wane and die she was somehow adopting the moral high ground over her husband, who continued his liaison with Camilla Parker Bowles. She and Hewitt scarcely spoke for the rest of the year as he trained his tank crews in Germany. In the dying days of the year Berlin's youth at last tore down the Wall, and the curtain literally came down on the old political order. Meanwhile, in Iraq, Saddam Hussein plotted his next move.

With Hewitt out of the way, and largely out of mind, Diana threw herself into her work. She took all her patronages – and she was patron to a good number of causes – very seriously, but none more so than the English National Ballet. Significantly, after she quit public

* Primarily based in London and Windsor, the site of the monarch's two principal residences, the officers and men of the Household Cavalry perform many ceremonial functions, from mounting guard at Horse Guards in Whitehall to finding escorts for state occasions.

life in December 1993, giving up most of her causes, she remained patron of the charity, perhaps because of her girlhood ambitions. One night in December 1989 we left Kensington Palace at just after 8.10 pm and drove the short distance to the grand, white-fronted residence of the French Ambassador at 11, Kensington Park Gardens. The Princess was in an ebullient mood, full of laughter and excitement, and was particularly looking forward to the half-hour performance that had been specially arranged for the evening, and which was to take place after the opulent dinner, served in a giant marquee in the residence's garden, and before coffee was taken.

'I can't wait,' she gushed, her mind on the performance to come. 'Mr Gorlin [the then Chairman of English National Ballet] has told me it will be just exquisite.'

I have a great love of opera and classical music, but I have to admit that ballet is not my forte. In fact, I was considerably relieved that the performance was limited to thirty minutes, although I did not let the Princess know this. To her, ballet was a passion, and she regarded the fact that she was patron of the English National Ballet as an enormous privilege. Even the dreary realization that she would have to put on another public performance of her own for the English National Ballet's wealthy benefactors, like the Marchioness of Douro, the Honorary Chairman, or billionaire's wife Mrs Lemos, Co-Chair of the Gala Committee, for once did not burden her. Gracefully, she took her place at the top table after a short champagne reception in the residence's grand dining room.

One of the events of the evening was a prize draw, held after dinner and the ballet performance (which, I'm sorry to say, largely passed me by), and before the auction, designed to raise more money from well-fed patrons for the English National Ballet. At around 10.35 pm, therefore, the Earl of Gowrie drew the lucky prize ahead of the auction. As usual I had bought a few raffle tickets, some for me and some for the Princess who, like most royalty, rarely carried cash, but was oblivious of proceedings until my name was suddenly read out by Lord Gowrie. I had won second prize. Fully expecting to collect a bottle of mid-range vintage champagne, I was astonished to be told that my prize was a five-star, all-expenses-paid holiday to Malaysia, staying in one of that country's most lavish hotels. The Princess, predictably, collapsed into fits of giggles at my good fortune (and my predicament as to whether or not to accept it).

Still laughing, she edged away from the crowd around her and joined me. 'You could always take me, Ken,' she whispered, 'I could do with a good holiday.'

After some hesitation – well, who wouldn't think twice? – I decided to give the prize to the Princess, so that it could become one of the lots in the auction, and thereby raise more money for the charity. We drove home in high spirits, the Princess enthusing about the ballet performance that had been the high point of her evening, and I completely bemused by my good fortune (even if I had been unable to accept it). Sadly, a few weeks later I learned that the Ambassador's magnificent residence had burned down. The gala evening in aid of the English National Ballet was the last grand function ever held there.

James Hewitt's absence affected Diana to a considerable extent, despite her feeling that the affair should end. She was often moody, sometimes tearful, and occasionally furious, venting her rage against the unfairness of life in general and her situation in particular. Yet it exerted an even more self-destructive influence upon her, for with her lover no longer around to distract her, Diana's attention turned to Camilla Parker Bowles. Her antipathy for 'that woman' was absolute. Despite the fact that she had been involved in an illicit love affair herself, her frustration over Charles's relationship often caused the Princess to boil over into a rage. Moreover, while both our principals enjoyed their clandestine encounters the strain of keeping things secret fell upon Colin Trimming and me as, respectively, the Prince and Princess's protection officers. Looking back, I realize that this was probably our hardest test.

One memorable evening, Diana came to the realization that she could take it no longer. At a party for Camilla's sister, Prince Charles's thoughtless behavior ended in a confrontation between his mistress and his wife.

It was, according to the Princess herself, one of the bravest acts of her entire marriage; the moment when she finally faced her demons and confronted Camilla Parker Bowles face to face about her affair with Prince Charles, and her refusal to give it up.

The setting was a house on Ham Common in Richmond, on the south-western outskirts of London, the home of Lady Annabel Goldsmith, where, to use Diana's word, a 'ghastly' party was being held to mark the fortieth birthday of Camilla's sister, Annabel Elliot. Nobody, least of all the Prince himself, expected Diana to go, but she honestly believed that it was her duty to put on a show of unity with her husband, despite the fact that almost every guest at the party knew about his affair with Camilla.

The Prince was displeased that Diana had chosen to go, and in the car on the drive down to Ham Common he 'needled' (Diana's word) her constantly, questioning the sense of her attending. Sitting silently in the front passenger seat, I honestly did not know what to expect of the evening ahead. Nor did the Princess. She had told me beforehand that she had no intention of kissing Camilla when she greeted her, and I had agreed that that was her prerogative. 'I'll stick out my hand and see if she takes it,' she said, though more to reassure herself, I suspect, than to canvass my approval.

I honestly do not think that the Princess had planned to confront Camilla that night, but the way in which events unfolded left her – a proud woman – no choice. It was clear on our arrival that many of the guests were surprised at Diana's presence, but soon after the royal entrance the underlying hum of meaningless social chatter again filled the room. After a while dinner was served, and, satisfied of the safety of my principals, I left the party and retired to the kitchen, which I quite often did at private parties so that Diana could relax. By her own account (printed in the revised edition of Andrew Morton's *Diana: Her True Story* that appeared after her death), she kept her end up well during dinner, and her fears of a difficult evening began to seem unfounded. Then, after the meal, she noticed that neither her husband nor Camilla Parker Bowles were anywhere to be seen. She decided to find out what was going on, although several of the other guests tried to dissuade her.

I had been in the kitchen for about an hour and a half when I heard the Princess calling my name. I replied that I was in the kitchen and a few moments later she appeared at the door, tearful and clearly distressed. She told me that Prince Charles and Camilla Parker Bowles had been absent for some time, and she was adamant that she wanted to find them.

'Will you help me, Ken? I have had enough. This is just too much,' she said. 'I am not going to be shown up in this way. I want to talk to her – now.' It was not my job to persuade her otherwise. Nevertheless, I tried, questioning the wisdom of making a scene, but failed.

'Ma'am, are you sure that this is a good idea?' I replied – if I am honest, as much for my own sake as for hers. I had not the slightest

Diana and her former protection officer, Sergeant Barry Mannakee. Rumors claimed that they had an affair, and he was summarily moved from royalty protection in July 1986.

**Above:** Preparing to enter the fathers' race at the young princes' prep school, Wetherby. The Princess w[as] highly amused when she saw me being kissed by one of the mothers.

**Below:** The Princess with William and Harry in one of the photo calls I arranged on Necker Island in 19[  ]. Richard Branson's island may have looked private, but that did not deter the world's media when Dia[na] stayed there.

Despite an estrangement in the last year of her life, Diana enjoyed a close relationship with her mother, Frances Shand Kydd, whom she sometimes called her 'rock', as she did me and others close to her.

Diana leaving church at Sandringham in December 1989, a duty she did not enjoy. It was during this visit to the Queen's Norfolk residence that the infamous 'Squidgygate' telephone conversation took place.

**Above:** Charles recuperates aboard the *Fortuna*, the King of Spain's yacht, in Majorca, with Diana and Queen Sophia of Spain. On an earlier visit to King Juan Carlos's palace on the island, Diana had poured her heart out to me about her failing marriage.

**Right:** Keeping a close eye on Harry as we leave the Arlberg Hotel, Lech, in the Austrian Alps, for a day on the slopes. Unlike the ever-present journalists and photographers, we protection officers had to be able to ski to do our job properly.

**Above:** Leaving a state banquet in Islamabad after a long day. Diana was tired, although she rarely l
show, except in private.

**Facing page:** Diana at a low ebb, attending the funeral of her friend, Adrian Ward-Jackson, who die
from AIDS in 1991. During his long illness, she often spent hours at his bedside, while I waited outsi

Superintendent Colin Trimming, protection officer to the Prince of Wales, and their Royal Highnesses India in February 1992. He and I shared many such engagements. By now everyone close to the coup knew that their marriage was in trouble.

wish to be dragged into a marital row between the Prince and Princess, perhaps with Mrs Parker Bowles involved as well. But Diana would not be persuaded otherwise, and she immediately led me down some stairs to the basement of the house, which appeared to be a children's area or play room. Sitting in one softly lit corner, deep in conversation, were the Prince and Camilla. As soon as they saw Diana they leapt to their feet, perhaps acknowledging their guilt. As may be imagined, I felt particularly uncomfortable and made to leave, but the Princess softly urged me to stay.

'Please don't go, Ken,' she said, as though somehow my presence was helping to give her the strength for what she was about to do. But I felt it was wrong that I should be party to what was, after all, a supremely personal matter. Certain that no harm – physical harm, anyway – would come to the Princess, I replied, in the general direction of all three of them, that it was not my place to be there, and excused myself. With that I left the room, deeply embarrassed, to kick my heels at the foot of the basement stairs. Anxious for Diana, I decided to stay as close as possible without intruding.

The Princess remained there in conversation for a few minutes before joining me outside. She seemed elated. She had seized the moment and had confronted her husband's mistress, and she had done so without being anything other than calm and coolly polite.

She told me that she had asked Camilla if she wanted to sit down, and had then asked her what exactly was going on between her and Charles. Diana herself takes up the story: 'It wasn't a fight – calm, deathly calm and I said to Camilla: "I'm sorry I'm in the way, I obviously am in the way and it must be hell for both of you but I do know what is going on. Don't treat me like an idiot."' A few seconds later she composed herself and returned to the party, where the clash of the two women was already being discussed in hushed, conspiratorial tones.

Personally, I found the whole business extraordinary. Even allowing for the difficulties in the marriage, what possible need could there have been for the Prince and his mistress to conduct a clandestine meeting at a crowded party at which the Princess was also present? It was a terrible insult to Diana, and the only charitable interpretation I can put upon it is that both Charles and Camilla had believed that their absence from the party would not be noticed.

Diana walked back into the room with her head held high, and I admired her immensely for it. The Prince and Camilla returned a few minutes later, still shaken, as much by Diana's resolve as by her decision to confront them. For the rest of the evening they circulated separately as though nothing had happened.

By contrast, the journey back to Kensington Palace was, as can be imagined, chilly and tense, with Diana repeating to her silent husband, over and over again, 'How could you have done this to me? It was so humiliating. How could you?'

Diana was not strong emotionally. She had made her point succinctly and with dignity, but later, when she was alone, her fortitude deserted her and, by her own account, she 'cried and cried and cried and didn't sleep that night'. Seeing her that evening, my heart went out to her, a young woman desperate to be wanted by the one man whom, I believe, she loved completely.

Prince Charles is not a bad man, but in this instance his treatment of his wife, and especially his willingness to allow her to be humiliated virtually in public, was unforgivable. The fact that he and Mrs Parker Bowles had been privately conducting an adulterous affair was irrelevant. What tore the Princess in two, wrecking her emotionally, was their readiness to humble her publicly without apparent remorse. From that moment Camilla became 'the Rottweiler' – Diana's nickname from then on replacing her usual euphemisms like 'that woman' and 'his lady'. More importantly, however, Diana now knew, once and for all, that her marriage was over. After that close encounter her references to Camilla became fewer. It was not that she had given up what she privately called 'the struggle', just that she no longer had the stomach for it.

'Ken, there comes a time when you just don't care any more. That time has come. I just don't care any more,' she said. From the absolute calm of her manner, I knew that she meant it.

# Chapter 8

PERHAPS THE FUNNIEST (to me anyway) display of expensive bad taste on Sir Richard Branson's Necker Island was an open-air lavatory built out of chunks of rock. I stood inside it, for a moment wondering what a celebrity visitor like, say, Robert De Niro had thought as he sat there watching cruise liners go past. (Probably, 'You looking at me?') And many of the world's celebrities have stayed on this tiny speck in the British Virgin Islands, which its owner proudly boasts is unlike any other holiday destination in the world (and at somewhere in the region of $52,500 (£35,000) for seven days in 1989, telephone calls not included, one would hope not). For Necker Island has, it seems, magic powers. According to the blurb issued to those lucky enough to stay there, the island isn't pretty, it's 'enchanting', and its millionaire – if not billionaire – guests don't come for a holiday, but to 'rejuvenate mind, body and spirit'. Branson visited the island in the late 1970s, and bought it for roughly £200,000 ($300,000) in the 1980s, at which time it was not much more than a mosquito-infested atoll. So when, in 1989, the Virgin tycoon offered the Princess the chance to take a holiday on the island (free of cost, too) she leapt at the opportunity. At times of crisis Diana loved to escape to the sun with her children and, by this point in her life, without her husband.

A part of my job was to try to find her suitable private sanctuaries away from prying eyes. It was almost an impossible task, although we did achieve it on one or two occasions. A photograph of a bikini-clad Diana on a beach was worth thousands of pounds to the almost ever-present paparazzi, and such shots were deemed essential to Fleet Street's picture editors and their syndication departments, as well as to the foreign media. Finding the Princess was big business and big money. I had experienced the frenzied chase for the Diana holiday picture before, when she and Prince Charles had stayed in Majorca as the guests of King Juan Carlos of Spain.

Having spent a miserable Christmas at Sandringham, Diana decided to take Branson up on his generous offer for her to greet the New Year of 1989 on his private island after he had personally guaranteed her privacy. Prince Charles, of course, was not included. He probably would not have come even if he had been, but in any case he chose to stay with the rest of the royal family at Sandringham.

For this, the first of our two trips to Necker, the Princess brought her mother Frances, her sisters, Lady Sarah McCorquodale and Lady Jane Fellowes and their children, five in all, and her own two sons. She had provided herself with a perfect excuse for the trip by saying that she wanted to spend some time with her mother and sisters, but in reality she was desperate to escape the ice-cold reception she was getting at Sandringham from her husband's family. As the boat bringing us from nearby Tortola neared Necker, and the island's beautiful white beaches came into view, the entire party seemed to breathe a simultaneous sigh of relief. The boys, alive with anticipation, could not wait to explore.

The unassuming billionaire was there to welcome the Princess and the rest of her party as we stepped on to the island. Then, more than a decade ago, it would normally then have cost $7,500 (£5,000) per day for the privilege of staying on the island, so Branson's gift of a holiday to Diana was an extremely generous one.

Necker was not quite what I had expected. The Great House, the main accommodation, struck me as being a cross between the lobby of a luxury hotel and a Surrey barn conversion. Inside, a snooker table had pride of place beneath a Balinese-style beamed ceiling. There were some stylish touches, like an outdoor claw-foot bathtub, giant beanbags and fridges stuffed with champagne specially produced for Necker Island. For guests for whom being on a private island just isn't private enough, there were separate cottages built in South-East Asian pagoda style and each equipped with a meditation room, presumably to allow the hugely wealthy to play at being ascetic, Buddhist monks. There was also a gym and a swimming pool, as well as four exclusive beaches, with a speedboat and several jet-skis at the guests' disposal.

Not only had Branson refused to accept payment for Diana's quite large party, but he had instructed his staff to spare nothing to make her stay perfect. As an example, a few weeks before we left, one of his assistants had telephoned me and asked what food I liked; my preferred 'color, region and grape variety' of wine, and whether there were any books or records I particularly wanted. On the island itself, the staff were equally impressive, and obliging to a fault. I am sure that if the Princess had said she wanted freshly caught shark for supper, then one of the staff would have donned a wetsuit and set off to spear one single-handedly. On our first evening our host held a magnificent lobster barbecue. As soft Caribbean music played and we watched the sun setting, Diana was in paradise. And so, I have to say, was I.

While Diana and her family sunbathed on the beach and William, Harry and their five cousins romped around, I addressed my first official task which was to liaise with officers from the local police force and senior officials from the British Virgin Islands. I told them that above all the Princess and her family wanted privacy, and both assured us they would do their best to secure it, insisting that nobody would be allowed to sail within a mile of the island's shores. Even without the official backup, however, Necker was a protection officer's dream. As the Princess and the royal party wallowed under heavenly blue skies, the rest of the world was kept firmly away. There were no inhabitants on the island – other than the guests – and access was mainly by boat, from Virgin Gorda. Even most of the staff came ashore every morning by boat and left each evening after dinner. If anything unexpected were to happen all I had to do was to summon a helicopter from Tortola and we could escape.

Graham Smith had accompanied Diana on the first trip, but by January 1990, when we made a second visit, he had been struck down with the throat cancer that eventually killed him, and although he was in remission, he was no longer fit for protection duties. Diana was desperately worried; she had somehow convinced herself that the stress of guarding her had led to Graham's illness. She hoped the holiday would at least help to revive his spirits. On the first trip to Necker, both Graham and I had jointly headed up security. Although we had been able to keep the flight details secret – for the press couldn't follow if they didn't know where Diana was – I felt certain that she would leak details of our destination. True, she insisted that, 'All I want is peace and quiet and to be with my boys,' but I knew that she felt that this was just too good a PR opportunity to miss.

Sure enough, it was not long before our peace was broken. Scores of press photographers arrived at the airport on Tortola hungry for pictures of the Princess in a bikini. Round one went to the local police, who promptly confiscated a number of cameras as soon as the press men arrived. But snatching a few cameras from the least experienced photographers at the airport, and other measures like banning flights over Necker and barring boats within a seven-mile radius of the island, were never going to deter the paparazzi and the elite of Fleet Street's royal correspondents. Within days Diana's haven was besieged by little boats bobbing around on the sea, filled with photographers desperate for pictures. Although some long-lens shots were taken and sent around the world, the effectiveness of the security measures limited the intrusion, to grateful sighs from royal party and protection officers alike. The following year they were back with a vengeance; better equipped and more determined than ever, and with the benefit of what they had learned from the Princess's first trip.

In the five years since her death, it seems that Diana has increasingly been written out of history. So it is easy to forget that at the beginning of 1990 hers was the only story that mattered in Fleet Street. Editors, apparently, wanted nothing other than to fill their pages with the latest news of her. Pictures and stories about Diana sold millions of newspapers; circulation soared and that kept journalists and photographers in jobs, which is all that most of them really cared about. The royal reporting teams of the British tabloid press, nicknamed the 'Royal Ratpack', were tough and talented journalists. In particular, James Whitaker and Kent Gavin of the *Daily Mirror*, and Arthur Edwards and Harry Arnold of the *Sun*, lived and breathed their work. Yet they were reasonable men, and despite the very different nature of our respective jobs, we tended to get along, and even to enjoy a measure of mutual respect.

In March 1990 the Prince and Princess had just returned from an official visit to Nigeria and Cameroon. Exhausted, Diana had arranged it so that she had no more engagements until the end of April. She had also arranged another trip to Necker, once again through the generosity of Richard Branson. For her it was the perfect escape and she was buoyant with excitement at the thought of spending time with her sons away from the Prince. What she had not foreseen, however, was that her decision to take a pre-Easter break on the island, once again without Charles, would send Fleet Street into a frenzy. It became headline news. Charles was blamed, even though it was Diana who had arranged the solo holiday. He chose instead to spend the time in the Scottish Highlands, thereby accidentally emphasizing the gulf between the couple. The tabloids unfairly lambasted him as a bad father. One headline screamed, 'This Is Your Father – he's hardly seen the boys since Xmas' while a second read: 'Another Holiday Apart! They'll be forgetting what Dad looks like.' The accompanying articles labeled the Prince an absent father and reported that he had seen his sons for only two days in the previous two months. (In fact, it was three days).

For this visit to Necker, Diana had decided to play Cupid to her brother, then still Viscount Althorp, and his wife of a few months, Victoria, inviting them both along for a surprise second honeymoon. Once again, William and Harry, her mother and sisters, with their children, also joined her at the hideaway. I headed up the security team alone, for although Graham Smith was in the seventeen-strong party, he was there this time as the Princess's guest. She knew that he was seriously ill, and hoped that sun and relaxation might help his recovery. It was good for me to have Graham around, too, because I knew that this year the paparazzi were determined to win their prized pictures. With so much in the British press about the holiday before we left, there was not the remotest chance of keeping the trip a secret.

Within hours of our arrival the press and paparazzi were back. A small armada appeared on the horizon, with more than sixty journalists and photographers packed into chartered boats of all shapes and sizes, cameras primed and at the ready. Diana was furious, almost incandescent with rage. 'How did they know we were here?' she demanded. Then added, bitterly, 'Someone must have told them.' When I suggested that it would not have taken much working out, as the Princess was known to have a penchant for exotic islands in the Caribbean (especially if her holidays there were gratis) she flashed me one of her stony stares. She was not in any mood to see the funny side.

The presence of the journalists and paparazzi, albeit offshore, irritated her and the rest of the party enormously. No matter how much I urged them to try to put it out of their minds, assuring them that I would make sure that it would not affect their security, the

Princess became obsessed with the problem. She kept saying, not very helpfully, that I should 'do something' about it. She also insisted that the media were frightening her sons. I was not at all surprised, for she had filled the young princes' heads with a great deal of nonsense about the press, telling them that they were all 'bad, bad men', with the result that her sons' reaction to journalists and photographers was all too predictable. (She was not altogether unhypocritical in this. She would later maintain a friendship with the *Daily Mail* journalist Richard Kay, and it was she herself who secretly selected Andrew Morton, once a royal correspondent on the *Daily Star*, to write the book that would, in the end, help her to escape from her marriage.)

I weighed up the odds. There were three other protection officers and myself against the crack troops of the world's press. Even Custer had better odds than this, I thought. There was also Smudger – Graham Smith – and although he was a sick man, and was not there officially, I took a lead from him. He and I agreed that we had to be proactive. The media knew exactly where we were, and since they weren't going to go away until they got what they wanted, we had to try and strike a deal, or pack up and abandon the holiday.

Once again, Diana had not brought any staff with her. So, without the luxury of a private secretary or a press secretary, it was left to me to deal with the problem. Until then, no one had really ever had to face such a situation before. In the past, royal holidays had either been taken within the almost fortress-like royal estates, like Sandringham or Balmoral, or as the guests of foreign royalty, as when the Prince and Princess had stayed in Majorca. A combination of the large numbers of encroaching journalists and photographers, the absence of any effective means of deterring them, the Princess's ill-humor about the whole business, and my own desire not to see the holiday cut short, meant that I was going to have to act as a sort of press liaison officer.

I could have told the Princess that this was not really my problem. She had decided to come to this island for a holiday, she knew perfectly well that she was always going to be open to press intrusion wherever she went and whatever she did. I might have added that my job was simply to ensure her safety, and that although the presence of the media was an irritation, it did not present a major breach of security. But I did not.

After talking over the situation with Smudger, I decided to

arrange to meet some of the senior Fleet Street journalists to see if, between us, we could broker a deal in a bid not only to restrain the more intrusive hacks, but to clip the wings of the rogue elements among the foreign paparazzi, who tended to be a law unto themselves.

There is a piece of received wisdom in my line of work which, in effect, states that to ensure effective protection, information is essential. If I was to find out what the paparazzi were doing, I needed to secure allies from Fleet Street. The professionals tended to be more reasonable because, unlike the freelance photographers, their pay checks were assured whether they got the pictures of Diana or not (unless they got fired for failing, of course). They wanted the scoop for reasons of professional pride as much as from a desire to beat the competition; in other words, they were not just motivated by money alone.

With this in mind I climbed into a small boat with Dave Sharp and sailed out to where most of the press boats were. I spotted James Whitaker's rotund frame and pulled up alongside. As I looked out at the gathered photographers and reporters with their sun-reddened faces and ample bellies, binoculars slung round their necks, I could not help smiling. They reminded me of *Sun* reporter Harry Arnold's apt description of the royal ratpack when he had told Prince Charles, 'We may be scum, sir, but we are *la crème de la* scum.'

We sailed in among them, and by a mixture of yells and gestures I signaled that I wanted them to meet me at Biras Creek on Virgin Gorda, about fifteen minutes away by motor boat. Sensing a deal, Whitaker, who always tended to assume the mantle of commander-in-chief of the ratpack, gave the order for the rest to follow.

Settled in a calypso bar, cocktails or beers distributed to everyone, we talked over and around the situation. I knew that I was in dangerous territory here. Technically, dealing with the press was well beyond my remit, and doing so could cause problems for me with my superior officers back at Scotland Yard. Yet in the end I felt I had no choice. I made it clear to the gaggle of hacks and photographers that the Princess was here on a *private* holiday and was under no obligation to give a photo opportunity just because the media happened to be intruding on her privacy. To sweeten the pill, I told them a few minor details about the holiday, without giving too much away. The senior journalists there – Whitaker, Kent Gavin and Arthur Edwards – sat quietly surrounded by the rest, listening to what I had to say. There was a moment's silence after I delivered my 'leave-us-alone' speech, before James Whitaker delivered his response.

James's bark was worse than his bite. The Red Tomato, as the Princess had dubbed him after seeing him packed tightly into a red ski-suit as he tried to give chase on a royal holiday in the Alps, adopted the mantle of spokesman-in-chief for the royal ratpack. With a manner somewhere between that of a retired colonel from the heyday of the British Raj and a female pantomime character played by a man in drag, he put the case for the indefensible. Mercifully, he spared me any 'freedom-of-the-press-and-public-interest' cant, adopting instead a more realistic approach.

'Ken,' he rasped portentously. 'We have a bloody job to do, and if we work together we can make everybody's job, including yours, a damned sight easier.' I knew he had a point, though I kept quiet. 'If you could just persuade the Princess to go along with the idea of a photo call, she would get a peaceful holiday, you would not have to worry about security and we would have the editors off our backs, get the snaps and go fishing.' Everyone, including Dave and I, burst out laughing but James silenced us with a glare.

He went on to point out that the newspaper journalists and photographers were the least of my problems, as the real concern was the foreign paparazzi. I knew that it was true. James continued by saying that if I could persuade the Princess to do one photo call, then he and the other senior Fleet Street journalists would do their best to broker a deal with the paparazzi. If the Princess wanted to have a reasonable holiday, a compromise with the media had to be made. The problem lay in selling it not only to the paparazzi, but to Diana as well.

*Daily Mirror* photographer Kent Gavin, or 'Idle Jack', as he was known, 'Widow Twankey' Whitaker's pantomime partner-in-crime, was the quiet one of the team. Unlike James, however, whose loud protestations usually went over people's heads, when Gavin spoke he commanded respect from his peers. The Princess knew and liked him, indeed, he had even been invited to photograph Prince William's christening in 1982 (and in 1996, the year before the Princess was killed, he was voted Royal Photographer of the Decade). He loved the good life and covering royal holidays, as well as official events, was an important part of his professional jet set life. For once, Gavin backed Whitaker, pressing home the point that the

Fleet Street journalists were not really the problem. 'Tell the Princess she looks a million dollars, and I'll make sure the pictures of her in the *Daily Mirror* do her justice. She'll knock 'em dead back home.' Kent Gavin understood that the real impact of the Princess upon the public was in pictures of her. He also knew that she was vain, and that the idea of appearing on the front pages, showing off her beautiful and bronzed body, would secretly appeal to her.

For my part, I realized that the key to any deal depended on the Fleet Street journalists' ability to deliver full co-operation from the paparazzi, men who, in the slipperiness stakes, made the most active eel look positively inert. Nevertheless, the Fleet Street teams did wield significant power over the paparazzi back then, since it was their editors who would pay the big cash for any pictures the freelancers got if they ignored a deal and struck out on their own. Additionally, the paparazzi were not stupid, and knew that it was better to secure a deal that got them some pictures, than risk getting absolutely nothing at all. With some satisfaction, I noted that as Dave Sharp and I left the bar the royal ratpack were locked in discussions with their French, Italian and German rivals. 'It puts the UN into perspective,' I thought, as I glimpsed a red-faced Whitaker berating some unfortunate French photographer who had dared to challenge his authority.

On the journey back to Necker I mentally weighed up how I was going to win Diana's support for a deal with the media. I knew I would need allies, notably Charles Spencer and Graham Smith, if I was to persuade her to co-operate. We may have found paradise, but I was well aware that if I failed to win the Princess over then, as far as she was concerned, mine would be a paradise lost.

Smudger supported me, as I had known he would; so too did Charles Spencer. He told the Princess that in his expert opinion we had no choice; we either negotiated a truce or it would be all-out war, and the local police simply did not have the resources to drive off fifty or sixty determined press men. Even with help from the guests, I and the two other protection officers would never be able to prevent some of our unwanted visitors from landing on the island and trying to get pictures of Diana and her sons; meanwhile, others out in the boats would come as far as they could inshore and snap her whenever she appeared. That was not intrusion, but full-scale invasion. As a clincher, Graham added his belief that if she did not agree, then we might have to decamp and either look for another holiday destination, at very short notice and with no guarantee that the media would not find us again within a day or so, or return to Britain. While the Princess was considering this, I explained that if we arranged one photo call there was a good chance that once they had got the pictures they had come for, the press would leave her and her family alone for the rest of the holiday.

'But can you guarantee it, Ken?' she said. This, of course, was the question I least wanted to have to answer, and the crux of the whole problem. I had to admit that I could not, but that there was very little alternative. Unlike in the previous year, the local police could not provide the additional cover we needed to cope with the numbers of journalists and photographers homing in on the island. They were busy chasing drug dealers, and had already withdrawn the night boat patrol they had originally offered. This, coupled with the fact that, the year before, I had dispensed with the services of the local night-time beach patrol after I had found the police team asleep over their rifles, meant that my security team was stretched well beyond its capabilities. There was nothing we could do to stop the press invading Necker at any moment, day or night. True, their mission was to take photographs, and they were therefore not life-threatening, but it would still have been hugely embarrassing if any of them had made it up to the house. It would also have driven the Princess, and probably some of her guests, into a paroxysm of fury, with who knew what consequences. The last thing we wanted was a PR disaster brought on by complaints from aggrieved journalists or photographers. As it was, William and Harry were muttering darkly about exacting revenge from the intruders.

I explained to Diana that while I appreciated that she was on a private holiday and that she was entirely justified in complaining that her privacy was being shamefully invaded, we had to agree to the picture deal. I assured her that I would not allow any of the press to set foot on the island, and that she would not have to pose for the cameras in any way. I suggested that she should just go about her normal business on the beach with the two boys, and I would do my best to oversee the operation from a boat alongside the press boats offshore. Once again she immediately grasped our main problem.

'But can they be trusted, Ken?' Of course, I had no way of knowing, but I tried to reassure her by saying that I felt the press could be relied on to deliver their side of the bargain, since it was in the interests of all parties for the deal to hold up. After a few minutes, and with a little gentle persuasion from her brother, for which I was extremely grateful, she agreed. I was almost certain that Kent Gavin was right, and that, deep down, she was quite looking forward to having pictures of her, looking sensational in a swimsuit, splashed across the front pages of the world's press, but she was not going to let me know that.

I called Kent at once and told him the deal was on, adding, as ominously as I could, that if he or his colleagues broke it I would never trust him or Fleet Street again. The laid-back photographer said that he would do his very best to deliver what he had promised. So at eleven the next morning I boarded a small boat and sailed out to the press launches moored offshore. When I arrived the hacks and photographers were in fine form, jostling for the best position and joking with each other. They were obviously relieved that their expensive journey had not been wasted, and that their editors – and ultimately the public – were going to get the pictures and stories they wanted.

The paparazzi were grouped together on a smaller boat moored a few yards away. They were deathly quiet, acknowledging my arrival with a nod almost in unison. Unlike the Fleet Street crew they were not interested in glory or lavish picture by-lines on the front pages. They were in it just for the money. I repeated the rules of engagement and briefed them all about what was going to happen. I then bluntly refreshed their memories about the deal we had struck, pressing the point that after this photo call they would leave the Princess alone. Again there were a few nods, this time of agreement, but I knew that in trusting them, I was going out on a limb.

Within a few minutes the Princess and her family appeared on the beach. She looked sensational, and played her role to perfection. I had suggested that she should play with her sons on the beach, within sight of the cameras, but what followed surprised even me. Surrounded by her sons and their five cousins, she proceeded to let them bury her in the sand, laughing all the while. Then, having extricated herself, she threw off her sundress, revealing her bikini underneath, and raced William and Harry, then aged eight and five, down to the sea to rinse off the sand. Her body gleamed with water in the hot sun, and the camera shutters clicked in frenzy. It was, as ever, a masterly display by the consummate public-relations professional.

After about twenty minutes I called a halt to the photo-shoot – if they hadn't got enough pictures by now, then they shouldn't be in the job. To a man, paparazzi included, they all stopped immediately, clearly elated at the photographs they had got. We fired up the boats' engines and headed for Biras Creek where I told them in no uncertain terms that this was the end and that, no matter how much I loved seeing their smiling faces normally, I did not want to see any of them again on this trip.

All of them agreed that it had been a fantastic photo call, one of the best they had ever had. They gave me credit for it, but it was the Princess who had made it work. Once again I asked them to leave us alone. I was convinced that some would stick around, but most of them, mainly the British freelancers, would leave. But somehow I knew that the French, who never took no for an answer, would be back for more. James Whitaker left me decidedly skeptical as he led Fleet Street's chorus of approval. 'Never mind all that, James – just deliver your side of the deal,' I said as I left.

Back home in Britain, the newspaper editors were delighted. Diana, looking absolutely wonderful, was splashed across the front pages of most papers, especially the tabloids. Under banner headlines, Diana sent her message back to her errant husband, who she suspected would have been enjoying secret trysts with his married lover, Camilla, while she was far away on Necker. 'I'm here without you, and I'm having a wonderful time,' it might have read.

However happy the press and the Princess may have been, my superiors at Scotland Yard were furious. When I contacted head office by telephone, I was told that the photo call had caused quite a stir back in London, and that senior officers were not happy about my involvement, which had been reported in the press. I was formally reminded by the Metropolitan Police's senior management that my role was not that of a press officer, but a protection officer. It was my turn to be incensed. I told them in no uncertain terms that I would be sending them a full report into what had happened on Necker, in which I would explain exactly why I had acted as I had done (with, I may say, Graham Smith's full support). Warming to my theme, I added that I was looking forward to hearing exactly how the geniuses who sit behind their desks in Scotland Yard would have handled the situation, a situation for which there had not, until then, been any precedent. Finally, I reminded them that I had a difficult job to do here, and that I was getting zero assistance or guidance from London, either from Scotland Yard or Buckingham Palace. I then stormed off in indignation to have a cocktail – virgin of course, since I was on duty – to calm myself down. It worked. As I watched a spectacular orange sunset sinking below the horizon I could not help laughing out loud at the way the whole business had turned out.

To my astonishment, and to their credit, the deal with the press held up for the next three days. I think the Princess was surprised, too, because she changed her swimsuit every day, just in case she should be photographed again. She was never one knowingly to disappoint her public. She and her party suffered no press intrusion whatsoever, and I basked in the glory of having brought about this almost unthinkable state of affairs. Diana and her family were able to walk on the beach, swim and snorkel without a press boat in sight. At last she was able to unwind.

There was no daily plan of activities, but William and Harry looked to the men in the party to organize their day. So while the Princess and the rest of the women lounged around the pool, watched over by Dave Sharp, I was tasked with keeping her two extremely active sons occupied. It was not an onerous task, not least because Richard Branson's island had everything in place to make this, for boys, the adventure holiday of a lifetime. One of William's favorite games involved the children unleashing billiard balls across the snooker table at high speed in a bid to smash their opponents' fingers, almost the only rule being that contestants had to leave their hands resting on the table's cushions until the ball was unleashed. I had to put a stop to this, as gently as I could. As a diversion, I took them snorkeling with their uncle Charles, but this was not enough to beguile the inquisitive prince. He wanted to explore. So he and I hatched a plan to reconnoiter the island, and one morning set off together armed with knives, and with only bottled water, fruit and some sandwiches to sustain us. William could not contain his excitement as we ventured deep into the island's interior.

For the next three hours the boy destined to be king and I hacked our way through the undergrowth, climbed rocks and forded streams, re-enacting our own version of *Robinson Crusoe*. William loved every minute of it. At one point I began to worry as the midday sun beat down on us and I realized that I had lost my bearings. I kept this to myself, however, and eventually, albeit two hours later than I had anticipated, we made it back to the main house. William raced in, desperate to tell his mother every detail of his great adventure.

Throughout the three-day truce I kept in daily touch with Kent Gavin by telephone. This was a way of briefing reporters, who had asked that I should let them know if anything untoward had happened to the Princess or any of her party that might constitute a legitimate story. I thought the tale of how the heir apparent had gone missing while exploring with his mother's police protection officer might make a good story, but for obvious reasons I said nothing.

I honored my side of the bargain, allowing the journalists harmless snippets about what the Princess and her party had been doing, and repeated that I expected the media to keep theirs. On the third day after the photo call, however, Gavin warned me that something was afoot. He told me that Fleet Street could no longer be held responsible for the French paparazzi who he feared would soon be out in force again. My heart sank. I knew that the Princess would be furious if their peace were to be broken by the media again. Gavin suggested that I should persuade her to do another photo call which, he thought, would probably placate the ever-hungry paparazzi.

When I put the proposal of a second photo call to Diana she was predictably reluctant.

'Ken, you said that if I did the first one they would leave us alone, so why have I got to do another one?' she complained. She had a point, but I reminded her that at least the deal I had struck had kept the press away for the last three days. I continued by saying that although many of the photographers had left the area, my information was that there were a few hardcore paparazzi preparing to invade her privacy once again. I then suggested that the best solution, however annoying, was for her to do a short, ten-minute photo call, at which point the deal would be reinstated, with any luck until the end of the holiday. After a few minutes' consideration she saw the logic of this and agreed, and the shoot went ahead the following day. She did not like being forced into a corner, but relaxed and beautifully tanned, she saw the advantages to both sides.

Yet even after this, a few paparazzi determined to try to get something different. The rest of the press honored the agreement and left the immediate area, but a handful of freelance photographers remained. They were, from a security viewpoint, considerably easier to handle than the original fifty or sixty, and I felt my decision to negotiate had been fully justified. But the young princes, in particular, still wanted their revenge on the ''tographers' as Harry called them. It was not long before they got their wish.

Richard Branson's manager on the island, Dan Reid, had returned from one of his business and supply trips to Tortola armed with three giant handheld catapults and hundreds of balloons, which he gave to the children. I have no idea where he found them, but they proved a big hit with the princes and their cousins. The catapults were huge. To fire the balloons, which for maximum effect would be filled with water to the size of cricket balls, the catapults had to be tied to posts or held by two people while the third loaded, aimed and fired the missile. Initially, they caused much hilarity as the children and the protection officers fought pitched mini-battles against each other. There was, however, one moment of slight anxiety when young Fellowes – son of Lady Jane and her husband, the Queen's private secretary, Sir Robert (now Lord) Fellowes – known as Beatle, received a direct hit in the chest when William launched an attack on him from the helicopter pad. Poor Beatle went down severely winded and was left with a huge bruise on his chest for the rest of the holiday. But after a brief cooling-off period during which the Princess considered a complete ban on our war games, the balloon battles were allowed to continue.

As the children perfected their warlike activities, William had a brainwave that he felt sure would get his mother's backing.

'Ken,' he said, his eyes lighting up with excitement, 'when the photographers come back in their boats, why don't we catapult them from the house?' There was a perfect vantage point, set upon rocks about eighty feet above the shoreline. William – whose ancestors had led troops into battle – was ready to get his revenge on the snoopers who had upset his beloved mother. Without me knowing he rallied his troops – Harry and their cousins – and they set about constructing two sites in readiness for the return of the press boats.

It didn't take me long to find out what they were up to. When I told the Princess what her sons were planning for the media she thought it was hilarious and approved it immediately. I was dispatched to supervise the battle plans, feeling rather like Captain Mainwaring from the British comedy *Dad's Army*, in charge of a unit of the Home Guard. I even adopted his catchphrases – 'Now gather round, everybody' and 'There's a war on, you know' when addressing my troops. Within hours, true to form, the press boats appeared on the horizon, which sent the children into frenzy. 'Steady lads,' I said, 'don't fire until you see the whites of their eyes.' It was not quite Britain in 1940, but to the two princes it was just as vital to defend their post from invaders.

As boats carrying the hardcore paparazzi approached, I gave the children the order to unleash their stack of colored water bombs. The unfortunate photographers did not know what had hit them, and after twenty minutes and several direct hits they retired hurt and did not return. To be fair, they had the grace to see the funny side. For William, protecting his mother was a matter of personal pride, and he rushed back to tell her of his victory, very much a hero in her eyes.

Everyone was in high spirits. The Princess, revitalized by her holiday, wanted to bid farewell to Necker in style, and to that end arranged a lavish beach party. That night, clad in a diaphanous blue silk dress, she was in real party mood. As the reggae band, the Bitter End Steel Orchestra, played, she grabbed me, looked me straight in the eyes and ordered, 'Ken, let's tango!'

As we swept away to the music of the steel band the rest of the party joined in. Diana's brother, Charles Spencer, had no choice but to follow our lead, being hauled onto the dance floor by his mother, Frances. Then, one after the other, Diana's sisters teamed up with the other detectives. Just to infuriate my Scotland Yard superiors even further, one of the band members sold the story of our last-night party to the *News of the World*. An article about our merry-making appeared on the following day, under the banner headline 'Di Tangos with Cop on Necker Island', and the accompanying text described me as a 'smoothie' who 'sees more of her than Charles'. For once, Diana joked when she saw the article, the Sunday tabloid had got it right.

# Chapter 9

Formal flowerbeds led out into an area of unkempt grass; green paths between tall cypresses planted at regular intervals ushered us into the cool darkness of the wood, where even the statues placed here and there were transformed. Outside in the formal garden statues of gods and heroes and characters from classical Greek drama stood in the carefully contrived vistas. Doubtless these sights were almost unchanged since they had been enjoyed by the ancestors of the noble Rizzardi family who, centuries earlier, had approved the original design of the grounds and the Roman-style garden theatre set within them. In the wood, however, the statues were of lions and wild boars, evoking memories of the wild animals which in classical times, wealthy Romans had kept in parks beside their villas.

'I am sure the air is different here, Ken. It tastes cleaner – crisper,' the Princess remarked as we strolled around magnificent grounds after our secret flight from London. The Villa Rizzardi, near Negrar, a few miles from the ancient city of Verona was, for Diana, the ultimate sanctuary, a place where she could abandon her innermost fears and just be herself – even if it was for only three days. I often thought that if she ever realized her dream and escaped from her life amid the palaces and courtiers and formal engagements, it would be to northern Italy that she would run, a place where she could find true happiness, if only she would let herself. It would have suited her perfectly, a place of great beauty, taste and culture.

The Princess and her mother, Frances Shand Kydd, were the guests of an old family friend, the Contessa Maria Cristina Guerrieri-

Rizzardi, owner of one of the most respected family wine estates in the province. To many she was known simply as the Countess of Verona. Frances and the handsome Contessa had been friends for some time, so when both she and her daughter were invited to hear Luciano Pavarotti perform in Verdi's *Requiem* in the open-air Roman Arena di Verona, Diana leapt at the chance. She was desperate to break away from the constant pressure and politicking of the Palace, and the chance of even a few days away from that world was as attractive to her as even a trip to Italy and a performance by the great tenor. Nor did it take her long to persuade me to go along with her plan. Without discussing the details with anyone I booked the flights in early August under the assumed names of Mr and Mrs Hargreaves, one of our favorite pseudonyms, and we headed for Italy.

Throughout her life, but particularly towards the end, Diana craved privacy. So on the occasions when we did 'get away with one', as she put it, it made the moment even sweeter. That weekend she was able to wander around the shore of the lake almost unnoticed and wholly unrecognized. She took the speedboat out on the lake and raced over the glass-like water. The family wine estate on the edge of Lake Garda was situated in the heart of the *classico* areas of the Veronese wines: Bardolino, Valpolicella and Soave (which we tasted and which were exquisite).

Yet the memory that will stay with me longest is of the night we spent in two of the most ancient cities in the world, Verona and Venice. Just before the performance was about to start Diana, Frances, the Contessa and myself slipped into the arena undetected and settled into our excellent – and expensive – seats, close to the front of the ancient theatre, which dates back many centuries to Roman times. In the minutes before the performance started, the Princess was tense with excitement – yet this was, apparently, the air-headed girl whom the media liked to dismiss as the 'Pop Princess'.

Pavarotti was simply magnificent, his commanding voice holding everyone spellbound. Then disaster struck. Halfway through the *Requiem* the heavens opened, and even our umbrellas could not stop the torrential rain from soaking us to the skin. Nothing, however, could dampen Diana's spirits that night. She was elated, by the music, the atmosphere, and the dramatic setting, and wanted the night to go on for ever. Sadly, however, the downpour meant that for the first time in the city's recent history the concert had to be cancelled. Pavarotti had spotted the Princess during the performance, and as he left the rain-drenched arena he invited our entire party back to his dressing room. There, in his broken English, the great tenor wooed the already smitten Diana.

'You were absolutely marvelous,' she told him. 'It was truly unforgettable. I was so profoundly moved.'

Then, even though her green flowered dress and matching hat were dripping wet, she spoke to the director and asked for the leaders of the chorus and the orchestra to be presented to her. After chatting with them for ten minutes, she turned to leave the Roman arena. Instead of the quiet exit she had imagined, however, she found her route lined by around one hundred and fifty members of the cast, who applauded her and sang 'Auld Lang Syne'.

By now Diana was on fire. In contrast to her mood, the rain was still falling so heavily that the emergency services had been called out to deal with serious flooding in the area. But nothing could deter the Princess. As we stood beneath a tarpaulin, sheltering from the rain, waiting for the cars, she suddenly declared that she wanted to go to Venice.

'Ken, we've got away with it. Nobody knows we're here, not even the local press. Let's live a little,' she beamed. It was close to ten o'clock, but I knew from her expression and her manner that nothing was going to stop her seeing Venice that night, even if she had to walk there. Much to the consternation of the local police assigned to us for the evening (I had contacted the Carabinieri on our arrival), I sanctioned it. The Italian officers said the rain made driving conditions dangerous and it would take at least two and a half hours to get there, although the distance was about seventy miles. They might just as well have saved their breath, for nothing was going to stop the Princess.

Within minutes, Diana, her mother, the Contessa's chauffeur, Tony Pezzo, who himself was related to the Rizzardi family, were heading for Venice, along with Sergeant Dave Sharp and myself. The flabbergasted British Consul, Martin Rickerd, also joined the party, somewhat bemused by our lapse into what appeared to be insanity. The Carabinieri provided an escort in a Saab, and I did my best to keep up with them all in a Fiat Punto, aquaplaning most of the way. After one of the most treacherous drives of my life we arrived at the headquarters of the Carabinieri in Venice just after midnight. The entire place was flooded with about a foot of water, and as the escorting police car turned the corner on the approach to the building the driver lost control and crashed into a brick wall. The Princess burst out laughing, which did not amuse the police officers who had gathered to greet her.

At that precise moment it stopped raining and the clouds obligingly parted to let the moon through. Diana jumped out of the Contessa's car and starting kicking the puddles, as if she were Gene Kelly in *Singing in the Rain*. The Venice Carabinieri then arranged for two motor boats to take us off to enjoy the astonishing beauty of Venice by moonlight. As we sped off along the canal, the driver of the crashed police car at last broke into a smile.

'I thought it was only we Italians who are crazy,' he said, his ill-humor evaporating in the wake of the Princess's mood.

There was no one else around. For the next hour we saw Venice as few have ever been privileged to do. We sailed along the Grand Canal, with the ancient city silhouetted against a stormy sky pierced by a full moon. Armed with a flask of coffee and a bottle of chilled Pinot Grigio, from which Diana would take the occasional swig as we had no glasses, we were midnight tourists in an empty city. She then announced that she wanted to walk through Saint Mark's Square. The Italian police, who by now had embraced the mood, agreed. We docked our launches at the Hotel Danieli and, still with the tarpaulin over our sodden heads since it had started to rain again, walked towards Saint Mark's Cathedral at the end of the square. It was an enchanting, if almost surreal experience. With the exception of a couple of vagrants dossed down above the water level near the famous landmark, we were the only people there. Then, from nowhere, Sergeant Dave Sharp appeared with a tray of hot croissants and small loaves of freshly cooked bread, which earned him a round of applause from the by now ecstatic Princess.

As she took another swig from the bottle of white wine, Diana, her eyes alight with pleasure, turned to me and said, 'Ken, if only I could have this freedom once a month, it would make the job worth it all the more.'

At last we had to depart. The Princess took graceful leave of the Venetian police officers who, being Italian, were equally charming in return. We returned to Lake Garda just in time for breakfast, snatched two hours' sleep, and set off for Milan's Linate airport for the flight home. It was there that the press finally caught up with us.

A lurking paparazzo snatched shots of the Princess, still animated after her three-day holiday, kissing the Contessa's chauffeur, Tony Pezzo, on the cheek as she made her goodbyes.

The *Sun*, which had printed the pictures, dispatched reporter Mike Sullivan (later to become one of Fleet Street's most respected crime correspondents) to Italy to find out anything he could about our trip. By this time, however, Diana was back at Kensington Palace, her private memories locked safely away. Sullivan did well, given that there was no real story for him to uncover. He talked to Pezzo, and wrote an exclusive based on their conversation. The paper was, of course, trying to suggest that Diana had tried to woo the handsome, thirty-one-year-old Italian. The story was as crass as it was untrue, for the truth was that the Princess had treated the Contessa's chauffeur with courtesy, and nothing more.

Sadly, moments of escape like these were rare, not only because of the pressures of Diana's duties and of her marriage, but because, in reality Diana craved public recognition almost as much as she cherished her privacy.

Since the start of her affair with James Hewitt, Diana had followed a demanding fitness regime, designed to tone her body and (she hoped) invigorate her soul. She swam most mornings, and worked out twice and sometimes three times a week as she honed herself into shape. There was also a seemingly endless stream of health instructors, gurus and alternative therapists in and out of Kensington Palace whose fields of expertise seemed to cover every inch of the body. She seemed to delight in parading around her apartment in front of staff in just her thong leotard, purely to invite a reaction. She would regularly clear her diary for what she called 'pamper days', when experts, from masseurs to manicurists would work on her, sometimes for hours.

At the end of 1989, a few days after Hewitt departed for Germany and the military life, the Princess told me that she wanted to detoxify herself, and fancied a visit to Champneys, one of the country's leading health resorts. With twenty complementary daily activities, more than a hundred treatments and therapies, and what many say is arguably the finest spa cuisine in the world, Champneys boasts that 'Nowhere else makes you feel this good'. Its treatments aim at addressing the whole person – mind, body and spirit – something almost calculated to catch Diana's interest.

So in January 1990, accompanied by three of her closest friends – Julia Samuel, Kate Menzies and Catherine Soames – and me, we booked into the resort, which is set in 170 acres of parkland near Tring in Hertfordshire, about an hour's drive north-west of London. It was bitterly cold when we arrived, but the local police were present in force and as vigilant as ever. In the event, however, I told their local commander to stand them down, as we wanted to avoid such a high-profile security presence. The truth was that, despite the Princess's good intentions, this was a girls' weekend rather than a concerted effort to keep fit, lose weight or tone up.

But one incident left the Princess and her girlfriends in fits of laughter. We had not been there long when the legendary singer Dame Vera Lynn, the British 'Forces' Sweetheart' of World War II who was there with her husband, came over to introduce herself to Diana. I thought that Dame Vera was being a little over-friendly, at least at first, but she soon got the message that the Princess was here to relax alone with her friends and left us. For the first time on a trip with Diana I remember dressing down, for we were in track suits in order to blend in with the other guests at the spa.

Later that morning, as I stood by the door of the reflexology room while the Princess was inside having treatment, I suddenly felt somebody touching my bottom. Startled and more than a little annoyed, I whirled around to find a man standing there, looking decidedly sheepish.

'What on earth are you doing?' I said. 'Don't touch me.'

'It's all right,' he said, 'I'm Vera Lynn's husband.' Quite why he might have thought that this explained everything mystifies me to this day.

'Does that give you any right to touch my backside?' I demanded.

'No, you're quite right,' he said, just as the Princess emerged from the reflexology room.

'I'm sorry, I was just testing to see where you kept your gun,' he said nervously, before scurrying off to join his wife.

'What on earth is going on, Ken?' Diana asked, glowing after having had her toes played with for an hour.

'I've just been touched up by Vera Lynn's husband,' I said indignantly. 'He was searching for my gun.'

Diana burst out laughing, as amused by my aggrieved manner as by the oddness of the incident. She regaled her girlfriends with the story over dinner that evening and they dissolved into laughter. Perhaps we were overheard, for a little later, an abashed Dame Vera came over and apologized to me for her husband's bizarre attempt to frisk me.

Diana's brave decision to be photographed sitting in on therapy sessions for the marriage-guidance counseling service Relate whenever she made official visits to the charity sent out a clear message. For her part, she felt that her involvement in sessions actually helped her cope with her own problems. I accompanied her on a number of private visits to Relate, during which she learned counseling skills, and took part in 'role-play of marital conflict' and discussions. Obviously her active participation had to remain secret, since the press, already alert to the strains in her marriage, would have plastered 'Diana Seeks Marriage Guidance' all over the front page.

A few days after her visit to Champneys we set off for Rugby, where Relate has its headquarters. I decided it would be quicker to go by train than to drive, so I had bought two first-class rail tickets and we sat in the front carriage with other passengers on the 8.20 am train out of Euston station. Diana read the *Daily Mail* as the other travelers, with typical British reserve, pretended not to notice us. She was in an ebullient mood, which always made her mischievous.

'Have we got any back-up with us today, Ken?' she asked, referring to the close-protection officers I had arranged in advance of the visit.

'Yes, ma'am,' I replied, wondering what was coming next. She looked at me a moment, then said, 'Why don't we give them the slip? It would be fun.'

'No, ma'am, we can't do that. It would be unprofessional,' I said. Disappointed, she slumped back in her seat, and I silently hoped that that was the last of her mischievous schemes for the day.

We were met by the chairman of Relate, David French, whom the Princess regarded not simply as the head of one of her patronages, but as a friend. He introduced her to the two course trainers, Irene Short and Moira Fryer, and she then joined them for a 'debriefing lunch' after sitting in on a counseling-skills exercise. Afterwards she joined in role-play of marital conflict and a discussion, telling me later that she had found both particularly enlightening.

Somehow though, she still found the means to play one of her customary practical jokes in between the drama of playing an abused wife. As I found out later, she had slipped out during the hour-long afternoon session and briefed the unsuspecting receptionist that if one of the back-up protection officers came back, they should tell him that she had already left for London by train. So when the unsuspecting PC Ron Haywood returned to Relate's offices to be greeted with the news that we had just left for the station, the poor chap panicked, since he was meant to be on the train with us. He was about to go sprinting through the streets of Rugby to the station when I managed to contact him. Diana the prankster had managed to work some mischief after all, despite the constraints of being on a formal visit to one of her most-admired charities. Such incidents – and there were many of them – were part of her playful nature, and show a character quite different from the self-obsessed depressive of so much of the popular mythology surrounding her memory.

Her visits to Relate and other charities demonstrated that despite her depression, fears and occasional fury over Charles's infidelity, Diana did her best to get on with her job. She toured Britain, winning over hearts and minds for a family which had already begun the process of repudiating her. With the public, unlike with her in-laws, she could do no wrong. Many of them seemed to have an unconscious gift for bringing her back to earth with a bump.

'You don't remember me, sir, do you?' the driver who met us at Manchester airport said in his strong local accent as we headed towards his home city on an 'awayday'. I was sitting in the front, with the Princess reading her briefing notes in the back, psyching herself up for the walkabout she was going to make. I was not in the mood for small talk, but the police driver persisted irritatingly.

'I said . . .' he began.

'I heard what you said,' I snapped. 'Just get on with it.'

'But I drove you the last time you were up here, sir,' he replied plaintively.

Before I had a chance to pull rank on the talkative constable, the Princess decided to engage him in conversation. Unlike me, she was polite.

'I remember you; you drove so very well,' she chimed in, although I was pretty certain she didn't know him from Adam. Unfortunately, this only encouraged him.

'Oh, really ma'am, I am honored. You must have so many people drive you and you remember me . . .' There was no stopping him now. I am also fairly sure that the Princess just engaged him in conversation because she knew it would exasperate me.

Eventually we arrived at our destination where, as always, a large crowd had gathered to greet her. As she made her way into the center of the throng, one woman seemed especially anxious to make Diana take notice of her, following her as she walked along a path cleared by local police, who held the onlookers back.

''Scuse me, Your Royal Highness . . . 'scuse me,' the elderly woman said as she frantically tried to catch the Princess's attention.

Diana stopped. 'Ken, there's an old lady over there,' she said, her signal for me to bring the woman to the front of the crowd. I nodded to a couple of the officers, and they cleared a space to let the gray-haired supplicant through.

'Hello, ma'am,' she said when she reached the Princess. 'You'll never guess what – my son's your driver.' Diana smiled and spoke to her for a few moments, and then the whole circus moved forward, protocol now re-established.

As soon as we got back in the car, her duties over, the Princess found the perfect solution to keeping our garrulous chauffeur quiet.

'You'll never guess what,' she said to him, trying not to laugh. Curious, the driver, who was beginning, rather presumptuously, to regard the Princess as a newfound friend, turned around, no doubt about to offer his next installment in inane chit-chat. Then the Princess struck her killer blow: 'I've just met your mother.'

'Bloody hell, no,' he said in alarm, flushing bright scarlet. He focused on his driving from then on, and we had a peaceful journey back to the airport.

Incidents like that underline one of the problems for members of the royal family, namely that although they are often keen to see 'real life', their status tends to prevent people from acting normally in their presence. Wherever they go walls are freshly painted, everything cleaned up or tidied away, and people stand awkwardly before them in their finest bib-and-tucker. So what royalty actually sees is a distorted, cleaned-up image of reality. Somehow, Diana managed to transcend this, her innate humanity putting people at their ease, letting them see beyond the trappings of royalty to the real person underneath.

On an 'awayday' to Whaley Bridge in Derbyshire in mid-June

she had attended the Festival of the Rose Queens, where she crowned the three 1990 Rose Queens at the local marina. With the ceremony over, she was then escorted to a narrow boat, the *Judith Mary*, moored on the canal, for lunch among the local notables who clog up such occasions. Once on board, she was introduced to the boat's owner, Rob Sharpe, who told her that he hired his narrow boat out for trips on the canal.

'You must get some funny people on here,' she innocently commented.

In a thick Midlands accent, Mr Sharpe, a no-nonsense sort of character, replied: 'Oh, we get some right funny people 'ere. I remember once we had a group of lads on a stag night, and they asked us to take 'em down canal, like, to local pub, like, which we did, but I said I want you back on boat by eleven o'clock.

'By eleven-fifteen nobody had shown, like, so I went in pub and I told 'em to get on boat, and they turned up a few minutes later with these three prostitutes . . .'

The Princess was enthralled, even as the collection of local dignitaries cringed in embarrassment. There was no stopping Mr Sharpe, however.

'That's when I told 'em, ma'am – told 'em straight, like, I did – I do not allow any shagging on my boat.'

Her laughter rang out clearly in the stunned silence that followed this gem: 'Oh well, Mr Sharpe,' she replied. 'Boys will be boys.' By then I turned away, almost bursting with the effort of trying not to laugh myself.

Two weeks later, on 28 June, Charles broke his arm badly in a fall while playing polo locally. In terrible pain, he was taken to the hospital in Cirencester, not far from Highgrove, where doctors decided to set the double fracture without pinning it. On leaving hospital he posed for photographers with Diana at his side, before she drove him back to Highgrove. Within minutes of dropping him off, however, she left again – with me, since I or one of my officers had to be with her at all times – for Kensington Palace. I understand that, shortly afterwards, Camilla Parker Bowles arrived to look after her injured man.

As we drove back to London, Diana confessed, quietly and sadly, without any hysterics but with absolute determination, that this was the final straw. She had wanted, she said, to care for her husband, but he had made it clear that during his convalescence, which was likely to be a long one, since the bones were not pinned, he did not want anyone near him. After that, Diana said she was simply no longer prepared to try to make anything of her marriage. Camilla effectively moved into Highgrove and the Prince allowed her a free rein; a fervent anti-smoker himself, he even allowed his mistress to smoke anywhere in the house.

I have absolutely no doubt that Diana desperately wanted at least to play the part of the caring wife, nursing her injured husband through his pain. He simply would not allow it. Perhaps it was a godsend. Throughout July and August Charles's temper worsened as his arm failed to heal properly. Eventually, a second opinion was sought, and a new treatment suggested, which would involve an operation on the arm. After much lobbying the Prince agreed, and he was booked into the Queen's Medical Centre, Nottingham. Diana was not consulted about this, nor did I ever hear her offer an opinion of any kind about Charles's decision. He arrived at the hospital in early September 1990 and his entire entourage followed, decamping from St James's Palace to set up office there, much to his wife's distaste, and even greater distrust. I drove her to Nottingham to visit him, but from the moment she arrived his obsequious aides made it clear that she was neither needed nor wanted.

Whatever happened now, the marriage was, to anyone on the inside, clearly beyond salvation.

They did not have much to say. Charles lay in his hospital bed, bemoaning his fate, and Diana simply sat and listened. Neither wanted to be in the other's company, and after the briefest of periods (long enough to be seen as acceptable when, inevitably, her visit was reported in the media) the Princess left his private room and walked along the hospital corridor. It was then that she found a middle-aged woman sitting outside the intensive-care ward, sobbing. Her name was Ivy Woodward. Diana's ability to interact with people she had never met before was extraordinary. In one natural motion she knelt beside the woman and then put her arm around her to comfort her.

'Do you mind if I come in?' she asked. In the ward, Ivy's son Dean lay oblivious to his royal visitor. He had been involved in a serious road accident on 30 August, and had been rushed to the Queen's Medical Centre by ambulance. Doctors there had done their best to revive him, but had just told his family that his chances of recovery were not considered good. His wife, Jane, sat by his bedside, lost in her own thoughts.

'He'll pull through. I know he'll pull through,' Diana told the two women. She could have left it at that, just a kindly and comforting word from a passing celebrity. For some reason of her own, however, she insisted on going back to comfort Ivy and her family. Every time she went to visit Charles, she also visited Dean. The story soon leaked out to the press, but Diana was not doing this for publicity. She genuinely wanted to help a family in need. On one of our trips to Nottingham, she did not even bother to visit her husband, but instead went to the Woodwards' home. In the late autumn Ivy's prayers were answered when her son came out of the coma that had claimed him for so long. Diana telephoned him as he convalesced in the City Hospital, to which he'd been moved after he began to recover, and promised to visit again.

The bitter irony of this curious interlude did not escape me, although I'm not sure the Princess saw it. She had tried to comfort and care for her husband, and had been unfeelingly rejected. At the same time, she had offered her sympathy and comfort to a family of strangers, and had been welcomed. Beyond that, however, she had genuinely 'made a difference'.

Diana's relations with other royals is best described as tricky. I have already said that she was in awe of the Queen, who remained a remote, if powerful, presence to her. She was nervous around the Queen Mother, always conscious that her grandmother, Ruth, Lady Fermoy, a close friend of the Queen Mother, had, as she put it, 'done a good hatchet job on her'. Lady Fermoy had been, however, right in her advice that royal life would not suit Diana; their outlook, lifestyle and sense of humor were very different from hers. Yet she might have coped even with these hurdles, had it not been for an incident during Charles's arduous recovery from his broken arm that confirmed her worst fears, as well as her increasing sense of isolation. In the autumn of 1990, while Diana carried on her life in London, Prince Charles escaped to the Queen Mother's Highland retreat, Birkhall, one of the houses on the Queen's Balmoral estate. While there, he was photographed, for the first and only time during his marriage to Diana, in the company of Camilla Parker Bowles. Photographer Jim Bennett captured the Prince of Wales and his mistress on film as they left the whitewashed mansion and stepped into a waiting car. What is not generally known, however, is that the Queen Mother was also staying at Birkhall at the same time, confirming Diana's belief that the royal family had sanctioned Charles's adultery at the highest level. It was a devastating blow and one that convinced her that she had to escape.

By now her relations with many of her husband's family were at an all-time low. The Queen was chilly and distant, as well as concerned about some of Diana's good works, notably AIDS. The Queen Mother, she commented once, seemed to regard her with a kind of detached pity. She found the Duke of Edinburgh impossible; although to be fair, in his own bluff way, he had tried to offer her an olive branch, only for her to slap it in his face. She liked Prince Andrew, whom she thought was underestimated, and Princess Anne she found stimulating, although she never felt that she could have a sisterly chat with her. She did, however, adore her Kensington Palace neighbor, Princess Margaret, who had been kind to her, as well as understanding, from the moment she had joined the Firm. Perhaps, with 'Margo's' extravagant lifestyle, her celebrated, sometimes tragic, love life and her occasionally almost bohemian independence, the two women empathized with each other.

As an aside, I once had the pleasure of accompanying Princess Margaret home after the State Banquet for the Italian President. It is an occasion indelibly etched on my memory. Diana had left early, but drink was still being taken, while President Cossigia continued an animated conversation with the Prime Minister, Margaret Thatcher.

As it happened, I was on duty for both Diana and Princess Margaret that night, having agreed to stand in for one of my colleagues and escort Margo, as well as Diana, from Kensington Palace and back again once the banquet was over. With Simon Solari driving the Rolls-Royce, I had escorted Diana home and returned for Princess Margaret. The champagne (and, it seemed, every other kind of drink) had flowed freely that evening. Margo, to assist her through the formalities of that lavish occasion, had had rather too much.

She also didn't want to leave. Eventually two Italian staff managed to prize her free, escort her to the car, and pour her into the back seat. Simon drove very carefully, but even so, she was so drunk that she twice fell into the well between the front and back seats. We eventually arrived outside her apartment at Kensington Palace, only to find that her butler had gone to bed and the place was in darkness. She, of course, had no key and neither had I.

Becoming desperate, I decided that Griffin, her chauffeur, must have a key. He had a flat in the palace, and I set off to rouse him. At that moment, the fluting voice of the Queen's sister drifted out of the back of the car.

'Don't bother with him,' she said. 'He'll be drunk.'

'Ken, the flashes are too bright, I can't see where I'm going,' the Princess said, with real alarm in her voice, as we stood at the top of the sweeping staircase. She was wearing a magnificent scarlet evening gown and a princess's ransom in jewelry, and looked a good deal more than a million dollars, but the incessant firing of flashguns from the foot of the stairs had almost blinded her.

It was an evening in October 1990, and Diana was in the process of leaving the Departmental Auditorium in Washington, DC, where she had attended a gala evening in her honor. Velvet ropes slung between stanchions controlled by two liveried footmen had been used to ease her passage through the packed reception, where the great and the good of America's capital had paid a small fortune just to be in the same room as her. Now she had to negotiate the grand staircase to reach street level – and she didn't want to do so in an ungainly tangle of scarlet silk and scattered diamonds.

'Ken, I'm serious. I don't think I'm going to get down these stairs in one piece,' she hissed anxiously.

'Don't worry, ma'am,' I said, as I slipped my arm under hers. My American colleague, Lanny Bernier, a security officer from the State Department detached to assist me in guarding the Princess during her visit, followed my lead. Then, at a nod from me, we literally lifted her up and frogmarched her down the staircase and out of the building.

'Oh, boys, that was fun,' she breathed, when we reached the waiting limousine. Then she turned to Bernier and said, 'Thank you so much,' the direct look and warm smile immediately winning her another conquest. I then introduced him formally whereupon Lanny turned to her and said, 'Ma'am, may I tell you something?'

'Yes, Lanny.'

'Can I say you're looking great?'

Diana was a little taken aback at the compliment from this burly officer, but answered him with another wonderful smile. 'Oh, Ken, he's so sweet,' she said as we drove away. On the following day she called Lanny to her suite, and gave him a photograph of herself that she had signed for him.

That was her last engagement of that working visit, and on the following day she and I, traveling as Mr and Mrs Hargreaves, flew back to England by Concorde. The trip to Washington was her first real solo success, and on the flight home she was buzzing with excitement.

Diana loved practical jokes. Still exhilarated after her trip, she was in the mood for fun, and was determined to make a little mischief on the journey from Heathrow to Kensington Palace.

'Ken, do one of your funny voices,' she ordered suddenly. Unlike her, I was tired and keen to get home, so I demurred.

'Oh, *please*, Ken. I am a Princess, you know – I'm not supposed to beg,' she pleaded. For some reason, I have always had a knack for mimicry. I looked back at her with one eyebrow raised and playfully replied 'Oh really, ma'am?' in a deeply affected accent resembling that of her errant husband.

Diana laughed, then begged me again. 'Oh, please, Ken, let's try Richard. He'd be easy pickings.'

This was a trick we would occasionally play on some of her friends. I would call the selected friend, pretending to be somebody else, and leave the mobile phone in the cradle so that everyone in the car could hear as I teased the unsuspecting victim.

In the end, I relented, telling the Princess and Simon to keep absolutely quiet otherwise their voices would be heard. Diana's chosen victim was Richard Dalton, one of her hairdressers whose specialty was coloring her blonde locks. Richard, who had a salon at Claridges, the luxury hotel in London's Mayfair, could be a little precious, to say the least.

I dialed his number, and set the telephone down in the cradle. The phone was now 'hands-free', and Simon and Diana would be able to hear every word of the conversation relayed through the speaker.

'Can I speak to Richard Dalton?' I said, in what I hoped was an educated Boston accent, trying to sound like a deep version of JFK. There was a pause, then a man's voice said 'Hello?' rather impatiently.

'Is that Dick? Dick Dalton?' I asked.

'The name's Richard,' he pronounced rather grandly, clearly irritated by my impertinence at abbreviating his forename.

'Whatever,' I responded, as Diana and Simon tried to stifle their giggles.

'Who is this?' Richard demanded, clearly growing more piqued by the second.

'It's Jack, Jack Sveltzer from the *Washington Post* – I'm the beauty fashion editor with the *Post*.'

Richard was deeply unimpressed. 'So, what do you want?' he asked bluntly.

'Well Dick, I understand you don't like Dick – or being called Dick, that is?' At this point Diana was practically on the floor of the car, she was laughing so much.

'No, I don't like being called Dick, Mr Sveltzer. Now what is this all about?'

'Well, Dick, don't let's worry about names. I deal in beauty – I am the beauty fashion editor, as I've said – and I understand you gave Princess Diana a makeover on her hair?'

'That's right,' he said, his tone becoming even more aggressive. 'What about it?'

'Well, she has great hair, but when was the last time you did her roots?

At this the Princess exploded with laughter, unable to suppress it any longer.

'No more, Ken, no more,' she pleaded, tears of laughter rolling down her face.

'What's all that noise?' Richard demanded, growing increasingly upset.

'Well, it's simple, Dick, I am doing a big feature on the Princess, and I am looking at pictures of her showing at least three inches of roots.'

'This is nonsense!' he roared.

It was then, fearing that Simon, who was literally shaking with laughter as he drove, might veer off the road, that I decided to come clean.

'Richard, it's Ken!' I said in my own voice. There was a moment's silence, followed by a series of expletives as we drove down the motorway towards London. It didn't seem to matter to Richard when I tried to tell him that the phone was on hands-free and that the Princess could hear every four-letter word uttered.

At Kensington Palace, just as the Princess was about to enter her apartments, I stopped her with a confiding, 'Ma'am?'

'Yes, Ken,' she replied.

'Don't forget to get those roots done in the morning.'

She paused for a second, put her hands on her hips and tilted her head to one side as if in royal indignation, before replying, 'I'll book an appointment for the both of us, shall I?'

James Hewitt had not spoken to Diana for more than a year when the Princess suddenly called him at his barracks in Germany. British troops stationed there were being mobilized as part of the Allied force preparing, under a UN resolution, to go to the Gulf to drive Saddam Hussein out of Kuwait, which Iraqi forces had invaded and taken over in August. She asked if he was going to be sent to the Gulf and he told her that he was. The Princess then asked if she could see him before he went. Hewitt was due back in Britain for his sister's wedding before flying to Canada for army maneuvers; after that he would leave for Saudi Arabia, where the Coalition forces were assembling and training. She invited him to stay at Highgrove while he was in the country and he accepted. That night, with her husband, as ever, away from Highgrove while she was there, her romance with James was rekindled. It was during that weekend that she told him that she was more than ever determined to divorce Prince Charles and walk away from the royal family, echoing what she had told me some months earlier after Charles had broken his arm

James flew out to Saudi Arabia on 26 December 1990, where he rejoined his squadron of the Life Guards. From then on Diana wrote to him every day, sometimes twice a day, doing her best to be supportive as he prepared to go to war. She also sent him hampers from Fortnum and Mason, the upmarket London department store, and bottles of whisky, which he duly shared among his squadron. She even sent him copies of 'adult' magazines like *Playboy*, *Mayfair* and *Penthouse* through the diplomatic bag, knowing that Saudi Arabia, like most Muslim states, banned publications that carried any hint of promiscuity.

Diana also remained in constant touch with James's mother, Shirley, and she and I would sometimes drive down to Devon to see her, with one or both of her sons, just for the day. There was another reason for these visits, however, for James used to send his letters to the Princess via his mother and Diana was always desperate to read them. I could understand her concern for her lover, but I again advised her to be cautious about her copious letter-writing. If the letters were to fall into the wrong hands, I said, the true nature of her friendship with Hewitt would become public property. But Diana, in love with the idea of being in love with a war hero, was in no mood to listen, and much less to worry over such trifling considerations.

# Chapter 10

On 3 June 1991 I received a bleep from Sergeant Reg Spinney, Prince William's personal protection officer, while I was lunching with the Princess at one of her favorite restaurants, San Lorenzo in Beauchamp Place, close to Harrods. The message on the pager's screen stated that William had been injured in an accident at Ludgrove, the prep school in Berkshire to which he had gone as a boarder when he was eight. The injury was serious. Before telling the Princess I excused myself to her, found a telephone and contacted Reg to find out exactly what the situation was. He told me that William had been struck a serious blow on the head by a golf club wielded by a friend, and had been taken for tests at the Royal Berkshire Hospital in Reading.

Diana went white when I told her. Abandoning lunch, she and I fled the restaurant and set off for Reading, with me driving and the Princess agonizing over the injury to her son. When we arrived at the hospital Prince Charles was already there. William was having a computerized tomography (CT) scan, after which the doctors suggested that he be transferred to the Great Ormond Street Hospital for Sick Children in London. Off we set again. Diana accompanied William in the ambulance while Charles followed behind in his Aston-Martin. Once there, tests confirmed that William had suffered a serious depressed fracture of the skull, and that there was a real possibility of brain damage. The young prince would have to undergo a difficult operation to pull the depressed bones out and smooth them off. The doctors told his parents that there was no need for both of them to wait in the ward while William was in surgery. To be fair to Prince Charles, Diana made it clear that she did not want him around and he therefore decided, there being nothing else to do but hope for his son's full recovery, to attend a performance of *Tosca* at the Royal Opera House, Covent Garden, in company with the European and Agricultural Commissioners and a group of Brussels officials. He was to pay dearly for that decision. Next day, the *Sun's* front-page headline bellowed; 'What Kind Of A Dad Are You?', going on to deliver a sententious sermon on the theme that a fractured skull is not a trivial matter. Once again, Charles had made a fatally wrong choice, not only in the eyes of the media, but also in those of his wife, for his decision to put duty before family further divided the couple. The only ray of light in the whole miserable business was that William was quickly on his feet again, without any danger of brain damage.

Adrian Ward-Jackson, an art dealer and a Governor of the Royal Ballet, was a great friend of Diana's. He was also deputy Chairman of the AIDS Crisis Trust, and it was through that charity that they had first met. Tragically, by 1991 he was dying of AIDS, the disease that she had worked so hard to 'de-demonize' in the light of the public taboos against it. Diana and Adrian had developed a special relationship over the years, and it is fair to say that he did more than anyone in helping her to launch her public crusade for a better understanding of the disease that he himself was stricken with.

In the spring of 1991 his condition began to deteriorate rapidly, and he was confined to his flat in Mount Street, Mayfair. Angela Serota, wife of Adrian's close friend Nicholas Serota, director of the Tate Gallery, and herself a good friend of the Princess, was constantly at his bedside, and I accompanied Diana on her numerous visits there to see her dying friend.

Adrian's worsening condition added impetus to Diana's mission to wake up the world to the AIDS crisis. In July she asked the wife of the US President, Barbara Bush, who was in London at the time, to accompany her on a visit to Professor Mike Adler's AIDS unit at the Middlesex Hospital. Diana saw this as an important milestone. In private, she told me that she always wanted to hug people she visited, not just touch them – something that some cynics now claim was simply a gimmick she employed to raise her own profile. It is an unworthy accusation, for she was genuinely moved by their plight, and desperately anxious to do all she could to alleviate their suffering.

On this visit, the Princess stopped by a man who was sitting, crying, on the end of his bed. In front of the First Lady, she took him in her arms. Afterwards the man, who told her that he had only a few months to live, said that he sensed a great deal of anger inside her. She listened to his comments intently, but said nothing, although I noted that she did not contradict him.

As we drove away from the hospital Diana was clearly very moved. She was not crying, but I could see that she was close to tears. After a while she found her voice again.

'I do what is expected of me, Ken – nobody can accuse me of not doing my best. That man said I was angry. Do you think I am angry?' she asked. Diplomatically, I elected not to answer. She did so for me.

'Surely it should be the other way round? What have I got to be unhappy about? God, he's the one who will be dead by Christmas . . .'

For all the work she did for worthy, and sometimes unpopular or unfashionable, causes, the Princess's image was starting to slip a little. The media, although in general sympathetic towards her, were no longer treating her like a saint by the beginning of 1991. For some time she had been the darling of the press, a kind of cross between Mother Teresa and a super-model. It was an image that she enjoyed, but as the whispers and rumors about her disintegrating marriage spread further and further afield, the press, aware that all was not well, focused more and more on the relationship between the Prince and Princess of Wales.

In May 1991, after the unceremonious departure of the Prince and Princess of Wales's private secretary, the affable Sir Christopher Airy, came the decisive moment when Charles and Diana's formal offices separated – a clear signal to anyone well up in Palace circles of the Princess's intent. Her equerry, Patrick Jephson, took over as her private secretary, while his friend Commander Richard Aylard headed up Charles's now separate office. From that point Diana was set upon her own distinct and divergent path. Members of both their staffs had to choose to be in either one camp or the other. There was no halfway house. Luckily, the policemen attached to the households did not technically work for the individuals concerned, so for us at least that problem did not arise.

But as the two sides in the 'War of the Waleses' drew up battle plans, Diana was inevitably caught in the spotlight, and her image tarnished as a result. By this time it was virtually impossible to hide the truth from the public. On her thirtieth birthday in July the *Daily Mail's* gossip columnist, Nigel Dempster, broke a story that perfectly summed up the situation. 'Charles and Diana: Cause For Concern' ran the headline above Dempster's piece, which brought consternation to both camps.

What the gossip columnist had written was a detailed and well-sourced account of the row over the plans for the Princess's birthday, in which he attacked Diana's petulance in rejecting Prince Charles's proposals for her birthday celebrations. Yet given the state of their marriage, it is difficult to see how she could have accepted a birthday party which amounted to little more than a publicity stunt.

In releasing details of the row, Prince Charles's supporters had plunged the knife into Diana in a pre-emptive strike, giving her a birthday present she surely did not deserve. It was the first time the two sides had clashed so publicly. Diana hit back, using the *Sun*, by claiming that she would be staying in to watch television on her milestone birthday. The gloves were off.

If Charles and his faction wanted a fight, then Diana was ready and willing to give them one. There was by then an agreement that she should not undertake an engagement that might clash with one of Prince Charles's, especially if he was to make what his people termed a major speech. Technically he had precedence, but Diana was in no mood to bow to him. She therefore told her private secretary, Patrick Jephson, that she had no intention of rearranging an invitation she had received to attend a combined National Aids Trust and National Children's Bureau conference. To add insult to injury, knowing full well that it would infuriate her husband and his growing army of aides, she agreed to make a speech at the conference. She knew that whatever she had to say would receive far more press attention than Charles's comments, no matter how worthy. This was the warning shot across the bows, Diana's way of throwing down the gauntlet. Inevitably, she achieved her objective, leaving Prince Charles and his advisers seething.

Although experience has taught me never to underestimate the British press, it never fails to amaze me how gullible journalists can be. True, some try harder than others to find out what is actually happening behind palace doors, usually to be rewarded with a barrage of abuse from courtiers whose job it is to offer the best possible gloss, and sometimes even to lie, for their employers. Other reporters, seeking an easy life, seem content to swallow the anodyne doses offered by spin-doctors and other aides or spokesmen. Acceptance of this spoon feeding was never more evident than in the British media's reporting of the Princess's supposed 'love cruise' with Charles in the summer of 1991, at the height of their marital problems. Bizarrely, most of the journalists who penned this 'love boat' rubbish knew perfectly well that the Prince and Princess were at loggerheads. Yet some, no doubt to keep in with Palace circles, chose to go into print with Richard Aylard's rosy briefings about the trip.

After I had accompanied the Princess as she inspected her regiment (the Princess of Wales's Royal Regiment, later nicknamed, rather cruelly, the 'Squidgys'), Arthur Edwards of the *Sun*, was plaguing me about the royal couple's destination, as news of the fact that they were taking a holiday together, with their sons, had leaked out. 'Is it Majorca? I've heard it's off this year,' he said.

'You might be right, Arthur, but I can't tell you even if you are,' I insisted.

'I've heard they are going to Italy aboard some Greek billionaire's yacht, Ken. Is that right?' he persisted. My silence was enough to make him realize something different was afoot this year. All I could tell him was to follow his instincts.

Fleet Street pooled information. With the notable exception of the *Daily Express* team of photographer Steve Wood and correspondent Ashley Walton, who flew to Majorca on a rumor or a whim, the rest of the hacks headed for the Italian port of Naples. They rightly deduced that the Prince and Princess were taking their holiday aboard the yacht owned by the Greek tycoon John Latsis – as Arthur Edwards had surmised – and that the royal party would board the yacht, the *Alexander*, from a military port, where security would make sure that no journalist or photographer got even close.

The *Alexander* is one of the world's largest and most luxurious private yachts. Worth more than $45 million (£30 million), the 350-foot yacht was equipped with every possible luxury, including vintage Dom Pérignon seemingly on tap. For Diana, however, the trip was nothing but a chore. The benefit for her was that she had a chance to be with her sons, but most of the other guests on board were people she termed 'Charles's cronies'. In this she was being a little unfair, since those who accompanied the Prince and Princess on such a holiday at such a time, given the state of relations between them, deserved a medal, not criticism, even if the guest list did somewhat favor the Prince and his friends. On board were the Queen's cousin, Princess Alexandra, her husband, the Hon. Sir Angus Ogilvy, and the Prince's relations and close friends, Lord and Lady Romsey, whom Diana despised because she knew they were also close to Camilla Parker Bowles.

Yet, as with the holiday on Necker the previous year, the Princess had invited Graham Smith to join the cruise. Her former protection officer was very ill by now, and both Diana and I feared the worst. In the event he enjoyed the trip, but within months he would be forced to retire.

In terms of Palace public relations, the cruise was a complete success, the media content to dub it the 'second honeymoon'. This was laughable, for in reality the couple were at loggerheads the entire time. The Princess, at her most petulant and spoilt, made it clear to everyone that she was unhappy at being cooped up on the yacht with her husband. At the start of the cruise the press, in hot pursuit, did indeed track the yacht down to a military port in Naples, but the powerful *Alexander* soon disappeared over the horizon, with the press boats falling far behind. The only time the royal party was disturbed again was off the coast of Sardinia, when a local photographer, Massimo Sestini, got lucky and scooped the ratpack. To make matters worse, he had also photographed some of Fleet Street's finest aboard their chartered speedboat, complete with posing pouches, allegedly looking for the royal love-boat. He promptly sold the shots to a Sunday newspaper, thereby making a number of enemies among the journalists he had snapped.

Diana was at Balmoral when, on 19 August, Angela Serota telephoned to say that the last rites had been administered to Adrian Ward-Jackson who was by now gravely ill in St Mary's Hospital. At once she and I left for London without, as was customary (and expected), asking permission of the Queen, traveling by car as we could not get a flight soon enough. We drove through the night the 550 miles from north-east Scotland to London so she could share Adrian's last moments. Diana slept most of the way, but spent hours with her friend once we reached the hospital. In the end he clung on to life until 23 August, and Diana, summoned by the faithful Angela, arrived to see him for the last time not long before he died. His death had a profound effect on her, and she dedicated her AIDS Crusade to him, the man who had first inspired her to support the cause.

Out of the blue, I received a call from James Hewitt. He said that he did not know what to do about his relationship with the Princess, and he wanted my advice. I knew that there was nothing I could do to help him, but I liked the man, so I agreed to meet. He had recently returned from the Gulf and their affair had been briefly rekindled; he stayed at Kensington Palace a couple of times, but, as he told me, the intimacy they had shared in their love letters to and from the front was completely absent in their face-to-face meetings. Now Diana was not answering his calls. He was confused. It was a difficult situation, and although I told him that I could see that he was in a dilemma, I insisted that I was in no position to help. What went on between him and Diana, I reminded him, was their business, and theirs alone. I could not and would not intervene. After the *News of the World* story in March 1991 which exposed their close friendship for the first time, the Princess had wisely decreed that they could not be seen in public together.

Hewitt was still in love with Diana, or so it seemed to me. Rather naively, during the Gulf Campaign he had kept in touch with her by using the *Daily Mail* satellite phone, courtesy of reporter Richard Kay, who had been sent to the front line to cover the war for his newspaper. What Hewitt did not know was that even while he was there, Diana confided to me that she felt he was getting 'too serious'. He was, apparently, openly talking about them spending the rest of their lives together. This unnerved Diana, for the idea of giving up the trappings of royalty and her position to become an army wife was not a prospect that excited her at all.

She also told me that she had never been completely convinced that James's declarations of love were entirely genuine, perhaps believing that he was as attracted to the idea of snaring a princess – indeed, the most famous woman in the world – as he was to her for herself. In any event, not long after his return she told him over the phone that it would be best if they 'cooled things' for the time being.

And that was that. After a short leave Hewitt returned to Germany, a posting that would last for around six months. When he came back to London, stationed conveniently at Knightsbridge

Barracks, on the edge of Hyde Park, Diana had moved on. He blamed publicity for killing their relationship; to me, she openly blamed his stupidity.

Within days of her 'Dear John' phone call, Diana began the process of self-justification.

'Ken, do you know that when James was in the Gulf he even borrowed Richard Kay's satellite phone so he could speak to me and let others listen? How ridiculous is that?' she said. She had a point. From a security point of view, her decision to distance herself from Hewitt was a godsend. Blackmail was always a serious concern. I did not believe that James, as a Life Guards officer, would himself stoop so low, not least because he had too much to lose. None the less, I always feared that blackmail was a possibility, especially from someone who had seen them together or had taken photographs of them during one of their trysts.

After the affair ended, James seemed to lose all sense of perspective. His sense of honor as an officer did not prevent him from publishing his account of the affair during the Princess's lifetime. Later, all the nonsense he wrote about MI6 plotting to kill him struck me as the rantings of a man desperate to sell his story to the highest bidder. James knows the truth, as I do, and in my opinion he would do best to stick to it.

Diana found that ending her relationship with James Hewitt was far easier than she had anticipated. By the time she finally cut the cord she had lost her respect for him. On more than one occasion she told me of her concerns. She believed that, far from being in love with her, James was a maverick who may have been using her. She had also explained to him that she had to resolve the many problems in her life, and could not do so while conducting an adulterous affair. Typically, when James accepted this with good grace, she was slightly irritated, no doubt having hoped that he would beg her to reconsider, declaring yet again his undying love.

On my advice, she asked for the return of the love letters she had written to him while he was in the Gulf. He declined, however, insisting that he wanted to keep them as a memento of their deep love for each other, even though that love had not endured. I was suspicious of his motives, but the Princess accepted his explanation, albeit reluctantly. From that moment, however, she was always concerned that the letters would one day be published by her former lover and suffered more or less continual anxiety over leaving such incriminating evidence in Hewitt's safekeeping. As events would prove, she was of course right to worry.

Several years later, after Diana's death, Hewitt's girlfriend of the time allegedly stole the letters from him and tried to sell them to the *Daily Mirror*. Fortunately, the paper's editor, Piers Morgan, did the honorable thing and returned them to Diana's estate. They are in fact Hewitt's property (although the copyright in them belongs to her estate) but, as Andrew Morton has pointed out, it is unlikely that he will ever see them again.

By the end of 1991 it was clear to many people, and not just those on the inside, that the Prince of Wales's marriage was in desperate trouble. Ten years earlier, when he and Diana had married, the couple had seemed so full of happiness and hope that observers spoke of a new era in British royal life, less stuffy, more approachable, more in tune with the country in the last-but-one decade of the twentieth century. Now, it seemed, that dream would end, as would the marriage itself. The generally held view, however, was that divorce was not a possibility principally because the Queen would never sanction it – or so it was said. I did not agree; indeed, I saw divorce as the only possible conclusion. The 'new' Diana wanted to spread her wings, but she wanted to do so outside the confines of the royal family. I knew that she wanted above all to escape her marriage, and to live a life in which she could 'be herself', something that she had often confided to me. What I did not know, however, was the one secret, in the years that I was with her, that she kept from me. Without my knowledge or that of almost anyone else close to her, the Princess had laid secret plans which she hoped would prove the 'no divorce' pundits wrong. The project was eventually to evolve into a book called *Diana: Her True Story*, and its publication would effectively bring the marriage to an end.

# Chapter 11

SEPTEMBER 1991 finally saw the Palace approve plans for the Princess's first solo tour, an official visit to Pakistan. This was her big chance and she was anxious not to fail, for it provided a great opportunity to emerge from the shadow of her husband and be seen not only as a worthwhile member of the royal family, but as a person in her own right. Prince Charles, meanwhile, was undertaking a visit to Nepal, and would collect the Princess in Pakistan for the flight home.

At the end of August before I set off for the reconnaissance during which I hoped to pave the way for a safe and media-friendly tour, Diana asked me to do all that I could to ensure that her character was reflected in the working visit; she wanted to show the world what the Princess of Wales was all about. Her private secretary, Patrick Jephson, took directives from the Foreign Office about what they wanted the Princess to do, as well as seemingly endless instructions and advice from the Palace. Formal directives were all very well, but despite the fact that I was her protection officer I knew exactly what type of schedule she wanted, something that went far beyond the issue of security. 'I am a humanitarian, Ken,' she said before I left. 'I want to touch the people and I want them to touch me.' She had made it clear that she wanted to smash down old royal barriers and set a new and exciting agenda. Somehow I had to make sure that she was not put at risk.

In security terms, Diana had set me a tough task. The fact that she wanted the crowds to be able to get close to her meant that potentially she would be in danger from any disaffected or demented person intent on making a name or proving a point. The

Princess's instruction was not a request, however; it was an unequivocal order.

The Pakistani government and people could not have been more helpful or hospitable, and were clearly delighted – 'honored' was the word they used – to be hosting such a high-profile tour. I quickly found that nothing was too much trouble for them. I was put up in the old Government House in Lahore, a fantastic building dating from the days of the British Raj, and immensely comfortable, and was assured that nothing was too difficult for them. At one point I asked if they could arrange a back-up car for security use, and emphasized that it had to be reliable. At this, the eyes of one of the local organizers lit up with excitement. 'Don't you worry, Inspector, don't you worry. I have something very, very special for you.' A few hours later I was taken to see it, and could barely contain my laughter as I was proudly shown an old but classic pink Cadillac convertible. We used it.

On my return I gave the Princess a full briefing. She had received a formal outline of the visit from Patrick, but she wanted me to reassure her, not just that all the proper security measures were in place, but that the trip was going to be a huge success. I did my best to set her mind at rest on both points. From the snow-capped Himalayan setting of Chitral to the cauldron of Lahore, she was going to get her way. She would be a princess of the people.

Diana flew out to Muscat, in the Persian Gulf, on a scheduled British Airways plane, where the BAe146 of the RAF's Queen's Flight was waiting to take her on the last leg to Islamabad. On landing she went straight to her first engagement, giving the world, and her detractors back at Buckingham Palace, a clear message that she meant business.

Her first stop was at a ceremony at the Commonwealth War Cemetery in Rawalpindi. This, Diana wanted to stress, was official business, sanctioned by and undertaken on behalf of the Queen. She ended this exhausting first day by flying the flag for Britain, and delivering a pretty competent speech at an official dinner hosted by the Prime Minister. She handled herself well, and certainly did not let anyone down, although there were many lurking in the corridors at the Palace who would have loved her to fall flat on her face, as she was well aware. Diana was not a timid girl, however, but a determined woman. She may not have had much in the way of formal education, but she was extremely canny, and had a highly developed instinct for other people and their expectations. Before she retired after that first testing day, both elated and exhausted, she again sought reassurance from me.

'Ken, how did I do?' she asked, a little apprehensively. Sometimes I felt like a trusted uncle reassuring his precocious but nervous little niece.

'Ma'am, you were bloody marvelous,' I said, and meant it. She smiled, said goodnight, and went to her bed.

The Princess performed brilliantly the next day, carrying out her duties with energy and enthusiasm, but by the third day her sullen demeanor had returned. She did not want to attend some of the events planned for her, and was beginning to make things difficult for those around her, especially Patrick and her press secretary, Dickie Arbiter. Things came to the boil as we sat in the aircraft at Lahore airport, waiting to return to Islamabad for a dinner she was due to host at the High Commission. I tried, as diplomatically as I could, to snap her out of her petulant mood, but to no avail – everyone was out of step except Diana, it seemed. Then news reached us that a thunderstorm had hit Islamabad which meant that we would have to stay on the ground for perhaps as long as another hour. She spoke to the High Commissioner who was accompanying her, and learned that the dinner had to be cancelled, at which she brightened visibly. 'Oh dear, Nicholas, what a shame,' I heard her say, just about concealing her delight.

After we had finally reached Islamabad, and as Sir Nicholas Barrington moped over the empty tables for the banquet that never was, I realized that with no formal engagements, we now had the evening to ourselves, since my back-up protection officer was looking after the Princess. I therefore suggested a 'boys' night out' – after all, why waste the opportunity? Patrick Jephson agreed and so, with Dickie Arbiter in tow, the three of us embarked on what proved to be a riotous night. Next morning, a much brighter Diana could not wait to hear about our night on the tiles. 'How's your head, Ken? Did you boys get up to no good last night?' Naturally, I admitted nothing, beyond a knowing smile.

A small incident of little significance, perhaps, but it signaled a sea change in the Princess's manner and behavior. From then until the end of the visit she performed her duties with good humor and considerable élan, and people flocked to see her. Above all, her natural sympathy shone through on even the most formal of occasions, making her countless new admirers. Back home the newspapers lapped it up. The headlines screamed that Diana had taken Pakistan by storm, that her visit had been a resounding success. The tabloids predictably hailed her vociferously as the jewel in the royal family's crown, one of them claiming, employing a typically lame pun, that she was 'All the Raj'. The Princess could barely contain her elation. As far as she was concerned, she had arrived as a public figure on the world stage.

Diana may have been buoyed by her solo success, but the triumph of her visit to Pakistan was inevitably regarded in a different light by traditionalists at the Palace as well as by those in Prince Charles's camp. She undoubtedly had the private backing of the Queen, who had sanctioned the visit, as had the Foreign Office, but there were many in senior positions within the Palace who felt that it had been not only unwise, but foolhardy.

The Old Guard feared that once Diana's free spirit had escaped the confines of the Palace there would be no stopping her, much less controlling her, as once they had. In this they were absolutely right. Diana had no intention of looking fearfully over her shoulder ever again. Convinced that her errant husband would never love her, she was determined to chart her own course in life. As usual, however (as was perhaps my policeman's lot), I urged caution, extreme caution. As I knew only too well, she was prone to overexcitability, but on this issue there was no point in warning her to hold back. Her mind was made up, and I knew from the way she was speaking that life was never going to be the same from this moment on.

At one stage during the tour the Queen's Flight BAe146 arrived at Lahore to collect us, bringing Prince Charles with it. As we prepared to leave for Islamabad aboard the aircraft a curious incident happened that left the royal party vastly amused at my expense. The RAF group captain commanding the flight was ready for take-off and was going through his final checks when we heard a loud banging at the back of the jet. The noise was so alarming that the pilot aborted the take-off. But the banging on the fuselage continued. With the engines shut down, the steps were lowered so that the crew could investigate further. Suddenly the local Chief of Police, a large and imposing man with a huge handlebar moustache appeared at the door, clutching a furled umbrella, with which he had obviously been knocking on the aircraft's metal skin. He was badly out of breath and seemed quite alarmed. Had he, just before we took off, uncovered some sinister plot to blow up the flight? No. Apparently oblivious of the fact that he had halted the royal flight, he pantingly began to explain. 'I had to stop you,' he gasped, with all of us hanging on his every word, 'You see, I forgot to let my wife say goodbye to Inspector Wharfe and she made me promise that I would do it.' We all burst out laughing.

Prince Charles, who was sitting in the royal apartment at the rear of the aircraft, turned to me and said, deadpan: 'Do you know him, Ken?'

I thanked our visitor with as straight a face as I could manage, and he departed, his marital duty done, while the flight crew readied the aircraft for take-off once more. As we lifted off Diana turned and nudged me. 'Ken,' she whispered mischievously, 'you obviously made an impression with the Chief of Police's wife.'

Her success in Pakistan crystallized the Princess's determination to 'go solo', a phrase she loved to use. Nobody, and especially not her husband, was going to stop her now. As she repeatedly told me, she was still in love with Charles, but she was not going to let him get the better of her. Her optimism was one of the most attractive features of her character, and when she was in one of these moods she was pure joy to be with.

After Pakistan, however, Diana realized that she had more cards to play. She had wooed and won the media. Cynics had written her off as nothing but an upper-class girl who had left school with no qualifications, a pretty accessory for the Prince of Wales and a useful mother to his heirs, but they had missed the point. She had become adept not merely at surviving, but at flourishing, in the world in which she found herself. She knew who to flatter and how, even if it was sometimes to deceive. Above all, she knew how to get what she wanted. After the struggles and disputes of the previous months, she was primed and ready for the fight to come, in which she would take on not just her husband and his supporters and cronies, but the royal family and the Palace as well.

The Queen was suffering from a bad cold, and her voice, weary and hoarse, summed up the worst year in recent royal history when, in a speech she made at the Guildhall on 24 November 1992, she described that year as her '*annus horribilis*'. The Latin expression was her first public admission of failure, an acknowledgement that the state of affairs within the royal family was in many ways dire, and she knew it, although it was also a reference to the disastrous fire at Windsor Castle on 20 November.

At the beginning of the year, however, many in the Queen's circle believed that the Prince of Wales's marriage could be saved. There was a feeling that a working arrangement could be put in place that would suit both Charles and Diana. Yet those in Diana's camp knew that nothing could have been further from the truth.

By early 1992 the couple were effectively separated in everything but name. Charles was living his preferred life as a bachelor. He rarely saw his sons or wife, and threw himself into his work. Camilla Parker Bowles, of course, was the soulmate who consoled him, and seemed to attend to his every need. Effectively, he had made it clear to Diana that although she was his wife, the mother of his sons, and Her Royal Highness the Princess of Wales, she had no place in his heart, now or in the future. Diana, although resigned to this way of life, had long since decided that she was not prepared to abide by the rules he had laid down. True, she had engaged in extramarital affairs, as he had done, but she was not willing to make life easy for him. I felt that she was, in some ways, still in love with the idea of being in love with her husband, and when we were alone together she would often ask me what she should do.

I continually urged her to try to win Charles back, or at least, for the sake of the sons they both loved, to come to some kind of amicable arrangement that would keep the marriage intact. But in my heart I knew that this was never going to happen. I believe that if the Prince had offered her even the smallest morsel of love she would have clung to it, and tried to rescue their dysfunctional marriage; but he did not. To this day, I remain convinced that Diana never wanted to divorce him. In a fit of pique she would fly off the handle and say that divorce was her only way out, but she knew from her own experience as a child, when her parents had divorced so publicly and bitterly, as well as from her work with Relate, that to end the marriage might have a catastrophic impact on their two sons. There was, too, another factor, namely that the actress in her, bolstered by her occasional descents into self-pity, also found the chance to play the wronged wife too compelling to miss. As I have said, it never seemed to occur to her that she was just as guilty as the Prince, that her own adultery was just as relevant to the breakdown of their marriage. We would talk for hours about that breakdown and the conversation always came back to the same question: should she stay, or go? My answer was invariably that she should stay and fight from within, because it would be terribly cold on the outside. I knew, however, that the time would come when there would be no other option. More importantly, so did the Princess. To the outside world, the charade went on. Although their joint public appearances were rare, people essentially mistrusted what they read in the newspapers about the rifts in the marriage.

Even if I had not worked for the Princess, the lighter moments of the job would have made being a protection officer worthwhile. One memorable occasion made a particular impression, not merely because I found it funny, but because it summed up the distance between the couple, as well as Diana's absolute lack of appreciation of her husband and his sense of humor. It was the evening of the state banquet held for the King of Norway in London. The Prince's policeman, Colin Trimming, had the night off, and I had said I could handle security for both our principals. That night, Diana was in a particularly impatient mood. She was not above tutting and tapping her feet to express her frustrations, in this case at having to attend this most formal of functions, at her husband, at having to dress to the nines, at delays and any other irritations that came to her mind.

In complete contrast, the Prince was extremely relaxed. He knew the form on state occasions like this, when all the senior, and many of the so-called 'minor' members of the royal family were on parade. Everything had to be done in almost military fashion. Royalty would arrive according to ascending order of rank, with the most senior, the Queen herself, arriving last at exactly the time listed in the program. It may sound a little absurd, but this is how the business of monarchy works (and has done for a very long time), and state banquets, when the principals turn out in all their finery, tiaras, dress uniforms, evening dress, decorations and all, is when the business of royalty becomes very serious indeed. Diana did not quite see it like that. As far as she was concerned, a state banquet was just an irritation, something to go to, be seen at and then get home from as early and unscathed as possible. In the mood she was in tonight, this was doubly, or even trebly, the case.

The Princess and I, in full evening dress, were in the hall of the apartments at Kensington Palace, waiting for the moment when we would set off in the limousine according to the prescribed order of precedence. The Princess sighed and turned to me. 'Ken, can we go early? I don't want to hang around here any more,' she said. There was a faintly childish whine in her voice.

'Ma'am, it's really not as simple as that, there is an order . . .' but before I could finish she snapped back, 'Ken, I know all about their bloody orders. All about them. I want to go now. Simon [her chauffeur] is ready, and I want to go now.'

Fortunately, Charles, also in evening dress, appeared in the hall right on cue, tugging on his cuffs in his slightly nervous manner, like an actor in a West End comedy. He clearly sensed an impending tantrum from his volatile wife.

'Are we ready to go, Ken?' he asked. There was a stony silence from both of them as I pointed out that it was not our slot yet.

'Have I got time for another Martini then?' he asked politely. I don't know why, but I couldn't help smiling broadly. It struck me as vaguely absurd that the future King was asking me if he had time for another drink, even if the question was rhetorical. I told him that he probably did have time. The frost emanating from his wife became icier.

'Is anything the matter?' he asked, not directing his question to anyone in particular. I decided to say nothing, aware that the impending storm was about to break. Diana was ready for a fight, if not spoiling for one.

'Well, Charles, there is, actually. I want to go now. I don't want to hang around here. Why can't we go now?' There was a dangerous edge to her voice now.

'Diana,' he replied reasonably, 'you know the system. We have to go at the set time, so that we arrive just before Her Majesty.' He took a step back as though preparing himself for an onslaught. He was right to. Diana, drawing herself up in her high heels (or 'tart's trotters' as she called them) turned on him.

'But Charles, why can't you go on your own? I can get there earlier, nobody will worry about me,' she said. Of course, she knew that if she turned up without her husband the waiting media would plaster it all over the front pages, speculating, quite rightly, that the Prince and Princess had had yet another row. When Charles pointed this out to her, however, she became even more frustrated, angrily repeating that she wanted to go now, and that he could follow her when he wished.

The Prince, who clearly did not want a fight retreated, asking the butler, Harold Brown, for a Martini, his favorite tipple, en route to his study. As soon as he left I told the Princess that I thought the whole row was silly. It was not what she wanted to hear, and she sounded off again.

I was actually trying hard not to laugh, partly at the ridiculousness of the situation, and partly at her husband's antics. A few minutes later Charles emerged into the hall again, as his wife paced up and down like a caged animal. 'Charles, I have really had enough of this. I'm off,' she fumed. 'No, Diana, we really have to wait,' he insisted. Whereupon he ordered another Martini from Harold and departed again. At this point I let out a little chortle.

'Do you find my husband funny, Ken?' Diana snapped, by now extremely irritated with me, as well as everything else. 'Well, do you?'

I paused for a second, and then said, 'Well actually, I do, ma'am. I think he has a great sense of humor.' Foolishly, I then added, 'It's not too far removed from my own.' From her expression, Diana was clearly exasperated. At the moment she and I were simply not on the same comic wavelength.

'So, what kind of humor is that?' she retorted curtly. Too late I realized that I had said the wrong thing. The Princess did not find her husband funny, so nor should her protection officer. For the rest of that night she said not one word to me, other than a few perfunctory answers to my necessary questions. It was an amusing incident – to me, at least – but also a sad one. It demonstrated the extent to which the relationship between Charles and Diana had deteriorated, and how difficult that could be for members of their household. For by this stage, early 1992, Diana had to be handled very carefully. Not surprisingly, she had become increasingly unstable emotionally and felt betrayed if a member of her inner circle demonstrated any empathy with the Prince or his team of advisers.

The formal separation of the Duke and Duchess of York, announced on 18 March 1992, had a huge impact upon everyone in the Waleses' household. We all knew that if the Yorks' marriage was over – something the Queen must have sanctioned – then it could only be a matter of time before the inevitable happened, and the Prince and Princess of Wales followed suit. Whatever her emotional state, however, Diana kept a very cool head. As the Yorks' separation played out in public, she scanned the newspapers to learn how it was affecting her own popularity. Of course this was cynical, but in the prevailing climate, it was wholly understandable.

For the Prince and Princess, the first important public event of the year was their joint tour of India, planned for months and due to start in February. Diana knew that they would come under the microscope during the visit, but she no longer cared who knew – press or public – the depths to which her marriage had sunk. Even before the trip began, the press fired the first salvo when the *Sun* published an exclusive piece revealing that she would be visiting the Taj Mahal, the great marble mausoleum, near Agra, built in the seventeenth century by Shah Jahan in memory of his favorite wife, and perhaps the world's greatest monument to love, alone. 'Di To Visit Taj Mahal On Her Own', the newspaper trumpeted triumphantly, once more exposing the gulf between the Prince and Princess. Gleefully, the accompanying article quoted Prince Charles who, in accordance with the tradition that surrounds the Taj Mahal, had said during a previous visit in 1980 that he would return to the monument with the woman he loved. Could there ever be a more significant statement about the state of the royal marriage?

Despite the headlines, Charles did not change his schedule. After their arrival in India, he insisted that he would attend a business function in Delhi, 200 miles away, on the day when Diana went to the Taj Mahal. Everyone could see the symbolism of this decision, but the sycophants surrounding the Prince were simply not prepared to tell him how shortsighted he was being.

Back in Britain, the predictable headlines followed. The *Daily Express* criticized the Prince for his PR blunder, publishing a huge photograph of a demure Princess sitting alone in front of the Taj Mahal under the banner headline: 'Temple of Loneliness'. For her part, Diana had done her best to ensure that she got her message across, although it should be noted that it was not she who arranged that sad solo picture, but the press. When we arrived at the Taj Mahal photographers bellowed at me to keep her entourage and the accompanying dignitaries back. I obliged, and they got the picture they wanted, out of which they made such capital. Diana did not mind – as I have said, she was past caring – but it is wrong to describe the setting-up of the photograph as one of her guerrilla raids in the PR war against her husband. Had he wanted to, Prince

Charles could have turned the whole thing on its head, simply by going with her to the Taj Mahal. Instead, he chose to let matters run their course.

Even so, the Princess, who was genuinely upset by her husband's refusal to join her at the Taj Mahal, drove home the point with a few carefully chosen words, when, perhaps – in my opinion, at least – it would have been better to have said nothing at all. When Sky TV News reporter Simon McCoy asked the Princess what she had thought of the magnificent tomb, she paused for a few seconds before firing her first public shot across the Prince's bows.

'It was a fascinating experience – very healing.' Pressed to say exactly what she meant by that, she paused again. Then, 'Work it out for yourself,' she said with a glint in her eye. The press pack had their story, as well as their picture to go with it, and Diana had effectively given them *carte blanche* to write what they liked about the state of the royal marriage.

As soon as she had uttered these words I could visualize the headlines that would follow. Yet I could not help sympathizing with her. The Prince might very easily have made the visit to the Taj Mahal a positive statement about his marriage, and impressed his wife in the process. Instead, his refusal to accompany her made it clear that he did not care about her, and that he did not care what people thought about his marriage. Publicly, he admitted at the time that he had got it wrong, saying that some people might think that he had been a 'fool' for not going and adding that a wiser man would have accompanied his wife to the Taj Mahal. Privately, I knew that he never intended going along with what was in fact a complete charade, no matter what anybody did to try and make him see the wisdom of doing so. To have done so would have made him a hypocrite, and I believe that he drew the line at that.

Whatever the rights or wrongs surrounding the Princess's visit to the Taj Mahal, after it things went from bad to worse. The situation reached a head on Valentine's Day. The royal party was in the ancient city of Jaipur, the magnificent capital of Rajasthan said by some to have been painted pink in honor of a visit by the then Prince of Wales (later King Edward VII) in 1876. The Prince was asked to play in an exhibition polo match there and, buoyed up by the invitation, was looking forward to it keenly. At the same time, a PR exercise was organized. After the match, the Princess was to present the cup to her husband with a kiss. Diana, however, was in no mood to be used, something that Charles's aides should have foreseen – they had, after all, had enough warning.

On the day of the match thousands of local people ringed the polo field in the heat and dust, making it, in security terms, almost impossible to police. As far as any protection officer might have been concerned, a thousand assassins could have been lost in the crowd, and we would not have known until it was too late. I looked on anxiously, but everything went to plan. The Prince's team won, and everything was set for the presentation. At this point, however, the crowd invaded the pitch, so that the Prince and Princess were barely visible amid the colorful, frenzied mêlée, and completely inaudible in the din of voices. The Prince was triumphant, his face alive, flushed with success at having just scored a hat-trick, a fine feat for someone who admits his lack of prowess at the 'sport of kings'.

Nevertheless the Princess, who was never knowingly upstaged, was determined to have the last laugh. When her husband walked up to the rostrum, in his sweaty polo outfit to collect his prize and kiss his wife on the lips, she turned her head to the side, forcing him to air kiss, and worse, humiliating him in front of the world's press. He was furious. Diana had made him look a fool, and he was not about to forgive her for it. Later, when I asked why she had behaved as she did, she replied. 'Ken, I am not about to pander to him. Why the bloody hell should I? If he wants to make a fool out of me with that woman, he deserves it. But I am not about to make a fool of myself so all his friends can laugh at me.'

I could see her reasoning, and even sympathize with it, but that was not how the Prince and his staff saw it. They accused Diana of petulance – 'She is nothing but a spoilt schoolgirl,' one of his household said to me. I defended her position but tired of the argument, Charles's aide simply shrugged his shoulders and walked off, though not without a final sally: 'Surely she could put on a show just once!' he said bitterly. Actually, I thought, she has been doing just that for almost all her adult life. So surely she is allowed some time off for good behavior, to be herself?

On the following day the *Sun* published a front-page photograph by Arthur Edwards under the banner headline, 'The Kiss That Missed!' Charles was pictured grimacing as the Princess bluntly rejected his kiss. Inside the paper cruelly published a guide for the Prince, showing him how to kiss a woman properly. Diana had shown Charles up as unfeeling at the Taj Mahal; now she had made him look a fool.

There was no going back after that. The battle lines had been drawn up, and the Prince and Princess hardly spoke to each other during the rest of the tour. As Diana and her entourage headed for Calcutta to see at first hand the work of Mother Teresa, her husband, still seething over his humiliation at the polo match, flew instead to Nepal.

By now these joint tours were anything but joint. The Prince and Princess effectively ran their own shows, Diana acting the chief executive and publicity director of her own roadshow; her own 'tour within a tour'. As luck would have it, however, Mother Teresa was not in Calcutta. She was reported to be seriously ill and had to be taken for treatment at a hospital in Rome. Thus, to Diana, the perfect photo opportunity featuring the inspirational Albanian nun and the 'princess of hearts' could not happen after all. Not that it stopped others from saying that it did. So I can categorically state that Diana did not, as Patrick Jephson wrongly wrote in his memoirs, *Shadows of a Princess*, share several photo opportunities in Calcutta with Mother Teresa, as much as she would like to have done so.

I was not feeling in top form in Calcutta. I had a bad fever, having been struck down with a dose of malaria after a security review at the most appalling place I have ever visited in all my life, the mortuary attached to the hospice run by Mother Teresa's Sisters of Charity. Indeed, the hospice itself was effectively a mortuary. The wretched souls in there barely had a living cell in their emaciated bodies, while some of the assistants, many of whom had traveled from the West, were themselves infected with AIDS.

It may seem strange, then, to say that the actual royal visit to the hospice was a success, but it was. One desperately sick man, whom doctors said had just hours to live, had amazed everyone by staying alive for twenty-four hours after he was told that the Princess was coming. In her spotless pink dress, surrounded by the grime, dust and despair, she crouched beside the dying man and clasped his hand. It was an almost biblical scene, and the hordes of pressmen were quick to snap pictures when she knelt and prayed for him. The blackboard above the door that led to the mortuary read that fifteen of the hospice's patients had died that day.

Within half an hour of her departure, that figure had risen to sixteen as the poor man's wasted body was carried in to join the rest. The sisters had asked me on earlier, as they showed me into the mortuary, if the Princess would want to see it too. It was a depressing place, sad beyond words and with an atmosphere that seeped into every pore of one's body. I declined. Even Diana, I thought, would not want to go this far.

The tour of India plumbed new depths of despair for the Princess. For her there would be no turning back and a formal separation was now inevitable.

The strain of hiding the real story – the truth behind the relationship between the Prince and Princess of Wales – was taking its toll not only on the principals, but also on the staff of both households. After India, I personally vowed to try to sidestep these joint ventures. Frankly, the tension these trips caused was too much for anyone to cope with. It stressed Diana to such an extent that she became hell-bent on destroying everything to do with the tour that had been so carefully worked out and organized by advisers after months of planning. Like the little girl in the poem, 'When she was good, she was very, very good, but when she was bad she was horrid.' Yet on her own Diana was a different person, and her solo events were essentially pleasurable experiences. Holidays with her sons, too, which on the whole I was left to handle, were great fun, not least because they were often set in idyllic locations. With the Prince off the scene, Diana and her team of trusted members of her inner circle could relax. Since her death, and even before it, a lot of nonsense has been written about her mood swings. True, she could be petulant and, at the very least, changeable, but she could be damn good fun too, and had a graceful gift of knowing how to make people feel very special.

We returned from the Indian sub-continent. From this moment nothing would ever be the same in the royal world again. Accepting the inevitable, the Prince's team of advisers, which seemed to be growing by the second, began to take the first steps in preparation for a legal separation. The leading lawyer and government adviser Lord Goodman had been suggested to the Princess as a man who could be trusted when taking soundings of such an explosive subject.

Diana, from now on, had only one thing on her mind – escape. Before that process could be put in hand, however, relations with her husband were to deteriorate further.

# Chapter 12

Veteran royal watcher James Whitaker made his way towards me across the hard-packed snow. At the moment, he looked as though he was about to explode, his complexion matching the bright red ski suit that he always wore. Here was a man on a mission.

'How's the skiing, James – having fun?' I asked, in a bid to head him off at the pass.

'Well, as you've asked, Ken,' he replied, 'it's not all that good. I had to contend with solid ice in the morning, followed by slush after lunch. It was like skiing in a large vat of porridge.' Then, before I could even begin to feign sympathy for the lot of the royal reporter, he dropped his bombshell.

'Ken, I have some bloody serious news and I want you to be dead straight with me,' he said. His expression had become so austere that it was almost comical.

'Well, James, what on earth is it?' I said, trying not to be outdone in seriousness and sincerity. From my many dealings over the years with the Fleet Street legend, I knew that to him everything was always 'bloody serious'.

'It's the Princess's father, Ken. Earl Spencer. I have it on bloody good authority that he died last night.' Then he added, 'You see my predicament, don't you, Ken? I need this confirmed before I go to press.' If it were true, this was indeed 'bloody serious'. Worse, James would insist on confirmation, and would make a considerable nuisance of himself until he got it. I paused for a moment, trying to maintain my composure, before offering what I hoped was a suitably evasive response.

'Well, if that really is the case, James, it's the first I've heard of it. And I'm quite sure I would have been told,' I replied, trying to hide the feeling of panic creeping over me. I knew that if James's source was right, then all hell was going to break loose. By now feeling thoroughly anxious, I cut short our conversation, telling James that I would find out it he was right and assuring him that I would get back to him as soon as possible.

With that I returned to the hotel, where I telephoned the Princess's sister, Lady Sarah McCorquodale, in England. It was not the easiest of questions to ask a daughter and I was dreading the response. If the report was true, however, I knew that we would have to act decisively. There was a great deal at stake, and I did not know how Diana would cope. Sarah, however, assured me that although her father was not in the best of health she had seen him recently and had left him sitting up in his hospital bed; she added that he had been in quite good spirits. Relieved, I went back to James and assured him that the news of the earl's death had been grossly exaggerated. As was his wont, he shook his head knowingly and said, 'That's amazing, Ken, it came from a bloody good source. Bloody good.'

Yet within a day of our conversation Johnny, eighth Earl Spencer, the Princess's beloved father and a true gentleman, would be dead. And the ski resort of Lech in the Austrian Alps, where the Prince and Princess of Wales and their sons were on holiday together that March of 1992, would become the setting for one of the most dramatic and difficult episodes in my career with royalty.

Every country that offers good skiing has at least one ultra-smart resort that lures the so-called beautiful people to its manicured slopes, and Lech is one of the most exclusive resorts in Austria. It boasts some excellent intermediate skiing on its pistes and those of neighboring Zurs, and is perfect for families. Other benefits include short queues, even on the busiest weekends, and a number of exclusive hotels. Quite simply, the Princess had found a haven nestled in the Austrian Alps for her and her sons.

William and Harry had been plaguing their parents to take them skiing for some time. The Prince had promised to arrange it, but nothing ever materialized, although at least once a year he himself still made his annual pilgrimage to the Swiss Alps and his favorite resort, Klosters. The Princess, however, was determined that it would be she and not her husband who answered their sons' wish.

Diana's close friend Catherine Soames, the former wife of Charles's long-time crony, the erstwhile Tory minister (and grandson of Sir Winston Churchill), Nicholas 'Bunter' Soames, suggested that Lech would be the perfect place for the Princess and her sons to enjoy their first skiing holiday together. Overcome with excitement, Diana rather impetuously booked the holiday after Catherine showed her a brochure. A few days later she broached the subject with me, knowing that security would be a potential nightmare, given the inevitable press attention her holiday would attract. I told her that I would have to check the resort out as such a visit could have serious security implications. Then I booked a flight and headed for Austria.

Upon my arrival it was soon obvious to me that the location was perfect. The wooden chalets, the mountains dusted with snow and peppered with trees, and the people – protective, discreet and professional – made Lech an ideal royal retreat. It had been a haunt of European and Middle Eastern royal families for many years, but now it was about to be exposed to the ultimate test – Diana, Princess of Wales, the most famous and sought-after woman in the world. I knew it would not take long for the foreign paparazzi to find us. Tracking the Princess was like a military exercise to them, and a lucrative one at that; they were also extremely good at it. The British press was pretty quick to react, too, but from my perspective they were always easier to handle. The British newspaper reporters and photographers would always negotiate. For them, there was too much to lose if they overstepped the mark. But there were always a few photographers and journalists from the foreign press who simply did not care. You could make a deal with them and they would swear until they were blue in the face that they would honor it, but both you and they knew perfectly well that they never had any intention of doing so.

Diana had made it clear to her husband after the avalanche in Klosters that claimed the life of their friend Hugh Lindsay in 1988 that she would never return to his favored resort in Switzerland. The Prince, being a creature of habit, made it equally clear that he would do exactly what he wanted, and that if she did not care to join him in Klosters, that was her prerogative. None the less, her decision clearly annoyed him because, being a keen and proficient skier, he wanted to teach his sons to ski in the place where he had learned and had had so much fun over the years. But the Princess was in no mood to co-operate. Although she was a competent skier she was not in Charles's league, and so when she told him of her plans to take the two young princes to Lech it annoyed him that she was taking charge of training his sons in one of his favorite sports. For her part, Diana basked in his irritation. The fact that he wanted to see Princes William and Harry ski meant, figuratively speaking, that the mountain would have to come to Mohammed. In March 1992, Prince Charles agreed to make the effort and travel to Lech from Klosters to join his family. The Princess would have preferred him to stay away but, acutely aware that her sons would love to show off their new skills to their father, she agreed.

Until the point when the Prince arrived in Lech everything had been going so well. Every morning at around nine o'clock the Princess, in company with her friends Katie Menzies and Catherine Soames, would go to breakfast in the main restaurant of their exquisite five-star hotel, the Arlberg. The owners, the Schneider family, treated their royal guests perfectly, with complete discretion and just the right degree of deference. After a light breakfast the party would gather in the ski room in the hotel's basement and prepare to face the press. The previous evening I had met the ringleaders of the eighty or so reporters, camera crews and photographers who had descended on the resort for the royal holiday. Without a press officer on hand I arranged a photo call of sorts at the foot of the main ski-lift. From long experience we knew that the more experienced skiers among the media pack would give chase whatever we did, but I had to try to organize something to avoid the situation getting out of control. In reality I was fighting a losing battle. Some of the foreign photographers were so accomplished they could ski backwards down the piste in front of the Princess with their lenses trained on the royal party.

Sometimes though, the press would back off and Diana would then disappear for the morning with her two girlfriends, a guide, an Austrian policeman and a trained skier from Scotland Yard, before rejoining her sons for lunch in the mountains. As head of security for the trip I would remain at the hotel within radio contact. Occasionally I would join the Princess at one of her favored haunts on the Mohnenofluh near Oberlech, a refuge about 200 meters above the village, where the skiers would devour Austrian fare and the odd *Glühwein*. Diana would ski for another hour or so after lunch, but by mid-afternoon the warm spring weather made conditions slushy and difficult, so she would return to the hotel for a sauna and a swim before getting ready for supper.

The serenity was shattered by the announcement that Prince Charles and his entourage would be arriving the following night, although what happened next proved in the end to be the comic relief before the storm. The Prince had arrived late after snowdrifts blocked the Arlberg Pass, the only route into the village. Diana had made it clear that her husband would not be welcome in her private suite, and his personal arrangements had to be made through Hannes Schneider if he wanted rooms in the Arlberg for him and his entourage and I arranged his accommodation after consultation with his protection officer.

Members of the royal family expect everything to be perfect, down to the tiniest detail. So when the Prince arrived late that night, he immediately asked for his favorite drink, a stiff dry Martini. But when he went to his room he noticed there wasn't a refrigerator. At once he called in his policeman, Inspector Tony Parker, and pointed out that despite it being the dead of night he needed a refrigerator. And he needed it *now*. Enter Herr No Problem, Hannes, the son and heir of 'old man Schneider', as the Arlberg's owner was universally known.

'No refrigerator, no problem,' he replied in his slightly high-pitched, heavily accented English – even though there was not a spare one in the entire hotel. Twenty minutes later I saw, through a window, Hannes strolling purposefully through the snow with a mini- refrigerator on his back. I have no idea where he had got it, but to the Schneiders when a prince wants a refrigerator, no matter how inconvenient, a refrigerator he gets.

The rest of the stay in Lech was not so entertaining; indeed, it turned out to be an ordeal. Once more fate intervened, and as it turned out, the Prince never skied in Lech that year, or ever since. For on 29 March 1992 James Whitaker's grim prophecy was realized. The Princess's father, Lord Spencer, died at the Brompton Hospital in South Kensington, after years of ill health.

Before her husband's arrival the Princess had been completely relaxed, as well as determined to have fun. I had even arranged for another guest at the hotel, the British pop singer Sir Cliff Richard, to give a private concert for her. Cliff, an evergreen legend who has had Number One hits in Britain in each of the last five decades, knew Diana was in the hotel and thought it would be fun to perform for her. As a result, his friend, disc jockey Mike Read, approached me and asked if I could arrange it. I told the Princess, who agreed that it would be a great idea. In the event, the concert up in her suite never happened, for the news came through that her father had died. It was a time that was to test those around Diana and the Prince to the very limit, quite apart from the strain it placed upon her and her sons. For me, the tightrope that advisers have to walk between a royal couple's public and private lives has rarely been so slippery as when the Princess learned of her father's death.

On the afternoon of the 29th I received a telephone call from Diana's sister, Sarah. She was understandably distraught. Just twenty-four hours earlier she and I had laughed off reports of her father's death. Now it had become a sad reality. By this time the Prince was fully installed at the Arlberg with his entourage, consisting of his Private Secretary, Commander Richard Aylard, and his part-time Press Secretary, Philip Mackie, dubbed the 'Silly Ghillie' by the media. Armed with the news, I immediately went to Aylard so that he could formally tell the Prince and ask if him if he wanted to break the news to his wife. I assumed that on being told that Prince Charles himself would tell the Princess, but to my surprise I was asked to see him.

It was decided by all present that as I knew Diana best, the news would be better coming from me. I felt that it should be her husband who told her. I reasoned that the situation was difficult enough without me adding to its complications. Even so, I could not help thinking that these circumstances were in contrast to the touching moment in Kenya when Charles's father, Prince Philip – a man so often accused of insensitivity – broke the news to the then Princess Elizabeth that her father, King George VI, had died. The two of them had wandered through the grounds as the young Queen contemplated the enormity of her loss, and how it was going to change her life for ever. As Charles's aides were very anxious about the Princess's reaction, I thought that the only thing to do was to be exactly what I was – a policeman. If I could not take control in a moment of personal crisis, then who on earth could? Charles knew that his wife would be inconsolable over her father's death, and he was equally aware that he would bear the brunt of her grief and frustration. Eventually, it was agreed that I would break the news to the Princess.

As I made my way to Diana's suite I could not help reflecting that this was something I really did not want to do. True, the breaking of tragic news is part of a police officer's duty, but in most cases the officer involved does not know the people he has to tell. Diana was my principal, but I had also grown to respect and admire her. This was going to be one of the worst duties I could undertake for her.

As gently as I could, I broke the news to the Princess. She was calm at first. She had not expected it, nobody ever does, however much they may have readied themselves for bad news. But before long her eyes filled and tears began to stream down her face.

'Oh my God, Ken . . . oh my God. What am I to do?' she sobbed, over and over again. My heart went out to her. I sat beside her on the end of her bed, feeling helpless. Then I put my arms around her, trying in vain to comfort her in her terrible distress. At that moment, with all her defenses down, she looked like a lost little girl who has suddenly been made to realize that she is alone in the world.

After a while I tentatively broached the subject of what we had to do next. As delicately as I could, I introduced the subject of the Prince. In an atmosphere you could have cut with a knife, she proceeded to make it abundantly clear that she wanted to return to her dead father and her family as soon as possible, and most definitely alone. Under no circumstances, she said, did she want the Prince to accompany her.

'I mean it, Ken. I don't want him with me. He doesn't love me – he loves that woman. Why should I help save his face. Why the bloody hell should I? It's my father who has gone. It's a bit bloody late for Charles to start playing the caring husband, don't you think?' she said, every passionate word coming straight from the heart. Foreseeing trouble, I returned to the Prince and his staff, leaving my number two, Sergeant Dave Sharp, with Diana.

By this stage in their relationship there was absolutely no dialogue between the Prince and Princess. I was therefore not so much a conduit, as the last resort. To make matters worse, Diana bluntly refused to speak to Richard Aylard because he was the Prince's right-hand man, and, as far as she was concerned, public enemy number one, the chief supporter in Charles's camp. Nevertheless, I passed on the bad news to Aylard. The blood seemed to drain from his already pale face as he instantly anticipated the Prince's reaction. Seconds later Charles emerged from his suite, still clearly in shock. He was, of course, concerned for his wife, himself and his children.

In this extremely unhappy situation I decided to take control.

'I am going to put my police officer's hat on, sir. This is a very difficult and delicate situation. How do you think we should handle it?' But the Prince seemed by now to have come to a decision. I was left in no doubt that the task of getting the Princess back to Britain in a reasonable state and in company with her husband would be my responsibility.

Again I was asked to reason with her, on the grounds that I knew the Princess so well. There was little I could do about it, and I therefore promised to return to the Princess's suite, adding that I would do my best. As I left, I turned and told the Prince that I could make no guarantees. He, meanwhile, telephoned the Queen, who was at Windsor Castle, to break the news that the earl, a former equerry both to her and to her late father, King George VI, had died.

I was extremely apprehensive as I made my way back to Diana's suite, fully aware that there was a lot riding on this next conversation. If she decided to throw a hysterical fit and refuse her husband's request – and she was quite capable of doing so – we would be back to square one; moreover the press who would soon begin to mass outside the hotel would have a field day. Lord Spencer's death was a major news story, and if the Prince and Princess did not return to Britain together then nothing, not even compassion for the grief-stricken Diana, would stop the journalists from going for the jugular. The truth about the Waleses would be immediately and blindingly obvious to the most naive journalist. I made my decision in the light of all this. Returning to the Princess's room, I told her bluntly that this was not a matter for debate.

'Ma'am, you have to go back with the Prince. This one is not open for discussion. You just have to go with it.' At once her tears began to flow again. I tried to comfort her. We talked about how I had lost my father, Frank, and that I, like her, had not managed to get back in time to speak to him. Death, I assured her, was part of life. And as she continued to weep I told her that we all have to go on for our families' sake, as well as our own.

'Ma'am, your father would not have wanted this. He was a loyal man; he would not have wanted his death turned into a media circus, would he?'

I don't know what it was that struck a chord, but something did.

Her mood changed. She became calmer, and began to listen to reason. 'Okay Ken, I'll do it. Tell him I'll do it, but it is for my father, not for him – it is out of loyalty to my father.' Perhaps it was the word 'loyalty' that had made the difference, but whatever it was, the Princess was back on level ground. I had done the Prince's bidding, and on the face of it, at least, a potentially damaging situation had been averted. Diplomacy, common sense and Diana's own sense of pride had won the day.

Back I went to the Prince's quarters, where I told Richard Aylard that she had relented and agreed to travel back with the Prince. There was a palpable sense of relief all round. It was only then that Aylard and the 'Silly Ghillie' headed off to the Monzabon Hotel, opposite the Arlberg, where they had asked the media to assemble for the daily briefing.

While I sat at the foot of the Princess's bed, trying to comfort her, Aylard and Mackie broke the news to the press. It was around 7 pm local time, which meant that it was 6 pm in London, and nobody there knew that the Princess's father had died earlier that evening. At the Monzabon the press had all turned up to hear what the royal party had been doing that day and to make sure that none of them had been injured. So when Aylard told the gathered media the news, it was greeted with a respectful silence until the veteran *Sun* photographer Arthur Edwards asked the crucial question: 'Richard, has this gone out on the Press Association wires?'

Aylard and Mackie looked blankly at each other for a second, then replied in unison, 'No!'

All hell broke loose. There was a mass exodus, as if war had been declared or the three-minute warning for a nuclear strike had been sounded. Journalists, photographers, camera crews and anchormen were literally climbing over one another as they raced for the phones so they could tell their respective editors before the first editions went to bed, or the next news bulletins went out. Some of the journalists, perhaps understandably, did not really trouble themselves too much about the other guests as they shouted their stories down the telephone for the next hour or so.

The Princess refused to talk to anyone, and gave me strict instructions that nobody else, particularly her husband or members of his party, would be welcome in her suite. Charles, however, appeared unmoved by his wife's directive. Instead, he went outside to play snowballs with his two sons, where he gently broke the news to them that their grandfather was dead. Despite their sadness, the boys took it well. This was their first real experience of death, and the Prince, a sensitive and caring father, did his best to console them. There was nothing he could do to help the grief-stricken Princess.

For the next three hours I sat on the end of Diana's bed as her emotions raged. One minute she was lucid, in touch with reality, accepting of the situation. At other times she was angry at the world, shouting and screaming as the tears streamed down her face. She wanted to fly back immediately but given how late it was, a Royal Flight could not be arranged until the following morning. I could do nothing but try to calm her, telling her that it was only sensible to wait for morning. 'It makes sense, ma'am,' I kept saying. 'Trust me on this one, it is the right thing to do.'

The Prince of Wales is undeniably a good man, and I speak as someone who has known him at close quarters. His is a sensitive, caring, even spiritual character. Furthermore, his treatment of his wife during their marriage was in some ways understandable. As much as I liked and admired her, she could be an extremely difficult woman, and it is axiomatic – indeed, almost a cliché – that when relationships or marriages crumble there are always two sides to every story.

We left Lech by car for Zurich airport the following morning. It was a gloriously crisp day, with a beautiful clear blue sky and wonderful powder snow sprinkled on the slopes like a thick covering of icing sugar over a cake. The Prince, always a passionate skier, had never been to Lech before, and as it turned out would not return. Tony Parker, the Prince's personal protection officer on this trip, was driving, with me sitting in the passenger seat alongside him. Charles sat in the back seat, next to his wife.

The tension in the car was electric. I looked in the mirror in time to see the Princess's eyes rise heavenwards in a gesture of the purest exasperation at comments made by the Prince. There was an icy silence for the rest of the two-hour journey.

At the airport we boarded the BAe146 of the Queen's Flight that was waiting for us, while the media, who were out in force, scribbled notes and the photographers' flashguns fired. Nothing was said during the entire flight. The Princess did not want to speak to her husband and he, fearing a furious or even hysterical outburst, did not dare even to try to start a conversation.

Whatever the discomforts of the journey, however, it was soon clear that the PR spin had worked. The next day it was reported that Prince Charles was at Diana's side in her hour of need. Yet as soon as the Prince and Princess arrived at Kensington Palace they went their separate ways – he to Highgrove, and she to pay her last respects to her father.

I accompanied the Princess and her sisters when they went to see their father's body at the chapel of rest at Kenyon's, the funeral directors in Notting Hill, London. When we arrived Diana, who by now had become much calmer, asked me if I too wanted to pay my respects to the late earl. I demurred, saying that I thought that this was a supremely private moment, and one that belonged to the Spencer family, and to them alone. Diana smiled, then turned and joined Lady Sarah and Lady Jane inside the funeral directors' premises. I had met Lord Spencer on a number of occasions. He was an extremely courteous man, very much an English aristocrat of the old school. Despite claims in the media of rifts between them, he always enjoyed a very close relationship with his younger daughter, Diana. As a father he was very attentive, and was always conscious of the needs of his children. It was perhaps inevitable that there would be conflicts with his children over his second wife, Raine, Countess Spencer, but he never let these differences come between him and Diana.

Sadly, the same could not be said of the marriage of the Prince and Princess of Wales. On the day of the earl's funeral, two days later, the atmosphere between the royal couple had deteriorated yet further. Diana resembled nothing so much as a volcano that might erupt at any second. If she did, I thought, we would never get her back – the full force of her fury, grief and frustration would break upon everyone around her, and no one would be able to control the effects. Certainly everyone, including the Queen, was very concerned about how the Princess would cope during the funeral. They knew she was highly strung, and were fearful of the repercussions.

In the morning I drove the Princess to Althorp, the Spencer's family home in Northamptonshire, for the funeral. The Prince also attended, against his wife's wishes, arriving by helicopter. It was an intensely sad day for her, and Diana and I did not speak much on the journey, but when she did talk she kept returning to the same theme.

'He's going to turn my father's funeral into a charade, Ken,' she complained. 'It's so false.'

'Well, ma'am, just don't let him,' I responded. My heart went out to her, and I felt helpless that I could do so little to ease her grief.

The Spencer family as a whole also did not want the Prince to attend, but in the event Diana's brother, Charles, the new Earl Spencer, persuaded her to relent. The press, however, noted that the Prince was not there to comfort her on the long journey to Althorp. Although her husband was at the funeral in person, it was clear from the Princess's body language that she was alone.

Lord Spencer was cremated after a quiet, private family service. Afterwards the Princess was handed the urn containing the late earl's ashes and we returned to the Spencer family vault inside the church at Great Brington, just outside the estate walls. All the late earl's children were there, family feuds at last forgotten as they made their final farewells to their father. Then a great stone was lifted and I joined the Princess in the vault, surrounded by the remains of her ancestors, with a candle as our only light. There were cobwebs all around us, and the air was pervaded by a pungent dusty smell. With tears in her eyes, Diana said a prayer; then she too said her final farewell to her father.

It is hard to believe that, just over five years later, she herself would make her last journey to Althorp in her coffin, mourned by millions.

# Chapter 13

D IANA WENT FOR A SWIM in the pool at the British Ambassador's official residence in Cairo, where she was staying. Swimming helped her clear her head, and in May 1992 she had a lot on her mind.

Climbing out of the pool, she wrapped a towel around her shoulders and said, 'Ken, if anything happens to me you'll let people know what I was really like, won't you?'

'Are you sure, ma'am?' I replied lightly. 'You'll be taking a hell of a risk.' She playfully pushed me on the shoulder as if to reprimand me for my cheek, but some serious matter was clearly preying on her mind. She dived back into the pool and started an energetic workout but, after only a few minutes' crawl and backstroke and no more than ten lengths, I spotted a glint of reflected light from the building opposite. Camera lens, I thought. I told the Princess and she climbed from the pool, wrapped a towel over her one-piece swimsuit and went back inside. I followed her, and found that from the residence we could see men on the roof of the building where I had seen the flash.

As they continued to take picture after picture, even though there was now nothing of interest to photograph, Diana spoke of her feeling of total isolation. 'Ken,' she said calmly, 'I want out of this once and for all.' I could not help but agree with her, at least where this intrusion into her privacy was concerned.

I was angry, however. I had identified the building as a possible problem during the reconnaissance that had preceded this trip, but officials from the British Embassy had said that there was little they could do about it because some Egyptian in-house security staff were easily bribed. And that is exactly what had happened. I walked across and entered the building, playing the policeman to the limit. When I got to the roof some of the photographers were still there with their cameras trained on the pool. An ITN cameraman, a freelance named Mike Lloyd, was also there, although he was just preparing to leave. When I confronted them all they admitted that they had bribed the guard to let them on to the roof.

Although hardly welcome, such long-lens photography was to be expected on private holidays, but most of these photographers had official accreditation passes from the Palace to cover the royal tour – an *official* tour, during which they would attend scores of photo sessions – and I told them that their behaviour was a blatant intrusion into the Princess's privacy. They agreed to leave immediately, although whether swayed by my anger, or by their fear of losing their accreditation, I do not know.

Next morning, inevitably, the pictures appeared in most of the British newspapers, and ITN even ran the intrusive footage on the news. Diana, determined that her trip should not be trivialized, was concerned in case the pictures shown on British TV should offend Muslim sensitivities, given that they showed her in a swimsuit, and feared that they might create a false impression of her attitude to her official tour, following so closely on the row over the Duchess of York's island-hopping holiday in the Far East. Diana's press aide, Dickie Arbiter, sprang into action, issuing briefings and threatening action against those who had snatched the pictures. He told one newspaper, 'If the first thing people see of her in Egypt is her swimming around in a pool, it puts her in a frivolous light.' The principal result was that he insisted on Draconian punishment for the offending journalists and photographers, against the Princess's wishes, banning them from the upcoming visit to Korea, which turned out to be the last joint tour undertaken by Charles and Diana.

In reality Diana had far bigger concerns than some video footage and a few grainy, long-lens snapshots of her lapping a swimming pool. Andrew Morton's book, in which she had secretly collaborated, was about to be launched upon a largely unsuspecting world, and she was well aware that the mother of all rows would follow.

Diana knew the show had to go on nevertheless, and she was determined not to disappoint her hostess, the wife of Egypt's President Mubarak. To that end, she set about her official duties, which included a visit to a home for blind children that moved her terribly, with a good grace and astonishing energy.

Not for the first time, Fleet Street totally missed the real story and traduced the Princess, printing the swimming-pool shots rather than following her as she set about a full program of engagements. Not only that, but they had missed another opportunity to expose the truth. The fact that while she was promoting British industry and her own brand of caring abroad, her husband was on holiday in Turkey with another man's wife, was undoubtedly more in the public interest than a few cheap shots of Diana in a swimsuit. Worse, before arriving in Egypt, Diana's flight had first landed in Turkey, where Prince Charles left the aircraft to join a party of friends including Camilla Parker Bowles.

Diverting to Turkey to deliver her husband into his lover's arms had not only added considerable time to the Princess's journey, but had also increased the stress she was already under. Understandably, she broke down in tears as, very late at night, we approached Cairo. Somehow, though, she pulled herself together just when she needed to, vowing not to let her 'A' Team' down. Diana knew perfectly well the reason for her husband's trip to Turkey, but she was determined not to crack up while she was on official duty. For that she deserves enormous credit.

Although she handled the formal side of her duties with her usual charm and aplomb, Diana was in a very emotional state and had to be handled with care. With hindsight, her tears may have had more to do with the impending publication of Andrew Morton's book than with her frustration at her husband's blatant infidelity. Yet for her, the Egypt trip delivered all that it had promised: yet another solo triumph for the Princess. In terms of press coverage, the visit was also a true Diana media spectacular, which saw her agreeing to pose for photographs by the Pyramids, the Sphinx and the breathtaking temple at Luxor, to the delight of the hordes of pressmen. Unfortunately, the words that accompanied the stunning photographs when they appeared in the papers were beyond her or her assistants' control.

With the greatest secrecy, Diana had sealed her own fate and defined her future; but I am convinced that she would not have gone ahead with the deal with Andrew Morton and his publisher, Michael O'Mara, had she not truly believed that she could get away with it. In that she was right; it was only after her death that Morton revealed that she had not only secretly collaborated in the writing of *Diana: Her True Story*, but that it was she who had approached him in the first place. Many people had their suspicions about her part in the project, but she and the very few other people involved maintained their silence until the end. I was kept completely in the dark about the entire project – probably for my own good, for Diana knew that if I had found out about it I would have been compromised. Her decision to strike a deal with the independent journalist, writer and former royal correspondent Andrew Morton through her close friend, Doctor James Colthurst, was one that she took entirely herself. She wanted to be free of her marriage and of the stifling embrace of the Palace, and she had come to believe that if Morton could write her version of events, for all the world to read, then it would prove so damning of Prince Charles and his family that they would have no choice but to grant her, in effect, an exit visa.

It was strategy typical of Diana, naive, perhaps even childish, but almost brutally direct. Morton's account proved to be a brilliant and historic document – and perhaps the longest divorce petition on record. More importantly for Diana, it achieved what it set out to do – rocking the monarchy to its foundations and freeing her from its shackles. For the first time, too, the anonymous friends so often cited in newspaper stories were named and quoted on the record in the book. What infuriated the Palace and the royal family was that it was clear that, despite her protestations, they had at the very least spoken to Morton with Diana's consent and encouragement.

*Diana: Her True Story* broke when the first extract of the serialization of the book appeared in the *Sunday Times* on 7 June 1992. Then the book itself was published, immediately becoming a major and long-running bestseller. Clearly readers wanted to know about the Princess; thanks to Morton they now knew a good deal more than Prince Charles, the royal family and the Palace had ever wanted them to know. This was not throwing down the gauntlet; this was unhorsing an opponent before he had even reached for his lance. In the weeks that followed the royal family bluntly pointed a damning finger of blame at the Princess, but at no stage did she buckle under pressure. She stuck to her story, denying that she had co-operated with the book or encouraged its author in any way.

When questioned about Morton, her answer was invariably the same: 'I have never spoken to him.' She was, of course, not lying. She had not given face-to-face interviews to Morton; indeed, she never met him, but had provided him with tapes of her thoughts and memories recorded in private conversations with her old friend Colthurst at Kensington Palace. The Old Etonian doctor would then deliver the tapes secretly to the author.

When the Princess was questioned by her brother-in-law, Sir Robert Fellowes, the Queen's private secretary, on the question of her collaboration with Morton, she again categorically denied it. This led Sir Robert to tell Her Majesty that he believed Diana was telling the truth, and that the Palace's sole remaining option, given that it was impossible to prove that the book was a work of self-interest orchestrated by Diana herself, was to go all out and attack the book, questioning Morton's accuracy and motives, and denigrating his sources. It was too little, too late; the book had (and has) an authority that proved unshakeable. Some of the Prince's circle tried to intimate that Diana was at best hysterical, and at worst mad, but that too backfired. She was by now too popular, too visible, too beautiful – as well as too important to the media – ever to fall victim to such shabby denigration. When it later transpired that Diana had lied to him, Fellowes offered to fall on his sword, tendering his resignation, which the Queen, who liked and respected him, refused to accept.

I may not have been party to the *Her True Story* gunpowder plot, but I knew that something was afoot once the project got under way early in 1990. I have said that Diana may have wanted to keep me in the dark for my own protection, but on reflection it seems more likely that she knew that I would advise against such subversive tactics, knowing that they might very well backfire spectacularly. Throughout this time, her demeanor was sometimes that of a frightened child who believes she may have got away with some piece of mischief, but fears, too, that she may be caught.

Nor, I honestly believe, did the Princess realize that Morton's book would explode in the way it did. She had spoken often to me about her feeling of absolute isolation. In her own words, she was deeply unhappy and desperate to escape. I feared the worst. If she tried to escape, how could she continue to see her children? And if she were simply to run away, it would, I was sure, destroy her. All this changed with the publication of *Diana: Her True Story*. The royal family and the 'men in gray suits' in the Palace were placed firmly in the gaze of the book's millions of readers, most of them sympathetic to the Princess. In such a glare, to which the media added voluminously, the Palace's ability to control Diana or influence her marriage evaporated. Her plan had worked triumphantly.

I was never an avid reader of the *News of the World*, but on this particular Sunday – 14 June – I made an exception. Frenzied speculation about what was in Andrew Morton's forthcoming book *Diana: Her True Story* had reached fever pitch among the newspapers that had not acquired serialization, of which the second extract appeared in the *Sunday Times* that day. In reality only a few people, including publisher Michael O'Mara, Morton himself and, as it turned out, Diana knew what was actually in it. Yet that did not stop some journalists from writing what they thought, rather than what they actually knew.

'Diana Wept Every Time Charles Was Late Home', read the headline. That did not worry me; apart from typical exaggeration and spin it was true that there had been occasions when Diana had cried with pent-up frustration when her husband failed to appear. Even if he had a genuine reason for being late, she always thought that it was because he had been with 'his lady'. No, what concerned me was the sub-heading: 'She told bodyguard to tap Camilla phone calls.'

The thrust of the article dealt with speculation inspired by the Morton book and in particular its most damning truth – the affair between the Prince and Camilla. The reporter, Clive Goodman, dubbed by the paper its 'royal man in the know', wrongly alleged that 'the book claims Diana turned detective and asked her trusted bodyguard, Ken Wharfe, to check Charles's telephone records. He allegedly found that the Prince was ringing the Parker Bowles's London home up to four times a week.' The article also stated that 'she'd get her bodyguard to take note of the mileage on the car she thought he'd be using then check it again the next morning.' The allegations, which I need hardly say do not appear in Morton's book, were completely untrue. But the report alleged that I colluded in and actually committed a criminal offence (illegal phone tapping), and otherwise engaged in unauthorized activities that were wholly unprofessional and a breach of trust. I had no choice but to sue. The *News of the World* printed an unreserved apology, accepting that there had been no truth in the allegations the paper had made against me.

Everyone in the inner circle knew that divorce was now inevitable. Yet, as the world held its breath for one of the most dramatic royal episodes in recent times, Diana herself, still in Egypt as speculation about the Morton story ran wild before any of the book had appeared in print, was close to breaking point. At a press reception just after the *Sunday Times* serialization began, she openly lied (as it turned out later) about her involvement in the book, telling James Whitaker and photographer Kent Gavin – who, like most of the media, had got wind of the impending story – that she had had nothing whatsoever to do with it. I could see the naked disbelief on their faces, but her lie would be enough to stop them 'off the record' across their front pages next day, trumpeting how the Princess had opened her heart to the *Mirror*.

In Egypt, to her credit, as she prepared to face the tornado about to hit the monarchy, Diana was able to find calm in the eye of the storm. She knew that everyone who worked with her was also under strain, and she did her best to lighten the mood, insisting that we take time out to 'de-stress' ourselves. On the last night of the trip she invited everyone to join her for a swim at the British Ambassador's pool. All of her staff were there, from baggage master Ron Lewis to her secretary Victoria 'Ralphie' Mendham (so nicknamed because she was always decked out in clothes by the designer Ralph Lauren). The tour doctor, Surgeon Commander Robin Clark, Royal Navy, a congenial but rather shy man with a sweep of hair covering his balding scalp, was rather reluctant to strip off and join in the fun, preferring instead to loiter rather precariously at the pool's edge. For some reason he was wearing a camel suit which, in the searing heat of Cairo, must have been incredibly hot. From the pool, Diana eyed him menacingly.

She swam over to me and said, 'Ken, is he going to come in for a swim?' pointing at the unsuspecting Robin.

'No, I don't think he is, ma'am,' I replied.

'Well, I think he ought to go in in that suit.'

'I think that would be better coming from you, ma'am, not me.'

She was not giving up that easily.

'If he agrees to go in in that ridiculous suit, will you help me put him in the water?' In fact, she had no intention of asking his agreement.

'As long as I don't get sued by the Royal Navy, ma'am, it would be a pleasure,' I said. With that we attacked Robin with a pincer formation and tossed him in the pool head first, his glasses flying off in the process.

What we failed to realize, of course, was that his suit was heavy wool, and by the morning it had shrunk by about a foot all round. Diana, of course, offered to buy the unfortunate man a replacement – and did so.

The Prince and Princess of Wales returned to Britain, and to the echoes of the media-fuelled row over *Diana: Her True Story*. With the prospect of separation looming the Queen summoned them both to a private meeting. They discussed a formal separation, but the Queen urged caution and asked them to go, with their sons, on holiday together one last time and to 'at least try'. Both agreed, although Diana fully expected a holiday from Hell.

Buoyed by what, for him, had been the success of the previous year's cruise, especially in giving the pursuing media the slip, Charles accepted an invitation from John Latsis to use his yacht again, despite criticism of him in the press about accepting free trips. It did not worry the Prince. Since using the Royal Yacht *Britannia* for such frivolity was out of the question, it seemed perfectly acceptable to him that he should make use of a friend's yacht.

Even before the royal couple and their sons set off, accurate stories about this second sham 'love-boat cruise' appeared in the press, which gleefully reported that the couple had been ordered to make a go of their marriage.

The royal ratpack is not for the faint-hearted. This time, they were determined that they would track down their prey and win their stories and photographs. Kent Gavin was in charge of hiring the boat, which he somehow convinced his colleagues from other newspapers was equipped with the latest electronic devices for finding and tracking members of the royal family. As it turned out, just about the only thing it was equipped with was enough drink to have kept the Royal Navy afloat in both world wars. Moreover, with Mr Latsis's yacht, his money, and his influence in the region, even the ratpack were doomed to failure. In truth, we never even saw them. None the less, our voyage was far from uneventful, although it was perhaps a blessing that what happened on the cruise did so well away from the intrusive gaze of the press.

Diana was in no mood to put on a show in her phony marriage, for the Queen or anyone else. By now the plans she had made for her escape were already bearing fruit. The only voyage she wanted to make was on a straight course away from the royal family. Her attitude and behavior made the trip, in the summer of 1992, almost impossible for those, like myself, whose job it was to look after her. A couple of weeks before we were due to sail she suddenly refused point blank to go, and told the Prince she would also stop her sons from joining him on the trip. This infuriated Charles, not least because he was keenly looking forward to a private summer holiday with the sons he adored. The Princess had successfully fired the first salvo. In fact, she had every intention of going on the cruise, but she took considerable pleasure in unsettling her husband.

By this time the Prince and Princess were barely speaking to each other, mustering a civil nod in public being about as far as relations between them went. So the prospect of a ten-day cruise was a dreadful one for all concerned, including the warring couple. The guest list was much the same as the previous year: the Romseys again, this time with their children, ex-King Constantine and ex-Queen Anne-Marie of Greece, and the Ogilvys again. Everyone on board, guests, staff or crew, knew that the Prince and Princess were at loggerheads. This was going to be a stormy voyage, even if the Aegean remained calm.

Initially, however, the Princess was surprisingly restrained. She and the Prince made certain that they saw very little of each other from the moment we set sail. If, as the press was reporting, this trip was designed to rekindle the embers of a dying marriage, it would need a miracle. Yet ironically, the royal party charted a route that they had taken on their honeymoon aboard *Britannia* eleven years earlier, taking in the Greek islands of the Aegean and the Ionian Seas on their ten-day cruise. Winds gusting up to Force 9 prevented them from sailing into the Aegean and instead the royal party flew by Queen's Flight BAe146 to Aktion, opposite Lefkada in the Ionian Sea, about two hundred miles from Athens, where they joined the yacht.

Despite our fears for the cruise, Colin Trimming and I were consoled by the seemingly endless supply of caviar and vintage Dom Pérignon champagne. Although our assignment was fraught with difficulties, especially as the Princess's behavior became increasingly erratic or irrational, there were distinct advantages to being on board the *Alexander*. The royal couple had separate cabins, and did not venture into each other's territory. Diana suspected that throughout the cruise her husband spent hours on the satellite telephone to his mistress. Her suspicions were well founded. What she would never know, mercifully, was that five years later, after her death, Camilla Parker Bowles would join the Prince aboard the same yacht.

The atmosphere was extremely tense. Diana wanted nothing to do with Charles and even her sons became concerned about their mother's strange behavior. On one occasion there was a bad scare when Colin raised the alarm after a real fear that she had jumped overboard. He came to my cabin and told me that the Princess had not been seen for a couple of hours. She was not in her cabin, and no one else had the least idea where she might be. Panic set in. The Prince was informed that his wife had apparently disappeared, and I saw genuine concern on his face. Colin and I conducted a thorough search, and found nothing. I then remembered that Diana had spent some time by the lifeboats, and went to investigate. In one of them, crouched beneath the canvas cover in floods of tears, I found the Princess. She had been sitting there alone for two hours sobbing. I was immensely relieved – at least she was alive.

After telling the others to call off the search, I spent the next two hours in the lifeboat locked in conversation with the Princess under the cover.

'Ken, they don't understand me. He's on the telephone to the Rottweiler, and everybody knows it. They are all in it with him. They think I'm mad and feel sorry for me, but they have no idea what I am going through,' she sobbed.

Quite certainly she had a point. Although Diana had been unfaithful too, she at least had the decency not to flaunt her affairs right under her husband's nose. Hurt and embarrassed, she had every right to feel humiliated and betrayed.

'If he wants her here, why doesn't he fly her here and leave me alone? It is a sham, Ken, a total sham. He is only here with me because his mummy has ordered him to. He is pathetic. Pathetic,' she fumed. She was right in that, too. It was as clear to her as it was to everyone else aboard that the Prince had no intention of even trying to make his wife feel wanted on this trip. Her reaction may have been childish, but in this instance it was entirely justified.

Having worked herself up to a fury, Diana then demanded that I arrange for her to be flown home immediately. She said she was not prepared to stay on the yacht for one second longer than she had to and, as a princess, she insisted that she could do what the bloody hell she liked. This was not the first time that I had had to deal with the Princess's petulance, nor would it be the last. I reminded her that I was fully aware of who she was and what authority she had. I also reminded her that I was only alongside her to protect her, not to be shouted at or ordered about like a subordinate, especially as I did not answer to her but to my seniors at Scotland Yard. Diana took the point and apologized, but still insisted that she wanted to get off what she described as a 'floating hell'.

She devised a plan whereby the captain of the *Alexander* would be instructed to sail to Cyprus, where she would get a helicopter flight to the nearest airport. From there, she said, she would board a cheap flight home, just like the thousands of holidaymakers from Britain enjoying their summer break on the Greek islands. I explained that getting a flight home at this time of year would be nearly impossible – everything would be pre-booked, with the result that it would take several days, at least, to arrange. At this she became furious again, saying that if she wanted excuses she would go to her husband. I tried to reason with her. If she, the most famous and photographed woman in the world were to arrive at Cyprus airport and sit in the departure lounge with hundreds of tourists, then it would be headline news. How on earth would she be able to explain her sudden decision to quit her family cruise? Surely, I said, appealing to her sense of reason, it would be better to tough it out aboard the *Alexander* for just a few more days? Then, with the final throw of the dice, I asked, 'And what about your sons?'

She paid me the compliment of listening to my arguments. Despite her occasional descents into immaturity, Diana actually had a firm grasp of the real world, even if at times she pretended not to. She knew that to make a show of defiance in front of her two beloved sons would be unforgivable. She was just deeply frustrated with living a lie and determined to have her freedom, but she realized to make a stand at this moment would send out the wrong signals. In the eyes of the media and the world she would be the quitter, not the wronged wife pushed almost beyond endurance. At last, to my relief, she agreed to remain aboard the yacht for the remainder of the cruise.

That relief must have been written across my face. She burst out laughing, both at my look, and at our situation, a policeman and a princess crouched in conversation in a covered lifeboat.

'Come on, Ken,' she said, 'we'd better get back to the rest of them. Otherwise that bloody husband of mine will be cracking open the champagne, hoping that I did actually jump overboard and he can make that hideous woman his Princess.' The determined glint was back in her blue eyes.

I knew, however, that we were not completely out of the woods yet. The Princess, although placated, was primed and ready to attack if her husband gave her sufficient reason. The Prince, sensibly, since otherwise he would have caught the full fury of her anger and frustration, ignored his wife's tantrum; in fact he did not even bother to speak to her that night. With several days of the holiday still to go, however, the rest of the party were living on their nerves.

It was the young princes who, in the end, provided the link with reality that everybody aboard this floating paradise needed. Harry, ever the daredevil, started it. With the *Alexander* at anchor off one of the Greek islands, the fearless boy took it into his head to leap more than thirty feet from the stern of the yacht into the sea below. Laughing as he trod water, he then dared his older brother to join him. William, never one to shirk a challenge, especially from Harry, followed. Both of them then tried to goad Colin into following them into the sea. It was at times like this that Colin, with magnificent timing, always managed to pull rank on me.

'In you go, Wharfey,' he ordered, absolutely deadpan. 'We can't have the second and third in line to the throne swimming around down there without protection.'

I looked at him in disbelief. Then, realizing that he was serious, I stripped to my shorts, shut my eyes and took the plunge. It was terrifying, and I had visions of smashing against the side of the yacht on the way down. As soon as I hit the water with an almighty splash, the two princes pounced. Harry adopted his usual fighting tactic, aiming below the belt, and when I managed to wrestle him off, his brother was on my shoulders within seconds, trying to grab me round the neck and duck me under the water. Everyone watched from the deck, laughing and shouting encouragement, and a breath of normality seemed to creep back into the atmosphere aboard the *Alexander*.

Even so, the young princes' leap caused a considerable stir. Prince Charles questioned Colin as to how they had been allowed to get away with it without being stopped. The Princess, however, thought the entire incident was extremely funny and praised her sons for their nerve, perhaps another swipe at her husband. But there were no reprisals. The Prince told his two sons that they were never to do it again and it was soon forgotten. It was a welcome break from the gloomy process of keeping the Prince and Princess apart, and for that most of us were extremely grateful.

Desperate to think of ways of keeping Diana occupied, I arranged a table-tennis competition involving all the party, including the protection officers. The Princess, who could be fiercely competitive, took the tournament extremely seriously, and with a combination of a naturally good eye for the ball and a certain amount of gentle persuasion she reached the final against ex-Queen Anne-Marie of Greece. Fortunately, the elegant former queen had the good grace (as well as the good sense) to lose the match to placate her younger opponent. Everyone, particularly Prince Charles, breathed a sigh of relief when Diana emerged victorious. It put her in a good mood for the rest of the voyage, and all talk of airlifts to an airport in Cyprus evaporated.

By the summer of 1992 the royal family seemed hell-bent on self-destruction. The Duke and Duchess of York had separated, and the infamous toe-sucking incident, in which the Duchess appeared in intimate photographs with her Texan 'financial adviser', John Bryan, had graced the front pages of the British tabloids. The Princess Royal was divorced from Mark Phillips, and was enjoying a new love affair with the Queen's former equerry, Commander Tim Laurence, Royal Navy (whom she would later marry) while Prince Edward was making headline news by announcing 'I'm not gay!' without, it seems, having been asked the question. Above all, the marriage of the Prince and Princess of Wales had been exposed as a charade, and many felt that it was only a matter of time before it was dissolved.

By the time the royal couple returned to Britain the marriage, far from being revived by the cruise, was on the verge of collapse. Now, however, the taped telephone conversation, recorded on the last day of 1989 between Diana and James Gilbey was at last released. Coming as it did so soon after the row over Andrew Morton's book, it proved to be, for the Princess, one scandal too many. Ultimately, the publication of her intimate conversation and deeply unflattering comments about the royal family was the catalyst for her exit from the House of Windsor. In my opinion, the tapes were more damning in the Palace's eyes, than even her suspected co-operation in the writing of *Diana: Her True Story*.

I had heard rumors of the tapes' existence several weeks before the transcripts were published. When I confronted the Princess with this less than welcome news she was understandably concerned. She had every reason to worry, for she of all people knew the nature of her relationship with James Gilbey.

What actually happened was this. On 25 August, not long after the Prince and Princess returned from the cruise aboard the *Alexander*, the editor of the *Sun*, Kelvin McKenzie, who always knew the tapes were a ticking time bomb in the newspaper's safe, published transcripts of the illegally recorded conversation after the existence of the tapes was mentioned in America's top-selling magazine, the *National Enquirer*. 'Dianagate' or 'Squidgygate', as the scandal came to be called, effectively exploded the myth of Diana the perfect princess. The *Sun* even put an extract from the tapes on a premium telephone number, so that readers could call and listen to Diana's unmistakable voice. Throughout the conversation the Princess, who was alone in her bedroom at Sandringham, desperate to escape the tension and hostility emanating from her husband's family, simpers as her admirer begs her to blow him a kiss over the phone. She describes life with her husband as 'real, real torture', and speaks of her frustration and resentment towards the royal family. Significantly, she also expresses fears about becoming pregnant with his child, a clear indication of the intensity of their relationship. In turn, Gilbey calls her 'darling' fifty-three times, and 'Squidgy' or 'Squidge' fourteen times. In one exchange he says, 'Oh Squidgy, I love you. Love you. Love you.'

Here was a typically foolish, if affectionate, conversation between two people involved in an intimate relationship. Adolescent sexual innuendo aside, the illegally taped conversation was significant because it confirmed to the public that the claims made in Andrew Morton's book that the Princess could no longer cope with her life as a member of the royal family, claims dismissed by the Palace as mere speculation, were true. At one point during her conversation with Gilbey, Diana says, 'I was very bad at lunch and I nearly started blubbing. I just felt really sad and empty and thought "Bloody hell after all I've done for that fucking family," it is so desperate.' Nobody, not even a Palace skilled at evasion and stonewalling, could call such a remark 'speculation'. Diana also told Gilbey how, at lunch, the Queen Mother had given her a strange look. 'It's not hatred, it's a sort of interest and pity,' Diana said.

Until that moment no one inside the royal family and its circle had ever publicly criticized the Queen Mother (although, to be fair, it was not Diana's fault that her private conversation was made public). Privately, however, being disrespectful about Her Majesty Queen Elizabeth the Queen Mother was a favorite pastime of the Princess's. Ironically, she would often speak with satisfaction of the disruption the death of 'the nation's favorite granny' would cause the officials at Buckingham Palace, and speculate irreverently on the choice of black clothes available to her to wear at the Queen Mother's funeral.

Perhaps Fate, like God, is not mocked. The grand old lady would outlive Diana by five years, and was there to pay her respects at the younger woman's funeral. Yet the extraordinary public reaction to Diana's death meant that she had the last word. No royal funeral, not even that of the Queen Mother in 2002, matched the public outpouring of grief for the Princess.

From the transcripts of what was said, Diana's words gave me all the confirmation I needed that the taped conversation was genuine. Although some commentators questioned whether the Princess would actually use expletives to describe her in-laws, I knew beyond doubt that the conversation was not a hoax. I had, after all, heard her use that same expression in the same context a hundred times and more.

I now know by whom the original recordings of the intimate conversations were made and why. True, they were picked up by amateur radio hams using basic scanners, but they were being transmitted regularly at different times to ensure the conversation was heard, knowing that it would eventually end up in the hands of the media. There are at least two sets of Diana tapes in existence; recordings of the same conversation made on different days by different radio buffs. A full investigation was carried out by the internal security services which identified all those involved, but for legal reasons I cannot expand further, nor is it necessary to do so. It does, however, lend credence to the Princess's belief, so often dismissed by her detractors as an example of her paranoia, that the Establishment was out to destroy her. She was aware that the intelligence agencies routinely monitored the daily lives of the royal family. Royalty Protection Department officers were categorically not involved in this surveillance. For my part, I simply accepted that any such steps would be a necessary part of her security, and warned the Princess to be aware, and went about my business.

I did not know until much later that they routinely taped the Princess's telephone conversations. We, her protection officers, were trained to be always careful, in case a terrorist organization was bugging her phones, to keep our conversations on the telephone short, and to speak, if necessary, in coded language. Not Diana, however, who used the telephone incessantly, and often spoke on it, literally, for hours. Nevertheless I was as shocked as she was when the tapes were made public.

In the end, the 'Dianagate' scandal was a pretty tawdry, if not squalid, affair that reflected little credit on most of those concerned: the Princess and Gilbey, Prince Charles and the senior members of the royal family, the media, and the eavesdroppers.

# Chapter 14

A N ESSENTIAL PART of ensuring Diana's security when she was
in my care was understanding her mood swings. While I
enjoyed her complete trust this was not too difficult, but it became
increasingly hard after she became involved in a police
investigation as a result of her close friendship with Oliver Hoare.

Hoare, an Old Etonian, was well known to the royal family, and a
friend of Prince Charles as well as of Diana; Charles often stayed in
the summer at the château belonging to Hoare's mother-in-law in
the heart of Provence.

By early 1992 Diana had become totally obsessed by Oliver
Hoare. They had first met during Ascot week in 1985, when he and
his wife were staying as guests of the Queen at Windsor Castle. She
was instantly attracted to him. Darkly good-looking, with thick,
wavy black hair that he wore quite long, he was confident around
the royal family, completely at ease, where others in the room were
nervous and anxious to please. By his side was an attractive woman
whom Diana, rightly, took to be his wife.

Hoare, a millionaire (or so it was said) art dealer specializing in
Iranian art and antiques, was then thirty-nine, his wife Diane, the
daughter of a hugely rich French heiress, Baroness Louise de
Waldner, two years his junior. The Princess later confessed to me
that she had felt a little shy when, at Windsor, she shook Hoare's
hand for the first time, and had blushed as she flirted with him. She
made polite conversation with Diane, both women talking of their
young families. That conversation ended abruptly when the Prince
of Wales and the Queen Mother joined them.

Hoare had certainly led an interesting life. His work had drawn him into some fascinating company, including a friendship with the great dancer Rudolf Nureyev. The two became close friends in the early 1970s and the Russian ballet star asked the young Hoare to decorate his apartment overlooking the Seine. They went through some wild times together. Diana was captivated, not least because of his connection with Nureyev, given her passion for ballet.

At that first meeting Diana saw a man who was everything the Prince of Wales was not, and, feeling rejected after the birth of Prince Harry, found herself drawn to him. The relationship between the Hoares and the Waleses flourished. Within a few weeks of their first encounter at Windsor Castle the Hoares were invited to dinner at Kensington Palace. They soon became firm friends. As the Waleses' marriage moved closer towards open warfare, both Diane and Oliver tried to help them resolve the crisis in their marriage. But when communication between the Prince and Princess finally broke down, Diana turned to Oliver Hoare for help and comfort. He spent hours with her in private at Kensington Palace. It is possible that Diana welcomed Hoare as an intermediary because she knew that he was a friend of Camilla Parker Bowles, and could therefore tell the Princess about her rival. Later, Charles and Camilla would dine with the Hoares at their London house, although Oliver never told Diana, knowing that she would have seen it as a betrayal.

As his friendship with the Princess deepened, Hoare found himself in an increasingly difficult position. He enjoyed a close friendship both with her and her husband (among other things, the Prince, too, is interested in Islamic culture), and as their marriage crumbled he did not want to be seen to be taking sides. The Princess added to his dilemma. She would question him endlessly about Charles's attraction to Camilla, something that she simply could not understand. In her desperation and sadness she came increasingly to depend on him. She could not get through a day or a night without at least speaking to him on the telephone. It was at around this time too, early in 1992, that Diana fell completely in love with Hoare. She had been physically attracted to him from the first moment she saw him, and believed that he possessed the strength and sophistication of a true man. She also knew that Hoare found her attractive but she was uncertain whether he felt the same for her as she did for him.

Diana absolutely adored him, as she confided to me. That admission did much to explain her behavior, and the humiliating events that followed. She craved him; she needed him at every conceivable moment. They used friends' safe houses in which to meet, and I would keep a watch from a respectful distance. Hoare, however, seemed to resent the fact that I was there, and probably suspected that I was reporting each meeting back to my superiors at Scotland Yard. Of course I was not, for I took the view that there was no need for them to know about the relationship as long as Hoare was not compromising Diana's security. I had taken the same line with Hewitt and Gilbey, who had both recognized the paramount need to keep the Princess safe, and had cheerfully accepted that I had to do my job.

What happened next would not have been out of place in a theatrical farce. I was on duty at Kensington Palace, since Diana was there. The Prince was away and Oliver Hoare was visiting. There was nothing new in this, but Diana maintained that the relationship was innocent.

'We just talk, Ken,' she told me. 'He is a very experienced, interesting man.' Quite, I thought acidly, 'experienced' being the telling word.

At around 3.30 am all hell broke loose as smoke alarms sent a piercing shrill around the apartments. I ran out of my room and headed straight for the Princess's. But before I reached it, like any good detective I traced the problem. It wasn't difficult. There, beside the huge plant in the hallway stood a disheveled Hoare, puffing on a cigar. Diana, who hated the smell of smoke, had obviously told him to smoke in the hallway, forgetting that this would set all the alarms off.

I knew that Hoare didn't like me – indeed, it was blindingly obvious. I honestly had nothing against him personally, but it was not entirely without satisfaction that I urged him to put out his cigar. He looked almost pathetic as he gathered himself together and left.

Next morning, I tried to make a joke of the incident. Diana, however, clearly did not want to talk about it. So when I suggested that she had been playing cards, perhaps strip poker, she flushed scarlet and went back to her room. No doubt I had overstepped the mark, but by this time she was already in danger of losing all sense of perspective. She knew this, yet she was not prepared to admit it, and I realized that, where I was concerned, it could only be a matter of time before there was a parting of the ways.

At the beginning of November 1992, Diana and Charles were forced to embark on an official visit to South Korea, a farcical trip which the press swiftly dubbed the 'Glums Tour'. Just days before she was due to set off with her husband, to whom she was not speaking, Diana declared, in the name of 'honesty', that she would not go. Fearing the worst, the Queen and Prince Charles urged Patrick Jephson to 'do something'. He therefore wrote Diana a letter which, in essence, said, that if she pulled out now, she could not expect the Foreign Office to help her when she wanted to embark on her solo career after her marriage was over (an example of the tacit acceptance in royal circles that separation, perhaps even divorce, was now only a matter of time).

I too was drafted in to try to 'talk sense' into the Princess. In the event, however, I simply told her to trust her instincts, although I reminded her that her father, Lord Spencer, had raised her to do her duty. Finally, the Queen personally intervened. What went on between the two women I don't know, but whatever was said, it certainly struck a chord, for the Princess eventually agreed to go along with what she privately called a farce.

Looking back, perhaps it would have been better if the entire tour had been cancelled and the Palace had come clean, rather than allowing the fiasco to unfold in public in the way it did. The press, who were circling the royal marriage in a feeding frenzy, were edging towards the hysterical. Newspaper editors sensed blood, and they sent their hounds in for the kill.

Nor was Diana, emotionally spent as she was in the aftermath of the row over Andrew Morton's book, in any mood to play games. 'It is bloody dishonest – it is just a damn farce,' she told me repeatedly. I could only agree. Nevertheless, Diana was determined to upstage, if not embarrass, her husband on this, their last foreign mission together. Whether it was flirting outrageously with a good-looking army officer, or storming ahead of Prince Charles as he courteously greeted people in the line-up at the opera, her behavior demonstrated at every turn that she could not have cared less whether he was with her or not. The Prince, ever the diplomat when on duty, was, however, beginning to lose patience.

The reporters covering the tour, hungry for the real story after years of being fobbed off with evasive or downright untruthful statements from Palace officials about the marriage, were taking no prisoners. Peter Westmacott, who had been seconded from the

Foreign Office to act as deputy private secretary to the Prince, was their first victim. Pressed by James Whitaker about the state of the marriage, he admitted under pressure that 'of course there were problems'. This was overheard by Simon McCoy from Sky TV, who immediately went on air with the story. It led the channel's news bulletin. Without naming Westmacott, McCoy said that a senior official had for the first time admitted that the marriage was on the rocks. The newspapers wanted the official identified, and one, the *Sun*, named Westmacott. Later, battered by his experience, he returned to the Foreign Office and was posted to Washington.

Not content with that, the royal reporters pressed harder. The next to suffer at their hands was Dickie Arbiter, who had the impossible job of acting as press secretary to both the Prince and Princess at a time when full-scale civil war was breaking out in their household. The newshounds, having tasted blood, told him that if he could not say where the Prince and Princess of Wales would take their next official trip together, they would write that South Korea was to be the last and that the marriage was doomed. Dickie pleaded for more time, promising to get back to them with an answer. Naturally, he could not – no such trip had even been suggested, let alone planned. The reporters ran their story. From their point of view, it was as well that they did, because if they had swallowed the Palace's line about the marriage they would have been made to look ridiculous when the truth came out. They were also right in saying that this was the Waleses' last tour together.

The Princess left Korea with her husband, but flew home without him. A photograph that appeared in most of the papers, which showed her looking out of the airplane window as Prince Charles disembarked at Hong Kong for an official solo visit, told the story. She was exhausted, and she knew that their marriage was finally over.

In Hong Kong the Prince was still smarting from the way his wife and the press had made a laughing stock out of him. He snapped bitterly at reporters for the next couple of days. At one stage he turned to the reporter he now regarded as Diana's apologist, Richard Kay, as he stood behind a staircase looking through the banisters, and grunted, 'That's where you belong – behind bars.' Striding past reporters and photographers on another occasion, he snapped sarcastically, 'And a merry Christmas to your editors!'

Back in Britain, the Princess was more determined to make a

stand than ever. She felt vindicated by the Korean débâcle. The disastrous tour had not, she insisted, been her fault. 'It should have bloody well been called off in the first place,' she told anyone who dared mention it.

She was desperately anxious to promote her own cause, and if she succeeded in doing so at the expense of her husband and the Palace, then so much the better. 'Ken, I want to get my shot in before they order the big guns to shoot me down,' she told me. I admired her spirit, but urged her to remain calm and keep a clear head.

'No, Ken, it's time I spread my wings. I'm going to fly and they cannot stop me,' she insisted. This was fighting talk, but dangerous.

'Be careful, ma'am. It's very difficult to take on the Establishment when you're an intrinsic part of it,' I warned. But my advice fell on deaf ears. She was determined to have her day, and determined, too, that everyone should see how she had been wronged.

A few days later, as we set out on an official solo visit to Paris and Lille, she declared, 'I'll bloody well show that family, Ken, you just watch me.' For me, the French trip epitomized her new spirit. She glowed, and she knew it, and for this brief moment the world was at her feet. Even before she arrived in Paris the French, who love a heroine, had rallied behind her. *Paris-Match* carried a front-page photograph by Patrick Dermarchelier (one of her favorite photographers) with a banner headline that screamed; '*Courage, Princesse*'. She did not need the French press to tell her anything, however. She had the courage and purpose of a lioness, and she was ready to roar.

It was a wonderful trip to be on. No longer shackled by her husband and his entourage, she showed the media – and the watching world – that this was the new Diana, and that nothing was going to hold her back. For her, the tour was about one thing: showing her public that as far as she was concerned she did not need her husband or his stuffy family. Diana, she believed, could stand alone.

The three-day visit was an overwhelming success, not only for her personally, but in terms of her official role: both the Foreign Office and the Queen congratulated her on her return. She and I even managed to sneak out without anyone knowing to see Paris by night. Diana was ecstatic; her face alive with pleasure and excitement. 'By God, Ken, this is living,' she declared as we drove along the Champs-Élysées.

The Princess returned to London on 15 November 1992 buoyed up by the success of her trip. She now truly believed that she could take on the royal family at their own game and win. Her mood, although still volatile, had improved out of recognition, and she no longer seemed weighed down by her troubles. She knew, however, that within a few days the Prime Minister, John Major, would get to his feet in the House of Commons to announce formally that the Prince and Princess of Wales had separated. Only hours before the announcement, and after all the protracted negotiations that had been going on between her advisers and Charles's since the publication of Andrew Morton's book, Diana told me that she still had her doubts about going through with it. She added that if the Prince had shown any remorse for his persistent relationship with the 'Rottweiler', she would, even then, have pulled back from the brink.

This may seem a curious remark, especially in the light of everything that happened that autumn, but I honestly think she was sincere. She had remonstrated with her private secretary, Patrick Jephson, about the negotiations for the separation, demanding action (and, ultimately, divorce). While the world waited for the next installment in the royal marriage saga, Jephson and Diana's other advisers had been thrashing out a deal with Prince Charles's team. A single small incident particularly upset her. At one point, the Prince's private secretary, Richard Aylard, had asked Jephson for the name of Diana's lawyers. This was little more than routine, especially given how far down the line to a formal separation the couple had gone. For some reason, however, it came as a surprise to Diana. She learned of it just before she and I set off for an official engagement, and when she got in the car she was furious.

'I don't want to speak to his bloody lawyers, Ken, I want to speak to him. Why won't he speak to me?' she raged, tears of pent-up frustration flowing down her cheeks. 'I have been that man's wife, I am the mother of our children and he cannot be bothered to talk to me face to face. What sort of person is he?' she screamed. I tried to calm her down, but she was still fuming when we reached our destination.

I felt desperately sorry for her, for at the time she seemed to be nearing breaking point. Typically, however, she soldiered on. She knew what her job was and nothing and nobody, not even the heir to the throne, was going to stop her from doing it. As she defiantly remarked, 'I am not going to have anybody say that I have let the side down. Nobody!'

Ironically, when the separation was formally announced in Parliament by the Prime Minister on 9 December 1992, I have never seen Diana so calm. She greeted this sad moment in her own and her country's history with a kind of fatalism.

'Oh well, Ken,' she said. 'I suppose that's that!' With that she began going through the paperwork for her next engagement, as though nothing had happened.

# Chapter 15

AT SIX MILES BY EIGHT, Nevis is one of the smallest islands in the northern Leeward chain in the eastern Caribbean. Nestled between Saint Kitts and Montserrat, it is dominated by a 3,500-foot dormant volcano, its peak shrouded with a blanket of cloud. The island's name derives from the Spanish word *nieves*, snow, for the volcano must have appeared, from a distance, to be snow-capped, to Christopher Columbus when he first sighted it in 1493. Exactly 500 years after Columbus, Diana and her sons made a voyage of discovery to the tiny island, on my recommendation, and fell in love with the place. As a result, it was to provide the backdrop to some of the most stunning photographs of the Princess ever taken.

To understand the importance that the Princess attached to this holiday, it has first to be seen in context. At the end of 1992 all hell was breaking out back home. The year had become not just an *annus horribilis* for the Queen, but for everyone connected with the royal family. On 9 December in the House of Commons, the Prime Minister, John Major, had stepped to the Despatch Box and announced the separation of the Prince and Princess of Wales to a hushed House. There was, he stated, no question of a divorce, and in the event of the Prince becoming King, Diana would be Queen Consort. Even then, as people close to the Princess tried to come to terms with the enormity of what was being said, no one really believed the Prime Minister. How could Charles reign with the wife from whom he was separated at his side? It was a preposterous idea.

Diana did her best to put a brave face on it, largely by hiding from the harsher realities of the situation, as she had so often done

**Above:** The leap of Lech – Diana deep in thought on hearing the news of her father's death in March 1992, which I had had to break to her. A year later she jumped from this balcony into the snow beneath for a night of freedom.

**Below:** The grief-stricken Princess leaving the Arlberg Hotel with Prince Charles, following the death of her father, Earl Spencer. She had not wanted her husband to fly back with her.

**Above left:** With Diana's equerry, Patrick Jephson, in Egypt, May 1992. His portrayal of the Princess in memoirs was tainted by bitterness.

**Above right:** The Princess of Wales staying cool despite the Egyptian sun – and the heat generated by serialization of Andrew Morton's book in Britain.

**Below:** Caught by a paparazzo's camera while keeping guard as Diana takes a swim in the pool at the British Ambassador's residence in Cairo, May 1992.

**ve:** With William at Thorpe Park in April 1993. Like his
**ther,** he was quick to laugh and great fun to be with.

**t:** Soaked to the skin after our amusement-park ride.
Diana always loved these days out with her sons.

**Left:** Diana comforts a leprosy patient in Nepal, just two months after her separation. She was convinced this would be her year as the government backed her still role as a roving ambassador.

**Below:** Serving the masses at the Mazerera Red Cross feeding centre in Zimbabwe. The scene was almost biblical, although the experience drained the Princess.

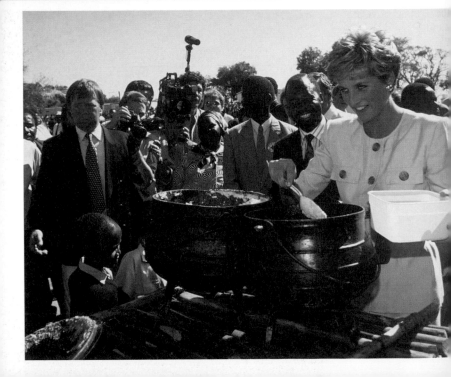

**Above:** On board the press launch off the Bahamas in August 1993. Co-writer Robert [Jackson] (far right), then a royal reporter, listens in; (**inset**) our rented police accommodation [at] Lyford Cay in the Bahamas. [The] press assumed it was [Diana's] holiday home, and so [never] photographed where she was actually staying.

**Right:** Diana disporting in the surf off Nevis — another arranged photo call. Not only the UK tabloids, but the world's press in general, all slavered over such images of the Princess.

**Above left:** James Gilbey attending a funeral in London in 1994. Diana turned to Gilbey late in 1989 as her relationship with Hewitt began to wane.

**Above right:** Oliver Hoare, the married man who was at the center of the 'phone pest' scandal.

**Right:** People labeled James Hewitt a cad, but I liked him and thought that he was good for Diana — whatever he may have done to make money from his affair with her after it had ended.

**Left:** Camilla Parker Bowles and her husband Andrew, major players in the royal divorce. I am convinced that the Prince of Wales believed that the Parker Bowleses would never divorce, but in fact their marriage ended in 1995.

**...ht:** Diana with her butler, Paul ...ell, during her visit to Bosnia in ...7. He became another so-called ...ck' – although I once saw her ...tremely displeased with him.

**Above:** Among the Prince's 'Highgrove set' — sandwiched between Charles and Patti Palmer-Tomkins, Camilla watches the Prince play polo. Two rows behind her, Jane Seymour looks on.

**Below:** A typical scene showing the media pack surrounding Diana. On this particular occasion, she was visiting the English National Ballet on the day her divorce was finalized in August 1996.

before. Within a few days of the announcement, however, it was clear that the strain was beginning to tell upon her. Decisions had to be made, and members of staff had to declare their allegiances – one wore the colors of the Prince or the Princess, not both. Unlike me, their respective staffs had their livelihoods to think about. Not surprisingly, in all this upheaval, the Princess became increasingly agitated. She admitted to me that she felt she was becoming paranoid, but said that she could not help feeling betrayed if any member of her inner circle showed signs of veering towards the Prince and his team of advisers.

'I can't help thinking of them [Charles and his staff] as the enemy, Ken. I know that's how they think of me – that madwoman who just keeps causing trouble,' she told me over one of our many lunches at San Lorenzo. In this atmosphere, working alongside her was like walking a tightrope. So when, in early December, she telephoned me at my office from Kensington Palace and implored me to help her find a Caribbean hideaway, I knew that it was imperative to act fast. Christmas at Sandringham with her estranged husband and his family, she said, was simply not an option.

'Ken, I need to get away. I cannot stand it here another day. I need some sun on my face.' There was a slightly frantic edge to her voice over the phone. She went on to tell me that she had heard about a resort in the north of Jamaica which she thought would be the perfect escape for her and the boys. 'But nobody, I mean *nobody*, must know about it, Ken. You are the only one who knows my plans and I need it to stay that way.' The line clicked and the phone went dead in my hand. Tightrope, I thought.

A few days later, on 16 December, without even telling my bosses in Royalty and Protection the precise details of what I was doing, I boarded a flight from Gatwick under an assumed name, bound for Jamaica. This was a part of my job that I loved. It was not exactly life-and-death stuff, but it was surely better than walking the beat in Tottenham.

After a ten-hour flight, we landed at Montego Bay airport and I hit the ground running. There was no time to lose. I hired a car and headed straight for Ochos Rios in the north of the island, to investigate the suitability of a hotel the Princess had asked me to investigate. Surfing through holiday brochures was one of her favorite pastimes, a form of escapism that somehow made her feel normal, as though she too could just jet away on an ordinary package holiday, like other people. As soon as I arrived at the Ramada Beach Hotel, however, I knew that it was not the right place for a royal holiday. There was no privacy, security was inadequate, and to cap it all soft drugs were being openly sold on the nearby beach. I visualized headlines: 'Di and the Drug Dealer'. I made some further enquiries, but they only confirmed my first impressions. There was nothing I could do but telephone the Princess and break the news to her as gently as possible, knowing that she would be deeply disappointed. She was clearly living on the edge of her nerves and needed to escape; she was also extremely anxious that the press should not find out about her projected holiday.

'Ken, I need to get away. I can't stand this dreary place any more. You must not come home until you've found somewhere.' This was a directive, not a request. It was a tall order, too, but I was perfectly certain that she meant it. I therefore called Colin Trimming back at the headquarters of the Royalty Protection Department to tell him, in the vaguest terms possible, what I was doing, and then headed back to the hotel to make a few calls, in the hope of finding a new destination for the Princess. As luck would have it, one of the people I spoke to told me about Nevis, and it sounded perfect. The only problem, for me, was getting there. Given the urgency in Diana's voice, I had to find somewhere that fitted her criteria as soon as possible. Unfortunately, though, I was traveling undercover, and could not tell a soul who I was and why I was in the area. So, posing as a British businessman, I contacted the airport and eventually located two Australian local-charter pilots who were willing to fly me to Nevis.

In their twin-engined, fly-by-the-seat-of-your-pants aircraft, which had clearly seen better days, we headed south in search of paradise, or the Princess's concept of it, anyway. The two pilots did not ask me what I was doing; they were simply happy to take the money. What was to happen next was typical of what could befall someone on a 'Diana mission'. Bad weather meant that we had to divert to Puerto Rico, which is a self-governing commonwealth (rather than state) of the United States. When we touched down on the island, however, my rollercoaster ride through the Caribbean was to come to an abrupt end. While the Australian pilots were refueling, a chisel-faced US Marine in uniform marched across the tarmac to where I was standing by the aircraft, glared at me accusingly and demanded to see my passport. 'You, sir, are on

American territory. Where are your papers and what is your business here?' he boomed. I tried my best to bluff my way through without giving anything away about my mission. I waffled on about being a businessman (I had dropped the false name, and my passport doesn't show my profession) and needing to get to Nevis as quickly as possible. It must have sounded incredibly suspicious, and in my by now rather frazzled state I hated to think what the shaven-headed marine thought I was up to or into. He was not interested in that, however. What he did not like was that I had flown into an American territory on business with no visa and no papers. As far as he was concerned I was an illegal alien, and he was not about to take any nonsense from me. At this point one of the pilots tried to intervene, but succeeded in making matters worse by winding the marine up even more.

'Why don't you loosen up, mate? It's not his fault we had to put down here and get some fuel, for Christ's sake!' the pilot drawled in an authentic Australian twang. This proved to be the final straw. I was duly frogmarched into the airport's security office and given the grilling of my life. The easiest way out would have been to have revealed who I was and what I was doing, but that would have meant that Diana's holiday plans could have leaked out, and the media would swiftly have arrived. Playing the businessman was a risk I had to take, but it was a close call. Eventually, they relented and admitted that there was not much point in throwing me in the cells, even though they told me that they did not believe a word I had said. With that I was fined $100 (£75) and ordered to leave American soil immediately. The final indignity came when the marine yet again demanded my passport. He flicked through it once more, studying every entry, which showed that on my royal missions I had crisscrossed the globe more times than Superman. He eventually located a blank page, and then rifled through a drawer in his desk for the appropriate stamp. Then, like a particularly small-minded Dickensian clerk, he thumped it down to mark my passport with the words 'Illegal Alien'. I boarded the plane and as we taxied along the runway I could not help wondering how I could explain the incident – and the stamp in my passport – to the Commander if he pulled me up on it.

A couple of hours later we touched down at the tiny aerodrome on Nevis. Unshaven and looking a little the worse for wear, I arrived at my sanctuary, the Montpelier Plantation Inn, which had been recommended to me by one of the contacts I had called from Jamaica. I had called ahead to say that I was on my way, and there to greet me were the owners, an English couple, James and Celia Milnes-Gaskill, who handed me a suitably refreshing Caribbean concoction and led me to my chalet, where I was able to shower and change. The Milnes-Gaskills had moved to Nevis in the 1960s and had begun to renovate the site, an old sugar plantation, in 1964; over the next thirty years they had managed to develop a small but successful hotel business. The main house stood on sixteen acres surrounded by secluded gardens and stone terraces, and there were sixteen chalets dotted around the grounds. Privacy seemed to be the watchword, and I knew instantly that this was the perfect retreat for the Princess and her sons. As a Caribbean hideaway it had everything she could want, but most significantly it offered a discreet haven into which she could disappear and no one would ever know she was there. That, at least, was the hope. I admit now I might have been a little too optimistic in my prediction.

I still could not say what I was doing on Nevis, so I kept up the pretence and told the owners that I was representing a VIP, but that I could not divulge any more details other than that the person insisted upon privacy and needed total security. The Milnes-Gaskills were charming people, the embodiment of unostentatious hospitality. Their business had been built on discretion and quality of service, and had thrived as a result. They therefore knew exactly what was required, and immediately set about preparing to accommodate the mystery VIP, at the same time providing me with all the information I needed. As I sat on the veranda of my chalet that evening, I could not help feeling a little pleased with myself. Mission impossible was now mission accomplished. In the privacy of my chalet I had telephoned the Princess to let her know the good news. I could hear the joy in her voice over all those thousands of miles between us. The stress seemed literally to melt away.

Before I flew home I had to complete the reconnaissance to make sure that everything was in place for a secure royal holiday. At this stage, however, I decided against discussing the operation with the West Indian Police Service, believing that it would be best to do so when I arrived as the advance guard just prior to the arrival of the Princess and her party. On my return to England on 21 December I sent the Princess a brochure about the hotel and a memorandum about the holiday. She was thrilled.

'Ken, you're so wonderful,' she gushed. 'If you recommend it then I know it will be perfect.' Her pleasure and excitement summed up our relationship. She would often say in her darkest moments, 'Nobody understands me,' but she knew in her heart that at least one person did his best to. Persuading Diana had been the easiest part of the operation. I now had to write a report to my senior officer, justifying the expense for the high level of protection, and therefore the cost to Scotland Yard. My reconnaissance report to the department had recommended a total of four personal protection officers; myself, Inspector Trevor Bettles and Sergeants Dave Sharp and Graham Craker, all to be under my operational control. While I would have overall responsibility for twenty-four-hour policing, Trevor would take charge of William, Graham would look after Harry, and Dave would assist me in protecting the Princess and would fly with her to the island, since I would travel ahead of them to ensure that effective security was in place from the moment of their arrival. In addition, I requested that PC Tony Knights should join the team as a night-corridor officer, which I felt was necessary because of the lack of any in-house night security. I also pointed out that during Diana's holiday on Necker in 1989 I had caught two locally based officers sleeping at their post at 2 am, and had sacked them on the spot after they had explained that they fell asleep on the job because they had to work during the day to supplement their low police income.

The final part of my report stressed that the separation announcement would only have intensified press interest in the holiday, and that although I had planned it on a 'need-to-know' basis it would be foolish to believe that the press would not find out. I reminded my superior that the Princess, as was usual, would not be taking a private or press secretary, and that I would therefore need all the help I could get to ensure that the holiday went smoothly and, above all, safely.

My recommendations were officially sanctioned once the usual rumblings about cost had subsided. So, on 28 December, armed with a Home Office radio (my Glock self-loading pistol would come out with the main party), I set off for Nevis for the second time. The Princess, with the boys, her old friend Catherine Soames and the rest of my police team, would follow two days later. Getting to Nevis without the press finding out that Diana and the boys were on the move was no easy feat. All the major newspapers have paid informants at airports to alert them when a famous person is traveling, and in late 1992 they did not come more famous than Diana. I had, of course, taken the precaution of making everyone travel under assumed names, and made use of the excellent Special Services Department of British Airways, but I knew there was still a better than good chance that the press would soon find out that the Princess was heading for the sun.

The Princess and her party arrived in Antigua some time after midday local time. I had arranged an aircraft from a charter airline, Carib Air, to be waiting for them there, which, after a discreet transfer, would take them on the twenty-five-minute island hop to Nevis. On arrival Dave Sharp reassured me that everything had gone smoothly. His addendum was more worrying: the press, he said, were definitely on their way; indeed, some journalists had been on the same flight from the UK. The duel between Diana and the media was about to start. As the Princess slipped away, most of the A-team royal journalists and photographers were already out of the country, covering a New Year skiing trip which the Duchess of York and her two daughters, Princesses Beatrice and Eugenie, were taking in Klosters. It took the press only a few hours to catch up with events, however. In the middle of the night they learned that Diana was on the move and predictably abandoned the Duchess, whose pulling power with the media was secondary to Diana's by a long way. They decamped *en masse* and headed for the Caribbean with their winter ski clothes, some complete with skis.

On Nevis, in the calm before the storm, Diana quickly settled into her holiday routine. With Catherine Soames and a few well-thumbed novels of the Jackie Collins type for company, she was able to relax in the sun and, wearing her bright orange bikini, splash in the surf with her sons, and generally revel in being, effectively, single again. She knew that it would not be long before the media pack arrived on the island, and as far as she was concerned if she was going to be photographed she was determined to look good. A golden tan was the first essential. After all, this would be the perfect opportunity to send back, in the form of front-page photographs, a 'glad-you're-not-here' postcard to her estranged husband as he endured the bleak winter chill.

Diana's daily routine was much the same as that of any other single woman on holiday with her children and a friend. She was never an early riser, and would emerge from her chalet with her patterned sarong wrapped around her waist for a private breakfast on the terrace at around 9.30 am. She did not eat much at breakfast when on holiday – a little fruit and some juice, and occasionally a cup of tea without milk – and after that would help her boys ready themselves for a morning on the beach. They would ask the hotel to prepare a picnic, and once it was ready would climb into the pickup and head for one of the deserted beaches on the island, a short distance away. An excellent swimmer, she would always be the first in the water. Although I or one of my team would be close by in case she ran into difficulties while swimming, it was never really a serious concern, but an officer would always accompany the boys as they swam and played in the warm sea. In the evenings she would eat a light meal, the menu on offer at the Montpelier being arguably the best in the region. We tended to dine all together, sharing jokes and discussing the day's events. The boys, exhausted by their strenuous activities, would retire after the meal, leaving Diana free to chat with Catherine and me about more serious issues.

The first day on the island was media-free, but all of us knew that it would not be long before they invaded our peace. Before that peace was broken, Diana relaxed. By contrast, William and Harry were always looking for different things to do on holiday while their mother was sunbathing. They loved playing in the surf with her, but she would soon return to her chosen spot to work on her tan. Restless, they decided to kidnap some of the island's indigenous population, although, mercifully, this did not involve abducting members of some lost tribe, but about a dozen giant toads. Harry was the instigator; he had spotted the creatures, which were about nine inches long, in the undergrowth and begged me to help him capture some. He and William had big plans for them. I told him to leave well alone, but he can be very persistent and eventually I relented, with the proviso that we put them back exactly where we found them. The boys became extremely excited and persuaded their mother and the Milnes-Gaskill children to join in the hunt in the vegetation around the Montpelier. The wretched toads proved to be difficult creatures to capture, but after several hilariously unsuccessful attempts we managed to ensnare about twelve of them. William and Harry tried to encourage their mother to help catch the toads, but she remained in the background, shrieking with laughter as we dived around the undergrowth in search of our prey.

'What are you going to do with them now you have caught them, boys?' Diana asked, almost dreading to think what the answer might be.

'You'll see, Mummy – just wait and see,' Harry replied.

The entire party were then instructed to rendezvous on the lush green lawn at the back of the Montpelier, where the princes' master plan was revealed – in essence, a chance for William and Harry to make some money. After selecting the most streamlined, athletic-looking toads for themselves, the rest of us were invited to pick our runners for the 'Nevis Toad Derby', a race they had devised to be run over fifteen feet, and place our bets. Seconds later the bewildered amphibians came under starter's orders, each held firmly on the start line by a hopeful gambler. At a shout of 'Go!' they were off, leaping the course in record time to the screams of encouragement from their backers. I am not even sure that any of the toads finished the course; most, I think, simply leapt into the undergrowth, no doubt hoping never to encounter royalty again.

This was no five-star holiday with over-attentive staff, fine cuisine and a luxury shuttle bus to and from the hotel, for Nevis then was a tropical island in its most rugged sense. Our daily treks to the beach were made in the back of the Milnes-Gaskills' open Toyota truck. Diana would pack a picnic of just basic snacks and cold drinks, and then we would pile into the truck with the boys' surfboards – Mr Eames at Harrods having done his stuff – sticking out the back. On the way to the white-sanded Indian Castle Beach or Pinnys Beach we would pass through ramshackle villages and wave at the local people going about their daily lives. Sadly, this serenity was about to be shattered.

I always felt it was a little absurd how, on receiving news of Diana, the royal ratpack would drop everything, collect thousands of pounds in cash dispatched to the nearest airport by their news-papers, and head off in search of her. They were essentially affable chaps, most of them, but ruthless when their quarry was in their sights. They were also experts in getting their own way. James Whitaker, Arthur Edwards and Kent Gavin were the leaders of the pack, but it was the quieter ones who were the most dangerous. Although the ratpack tended to work as a team (despite each being on the payroll of different news organizations), it could be a savage environment for any who defied the tribe, and God help anyone who broke their primal rules. In Klosters, as payback for having shown a certain individuality of spirit on a previous job, Arthur was given the slip by the group when they hit out for Nevis. So as the rest stole into the night, heading first for London, and then on to the Caribbean, Arthur, uninformed of the breaking story, was left to sleep on. He was apparently inconsolable the next morning when he made his usual diligent check call to the *Sun's* picture desk in London, only to be told that another team had been dispatched in search of Diana hours earlier. He was ordered to stay in Switzerland to photograph the Duchess and her daughters.

And now the ratpack was about to hit Nevis. Yet whatever my fears at the time, I must give credit where it's due: James Whitaker and his friend Kent Gavin were to be key figures in helping me arrange what the Princess herself described as one of the best holiday photo calls of her life, which saw some eighty journalists and photographers gathered on the public beaches of Nevis, frenziedly taking photographs or scribbling notes.

With the arrival of the ratpack, I found myself in an invidious position. With no press secretary or private staff I was left to mediate between the Princess and the worst excesses of the Fourth Estate. Diana, understandably sensitive to the criticism she would receive from the Palace old guard if she pandered to the press, was initially reluctant to concede a photo call. But since she had been tracked down, I told her I had to cut a deal. She asked for a couple of days' grace, but this was really so that she could perfect her tan in readiness for the bikini shots.

At first there had been a stand-off when the press arrived. I made it clear that the Princess regarded their presence as a gross intrusion of her privacy and that of her young sons. A few hours later, I had a taxing few minutes with James Whitaker and a *Daily Express* photographer, Micheal Dunlea. James was his usual robust self, but rather to my surprise it was Micheal, an excellent photojournalist with the tenacity to match his Irish name and nature, who caused me the most trouble on that day. By an unhappy chance the two of them had stumbled across Diana and her sons swimming off a public beach. Spotting the two hacks, I walked up and pleaded with them to back off, but as James plunged into one of his monologues about press freedom and public interest and I started ushering them away, Micheal fired off a few shots over my shoulder, which he was perfectly within his rights to do. It was the first minor skirmish in what would quite certainly become a full-scale battle if I did not act decisively.

At that moment I knew that the press had the upper hand. With only a handful of officers, I had no realistic method of controlling nearly a hundred journalists, and because this was a private holiday, Buckingham Palace had not sent out a press secretary, so I was left with the problem. My job was security but I knew, as on Necker, that unless I took charge of the situation the Princess would be exposed to the worst kind of press intrusion, and the holiday that she so desperately needed would be ruined. For her part, Diana, while sympathetic to the problem I faced, was not prepared to bow to the pressure, even though she knew that the ratpack had the upper hand.

'Nobody is going to stop me swimming with my sons, Ken. They will not ruin my holiday,' she said (subtext: not 'I, Diana, will put up with it', but 'You, Ken, will prevent it happening'). I agreed, adding that I would do everything in my power to avoid their stay on Nevis being wrecked. I therefore arranged to meet Kent Gavin in the bar of the island's Four Seasons Hotel. When we duly met a few hours later, I suggested a deal if he could guarantee that everyone present would stick to it. The alternative was that the press would be blamed for wrecking the holiday, forcing Diana and her sons to return to a bleak London winter. Gavin saw the sense of this, and agreed that Fleet Street's troops and the army of freelancers would back off, in exchange for a photo call next morning featuring the Princess and her sons in the surf. The deal was done.

It was a crucial moment. I am not and would never claim to be a public-relations expert, but I had learned a lot from working with the world's most famous woman, watching in admiration as she manipulated some of the most cynical journalists in that cynical profession until she had them eating out of her hand. I knew most of the key players among the journalists and photographers who danced attention on her, and felt that between us we could ensure that she was shown in the best possible light, and at the same time save her holiday. Besides, when the Princess insisted she wanted privacy, I knew her well enough to be able to tell when she really meant it, and when what she really meant was, 'Give them the pictures and cut a deal'.

For all her fame, Diana recognized that her success lay with her 'paying' public. If she did not appear in the British newspapers, then her star might wane. Being popular with the masses required hard work and dedication, and she shirked neither, but it also meant that she had to be seen as a glamorous figure as well, someone to inspire ordinary people to look beyond the mundane reality of their daily lives. She often told me that she felt a duty to the countless schoolchildren, elderly women, starstruck teenage girls and infatuated men whom she counted among her army of fans. She felt that to them she was not just a Princess, but an icon, and she was determined never to let them down.

'Ken, they expect to see me. They don't want to see me looking dowdy, they want to see me out there doing my thing,' she would say.

In all the years I was at her side, Diana never did fail her public. For her, maintaining her star status was worth all the effort. She never forgot, much less avoided, her responsibility to her loyal supporters. To have done so was simply not her style, not in her Spencer makeup. So even if she was parading on a sun-kissed beach before a horde of pressmen, she felt that she had to make an effort.

The Princess took some persuading, but once convinced, she was ready to take center-stage. After a couple of days sun-bathing, she looked magnificent on the morning of the first photo call. One memorable shot caught her as she emerged from the Caribbean surf, her bronzed skin contrasting with her orange bikini, looking absolutely sensational. Day after day she reappeared on the beach for a twenty-minute photo session, and to a man the media stuck to the deal; after each session they made themselves scarce, and the rest of the day was hers. In fact some left early so that they could send their photographs electronically back to their magazines and newspapers. 'It doesn't get any better than this,' Kent Gavin said to me one morning as he and some colleagues left the beach armed with rolls of lucrative film.

Back in Britain, the newspapers delightedly printed virtually every photograph and story about the Princess on Nevis that they could get. The legendary editor of the *Sun*, Kelvin McKenzie, wrote a leader in which he praised the press arrangements, named me and questioned the need for a Palace press officer when I seemed able both to protect and promote Diana at the same time. It was kind of him, but it was not something I had either asked for, or wanted, and retribution was not long in coming. My superiors at

Scotland Yard were not amused. They questioned why I was organizing the press, and reminded me, unnecessarily, that I was only there to protect the Princess, not to promote myself. This was a typical reaction at the time. Scotland Yard was no doubt being pressured by the Palace, which wanted to see the Princess's profile lowered considerably so that the Prince could shine, with the result that I was caught in the crossfire.

The reprimand infuriated me – after all, keeping the press happy contributed to my charges' security – but my colleagues advised me to remain cool. At a time when journalists and photographers are often condemned for their actions (indeed, photographers were to be initially blamed for causing Diana's death), I can only re-emphasize that every one of those on Nevis stuck to our agreement. Not one broke ranks; they knew that the deal with the Princess was a fair one, and that the pictures they were getting frankly could not have been bettered. There was no sneaking around in bushes, no following her and her sons, no stalking her from a distance, no invasion of the Montpelier. With the exception of a few archaic-thinking members of the royal household, who had an agenda of their own which involved trying to clip Diana's wings, and a couple of high-ranking officers at Scotland Yard, everyone was happy with the arrangement. These people were swift to criticize the deal with the press, but offered no practical advice, either to the Princess or to me, about how to handle the situation. Instead, they left me to deal with the problem, then complained that it was not my place to do so. Everything that my friend and Charles's protection officer, Colin Trimming, had once predicted was coming true. Nevertheless, and despite the flak I was getting back home, the deal was working, and I knew that it would continue to do so as long as Diana was on my side. Sadly, however, I knew her well enough by now to realize that it was likely only to be a matter of time before she and I parted. Her behavior during her association with Hoare, as well as her plans for her life in the wake of the separation, meant that she no longer wanted someone around her who constantly urged caution in her plans and actions. I had, however, always resolved that when that time came I stood a better chance if I jumped before I was pushed.

After a week in the sun, the Princess, relaxed and refreshed, returned to Britain. It was 6 January 1993, the start of one of the most momentous years of her life, and one that would ultimately lead to us parting. Yet for now our relationship was as good as it had ever been. As she stepped off the aircraft into the pale light of a winter morning, she turned and flashed a smile at me.

'Thanks, Ken, I really needed that. You saved my life. That was the best holiday I've ever had.'

'It was a pleasure, ma'am, a real pleasure,' I replied, not without a sense of satisfaction.

But these were dangerous times. The knives were being sharpened for the Princess, with powerful figures in Palace corridors whispering disparaging remarks about her flaunting her body to the press on Nevis. By association, they were out for me, too. When I returned to the office I was instructed that the Commander wanted a full report about what had happened on Nevis, and in particular about why I had adopted the role of the Princess's press secretary. I complied, although I never heard what happened to the report after I had submitted it.

A few days later I received a package from the *Daily Mirror's* Kent Gavin containing a full set of the photographs of Diana he had taken on Nevis. Inside was a note, which read: 'Many thanks for your kind assistance during the trip to Nevis. It was a difficult situation handled in a very professional manner.' Perhaps I was in the wrong job, but at least somebody other than Diana appreciated my efforts.

# Chapter 16

DIANA WAS CONVINCED THAT 1993 would be her year, and from the way it began she had every reason to believe this. Refreshed by her Caribbean holiday and no longer shackled by the wreck of a marriage, she was in high spirits. Nor was she in any mood to mope around her Kensington Palace apartment, even though she had removed from it all traces of her husband's existence. As for the Prince, he appeared to descend into gloom after the public declaration of his marital failure, just days after his wife returned from her holiday to rave press reviews. It seemed that there was just no stopping her.

'Everything is hunky-dory, Ken,' the Princess said as we drove through the police barrier at Kensington Palace. She was clutching a draft outline of the program for her forthcoming official visit to the Himalayan Kingdom of Nepal, sent to her by her private secretary, Patrick Jephson. Clearly excited, she read part of it out loud, as if to convince herself it was true.

'We await details of Lynda's [Baroness Chalker, the Minister for Overseas Development, who was also going] own program although it is expected that several of the engagements (especially on the first and second days) will be joint.'

She paused for a few moments, as if to check that I was listening.

'See, Ken? I am getting my way – the government is backing me,' she said, and there was a genuine excitement in her voice. She had been looking at me intently from the moment I had collected her, but I was distracted, and probably rather distant. I had other matters on my mind. The negative reaction I had received from higher ranking officers after Nevis still rankled, but more than that, it worried me. I knew that the more the Princess and the Establishment clashed, the more difficult my position would become. Oblivious of my mood, however, Diana continued. When she was on a high, nothing could get her down, and she seemed to think my quietness was due to concern for her.

'Honestly, you don't have to worry about me. I know what I'm doing. You watch – I'm going to write my own script from now on,' she smiled. I wasn't sure whether she was telling me, or reassuring herself.

'Ma'am, I have every confidence in you,' I replied diplomatically. 'You know I believe you can achieve whatever you want, as long as you truly believe what you're doing is right.' I had said it often enough before, but it was still the endorsement she was looking for.

'I promise you, Ken, the next few months are going to be fun,' she added before turning her attention back to the briefing notes that Patrick had prepared so meticulously. A few minutes later she suddenly roared with laughter.

'We'll be okay, we're staying at the British Ambassador's residence. Poor Patrick and the others are staying at some place called the Yak and Yeti. Sounds awful.' (In fact, it proved to be a splendid five-star hotel, with well-appointed rooms and excellent cooking, far superior to our spartan accommodation in the diplomatic enclave.) Rightly or wrongly, Diana honestly believed she could do the official job of Princess of Wales much better on her own, no longer hampered by the constant pressure of, and press references to, her failing marriage. She was not able to see that this formal position would inevitably have to change when her union with the heir to the throne was finally dissolved. Perhaps this was a little naive of her, but it was precisely that simplicity which made Diana so appealing – and so successful. She truly believed that she could remain within the system, yet break away at the same time, convinced that her affinity with the ordinary man or woman on the street would always be her savior. In a cynical world, such optimism was refreshing; moreover, from her point of view the year could not have got off to a better start. The writer and journalist Anthony Holden, a respected commentator on royal matters and one of her more sympathetic chroniclers, agreed. His cover article for the January 1993 edition of *Vanity Fair* trumpeted 'Di's Palace Coup', detailing how she had succeeded in securing her solo future at the 'expense of her detractors and her depressed husband'. The article continued: 'Since the announcement of the end of her marriage on 9 December, Diana, Princess of Wales, has been visibly reborn. There is a new bounce in her step, a cheekier smile on her face, a new gleam in those flirtatious blue eyes . . .' And of the separation: 'At long last the sham was over. For Diana it was a moment of triumph. For Prince Charles it was a crushing defeat . . .' The Princess was delighted when she read the article, and for a couple of days at least, it seemed that everywhere she went the magazine came too. Holden had hit the nail on the head for, reinvigorated, she was determined to show her estranged husband a clean pair of high heels in the battle for the hearts and minds of his future subjects.

It was now that something wholly unexpected happened which strengthened her position still further – 'Camillagate'. At the end of January, tabloid newspapers published extracts from an illicitly recorded telephone conversation between her husband and Camilla Parker Bowles, said to have taken place on 18 December 1989. It was both intimate and distasteful in its contents. Worse, with one eccentric reference during the call to wanting to become a tampon, Charles once again ceded the upper hand to the Princess, both legally and in terms of sympathy for her. The backlash was savage. Establishment figures normally loyal to future King and country were appalled, and some questioned the Prince's suitability to rule. Buckingham Palace was inundated with calls from reporters. Driven firmly on to the back foot, all Charles Anson, the Queen's press secretary, and Sir Robert Fellowes, her private secretary, could offer was the tired and often self-defeating 'no comment' response. The Prince's camp was devastated, and Charles himself personally humiliated. Those closest to him said that they had never seen him so low as at this time. One of his team confided, 'He has hit rock bottom.' Cartoonists lampooned him in the press; one cartoon, featuring him talking dirty to his plants, particularly amused the Princess, who collapsed into fits of giggles on seeing it. More importantly, however, Diana's lawyers had solid evidence to support a cross-petition for adultery should they need to. After all the Palace denials that had followed Andrew Morton's revelations in his book, which had effectively brought the Prince's affair with Camilla Parker Bowles to public notice, the taped conversation vindicated him, proving that Charles and Camilla had been lovers, if not throughout his entire marriage, then certainly from the end of 1989. (In actual fact, those on the inside knew that the love affair had been restarted earlier in the 1980s.)

There have been all kinds of views about the 'Camillagate' tape. Some commentators proffered theories that included a government plot to undermine the Prince, but I doubt that it was anything either so sophisticated or so sinister. As with 'Dianagate', when the tape was made, analogue phone technology gave amateur eavesdroppers the chance to listen in. I had consistently reminded the Princess of the importance of using codenames and nicknames, and of never to being too specific when using a mobile phone. It was a lesson she failed to learn, nor had her husband done so.

The Princess, once again reveling in the role of female victim, enjoyed the moment. 'Game, set and match, Ken,' she said, clutching a copy of the *Daily Mirror* containing a transcript of the 'Camillagate' tape to her as we talked in her sitting room at Kensington Palace. Later, however, she told me that she had been genuinely shocked by some of the baser comments, particular the Prince's tampon reference. 'It's just sick, Ken,' she said repeatedly.

It may be that she was genuinely offended by the tape, for she was ready to inflict more pain upon her husband. In February 1993, as the Prince set off, with only a handful of press in tow, on a worthy but, in media terms, dull trip to peasant farms in Mexico, she was taking the plaudits as she prepared for the next step in her career as a roving international ambassador. She knew that she was winning the PR battle hands down, and she was not about to relinquish her superiority. The contrast between Charles's tour of Mexico and her working visit to Nepal at the beginning of March could not have been starker.

The trip to the tiny mountain Kingdom of Nepal had been made even more attractive to Diana when the Prime Minister, John Major, confirmed that he was sending Baroness Chalker, the Minister for Overseas Development, to accompany her. The Princess was ecstatic at this very obvious declaration of official backing for her solo work. Her mercy mission to help the poor and sick in a Third-World country had now been afforded diplomatic status, and she herself had become an envoy for Her Majesty's Government. No matter how hard her detractors tried to denigrate her, nobody could take that away from her.

The press loved it, pointing out that this five-day visit was not to be Diana's normal hearts-and-flowers royal tour. Perhaps ironically, the Queen was credited with upgrading the trip, and the media reported that the Princess would for the first time be holding active discussions with the Nepalese government. Even so, she wanted it to be a low-key, no-frills working visit, conscious that she needed to keep the Queen on her side. The press went further, however, claiming that the Queen was determined to ensure that the Princess, despite her separation from Charles, would not be denied the privileges befitting her status as the mother of a future British king. Naturally, Diana lapped all this up, believing every word and seemingly oblivious of the pitfalls. For the Establishment, Tory grandee Lord (Alistair) McAlpine described the government's endorsement for the planned trip as 'sheer folly' in his *Sunday Express* column. 'This is all folly of the first order,' he thundered. 'It will do no good for either the Princess, the Baroness or for that matter for the refugees. The Princess is separated from the Prince and she no longer needs to undertake public duties that will cost the taxpayer large sums.'

The piece effectively parroted the views of the Palace old guard, and of Charles's staunchest allies, even if they were dressed up as a nod in the direction of saving public money. Diana duly took note. She was confident and riding high on a wave of support, but she was not a fool. As we drove to Gatwick for the flight to Nepal, she was in pensive mood. For all her bravado she was genuinely nervous. This was one of the most significant moments in her career and she was understandably anxious that she might make mistakes. During the nine-hour flight she read and re-read her briefing notes, before eventually taking my advice to sleep for a while. At last we landed in Delhi, where the party was to stay overnight at the High Commissioner's residence before continuing to Nepal the following day. After the normal pleasantries and a light meal, the Princess, tired after the flight, retired to her bedroom. Leaving the next morning, we flew into Kathmandu airport, a death-defying experience in itself as the plane approaches between treacherous cloud-covered mountains. From that moment we stepped back in time into the magical, almost medieval kingdom that is Nepal.

The British media were on the lookout for anything that might have been deemed evidence that the Princess's visit had been downgraded. At the airport, she was greeted by Crown Prince Dipendra and garlanded by small children. The press, however, were convinced that they already had their story when the unfortunate band that welcomed her failed to play the British national anthem when she appeared. This apparent lapse – or 'insult' as some papers chose to call it – made front-page headlines, although it did not seem to bother the same journalists that the same thing had occurred in Egypt, Pakistan and Hungary in accordance with the protocol governing working, as distinct from 'state', visits. Any royal reporter worth his expenses would have known perfectly well that the protocol for the visit would have been agreed between the two courts, British and Nepalese, months in advance. Still, no journalist lets the truth stand in the way of a good story. For the media, the apparent snub was enough to set the ball rolling. It did not seem to occur to them that in fact the Princess had herself requested that the working trip should be treated in a low-key, informal way, but the upshot was that the Nepalese authorities were furious. The article that upset them the most, however, was one by the *Daily Telegraph* correspondent Robert Hardman, who claimed they had laid a 'threadbare red carpet' with which to greet the Princess. One bemused official complained to me, 'Inspector, it is our best red carpet, and it is brand new.' I told the insulted official not to take it to heart and he seemed placated when I assured him that the Princess had thought his red carpet was one of the best she had ever walked on.

Crown Prince Dipendra made small talk with the Princess as we drove to the Ambassador's official residence, where she retired to her room to freshen up. A short while later she called me up to her room.

'Ken, I know you want me secure, but is it necessary to put me behind bars?' she asked, pointing to the barred windows. She was joking. Then she took a deep breath. 'Well, it's make-or-break time. By the way, Ken, do you think it's wise to give the Crown Prince an engraved hip flask for a present? He looks as though he likes a drink,' she said prophetically. Eight years later the Old Etonian Crown Prince would gun down his mother and father and other members of his family before turning the weapon on himself, in a drunken rage brought on because he had been banned from marrying his mistress. Luckily, he showed no homicidal tendencies on that trip, otherwise my Glock might have had to come out of its holster, and I am sure my shooting the Crown Prince would have been a difficult action to explain.

Quite early on in the trip the Princess turned to me and said: 'I hope we've got the *Gaget*, Ken. You know everything will go wrong without it.'

Much to her consternation, I had to admit that the said item had been left in a drawer back at Kensington Palace.

'It's no good,' she said. 'We've got to get it out here.'

*Le Gaget* was perhaps our finest wind-up, and an almost constant source of laughter. The small vibrator, bought as a practical joke after a staff night out in Paris during Diana's official visit there the previous November, had become her lucky omen. I had persuaded her sister Sarah, who was acting lady-in-waiting on the trip, to hide it in Diana's handbag the following morning, which she did. The Princess only discovered it while going through her bag in between meetings with President Chirac and Paul McCartney, and found the whole episode extremely funny. From that moment *Le Gaget* became her (secret) mascot for all future royal trips, and woe betide the secretary who forgot to pack it.

A telephone call was made to London and the secretary, Nicky Cockell, was asked to dispatch the vibrator by diplomatic bag to the British Embassy in Nepal. It arrived in a sealed packet, delivered on a silver tray by a Gurkha aide to the King of Nepal, just before the start of a press reception in honor of the visit that the Ambassador was holding in the grounds of his official residence. At that moment the Princess was preparing to go into the garden to meet the media who had been following her. The soldier had orders for the package to be delivered 'at once' to the Princess of Wales's equerry, Captain Ed Musto, Royal Marines, and nothing was going to deter him.

Musto, a self-effacing officer who towered over everyone present, not quite knowing what to expect, foolishly opened the packet and removed the offending item in front of everyone in the room (but, mercifully, not the press who were starting to gather outside). There was a stunned pause (and a few bemused glances from embassy dignitaries), until the silence was broken by Diana, who said, 'Oh, that must be for me,' and began to laugh. Musto graciously put the *Gaget* into his pocket and nothing more was said by the intrigued gathering of officials and dignitaries. With the delivery of our tour mascot there could be no question about the success of the trip after that.

The following day the Princess headed for the Nepalese countryside, dominated by steep slopes and rocky paths to see, against the backdrop of the Himalayas, conditions in which most of the country's inhabitants lived. Nepal is one of the poorest countries in the world, and her objective was simple – to try to remove the threat of hunger, or even starvation, by showing the public at home the terrible plight of most Nepalis, in the hope that money would pour in to the charities working to alleviate the problem. After a breathtaking flight over the foothills of the Himalayas aboard King Birenda's Chinook helicopter, we hovered over a giant open fire that was the centerpiece of a tiny, ramshackle collection of huts – the village of Majhuwa, our designated landing. We were in a mountain region famous as a recruiting area for the fearsome Gurkhas, the tough and valiant Nepalese hillmen who have provided regiments for the British Army for nearly two hundred years, and who have served the British Crown with undying loyalty. The Princess's visit came at a time when the British government had proposed cutting Gurkha regiments in British service (there are Gurkha regiments in the Indian Army, as well) by 2,500 of these warriors. There was a particularly poignant moment when she encountered a local hero – an old Gurkha, well into his nineties, who had joined the army in 1935 – standing in his frayed demob suit with his campaign medals glistening in the sun. As the Princess walked by he snapped to attention and gave her the smartest of salutes. What price such loyalty in the Palace, I thought sourly. Diana was taking all the strains of the tour in her stride, unfazed by the pressure, much of it self-inflicted, in the sense that she insisted on doing as much as she possibly could. She was exhilarating to be with, but always careful to heed advice so as not to put a foot wrong.

Meanwhile, the tension between the press and the Nepalese government continued to dominate the trip, at least in the British papers. It intensified when *Sun* photographer Arthur Edwards was accused of having made a racist remark to the Nepalese Prime Minister. Edwards, whose flattery of the Princess on tour was legendary, sparked a diplomatic incident as she arrived for a state dinner at the Royal Palace. When Diana walked past the press pen, Arthur smiled at her and said gushingly, 'You look fantastic tonight, ma'am.' My colleague, Inspector Peter Brown, who was on duty as her protection officer that night, smirked at the photographer, prompting him to say, 'You don't look too bad yourself, Brownie.' Unfortunately, at that precise moment the Nepalese Prime Minister was walking past and, hearing the comment, interpreted it as a racist insult directed at him. Once inside the banqueting hall he instructed his senior aide to complain to the British Embassy about the photographer's behavior, with the result that a bewildered – and innocent – Edwards was forced to explain himself and apologize. The consolation was that his editor, Kelvin McKenzie, thought the story was sensational and splashed it across the *Sun*'s front page on the following day.

Diana was beginning to stamp her mark on the trip. She had developed an excellent working relationship with Lady Chalker, whose down-to-earth approach and sense of humor matched her own. The Princess, who was in Nepal officially in her dual role as patron of the British Red Cross and the Leprosy Mission, now began making headlines for the right reasons in other newspapers. Even so, some of the tabloids continued to print trivia or dross. She made a flawless visit to the Lele Memorial Park, high in the Himalayan foothills, a gaunt, barren place that could only be approached by a winding, deeply potholed and crumbling road. It was a testing assignment for the Princess, and a sad one. She had been asked to pay her respects to the dead of PIA Flight 268, which, the year before, had smashed into the mountainside on its approach to Kathmandu airport, killing all 167 people on board, among them 34 mostly young Britons. When, a day earlier, I arrived on the advance reconnaissance the coffins of the victims, which had been disinterred for reburial in the park, lay uncovered in front of the semi-circular stone memorial, which had been built on a higher plateau overlooking the crash site. I told the organizer of the visit that these poor souls must be buried before the Princess arrived. Wobbling his head from side to side, he assured me that he understood the urgency. Nevertheless, I was convinced that my plea had fallen on deaf ears and that Diana would be faced with a gruesome scene when she came to the site on the next day. Over supper I raised my concerns with King Birendra's protection officer, Major Khandga Gurung, who assured me everything would be resolved by the morning. He was right, and I felt ashamed of my doubts.

Diana played her role faultlessly next day. Dignified and determined she was a perfect ambassador for the Queen. Unfortunately, the sunlight behind her meant that photographers took shots that showed her long legs silhouetted through her silk skirt. The following day, despite her solemnity at the ceremony, some of the newspapers ran those photographs, comparing them to the famous photograph of her as a teenage nanny at the Young England Kindergarten on the eve of her engagement to Prince Charles, in which the outline of her legs had also been visible. One tasteless headline, 'Legs We Forget', she found particularly galling, especially as she had performed her duty perfectly. She became upset, almost convinced that the media were doing their best to undermine her. I told her that she had nothing to worry about, and added that her legs looked great, which drew a smile.

Later that day the Princess visited the Anandaban leprosy hospital. The small, 120-bed hospital was crammed with victims, many with stumps where hands and feet should be, who seemed to accept their terrible affliction with gentle patience and great dignity. Once more Diana's humanity dominated the visit, and it was noticeable that when she walked through a ward without the cameras on her she spent just as much time with the sufferers, as she had when the press had been snapping away. She came away deeply moved, and more determined than ever to do whatever she could to help.

One of the trip's most memorable moments came on the day when we flew over the spectacular Himalyas in the King of Nepal's helicopter to visit a project to provide water for a spartan hillside village high in eastern Nepal. At one point the Princess disappeared into a desperately run-down one-roomed shack, home to an entire Nepalese peasant family. She emerged, clearly shocked, after spending several minutes inside with the hut's simple occupants. Moved by the extent of their poverty, she set aside her own problems and put into perspective the true worth of her trip to Nepal in one crisp phrase. Sighing deeply as she left the shack, she said, 'I will never complain again.' It was a great sound bite for the media, and I am sure that at the moment she said it she truly believed it. I knew from years of experience, however, that it was not a promise she would, or could possibly, keep. Alarmingly, it struck me that Diana appeared to be coming to believe her own propaganda.

After Nepal the Princess was determined to expand her schedule further, and in this respect the International Red Cross perfectly suited her interest and her ambition. There followed a series of personal meetings with John Major, whom she found sympathetic and engaging, very different from his rather gray public persona. She liked and trusted him. At first, she was anxious, but once the Prime Minister had put her at ease she opened up to him. He knew, from Foreign Office feedback after overseas visits she had made, that the Princess was a real asset, and one that should be nurtured. She was elated after these meetings – at last she was being recognized for what she could do, rather than as simply the wife of the Prince of Wales. The men in gray suits at the Palace, however, had other ideas. Just as the government was acknowledging and acting on her considerable talents, they turned on her with a pettiness that defies logic. In a ridiculous and demeaning sideswipe someone in the Palace ruled that she no longer warranted an entry in the Court Circular, a daily report that lists the official engagements and activities of the sovereign and senior working members of the royal family. This was their way of telling her that her engagements were less royal – and less important – than those undertaken by other members of the family. She rose above the snub with remarkably good grace. 'Silly fools,' she said dismissively on the way back from the charity première of the film *Accidental Hero* at the Odeon, Leicester Square, in April. The occasion had been televised, she had chatted with the film's star, Dustin Hoffman, a military band had played, and the Chairman of the mental-health charity Mencap, Lord Rix, had been there to greet her.

'How much more official do they want my engagements to be?' she asked rhetorically. 'According to them, that job tonight was not an official engagement. Did you see all the people who turned up, Ken? And I suppose all the money we raised for charity was not real, either? It's just ridiculous. But at least they come to see me.'

She had a valid point. While her husband was officially receiving star royal billing, on the Court Circular at least, carrying out his official duties before a handful of loyal supporters, thousands turned up at her unlisted engagements just to catch a glimpse of the Princess. Now, however, the Palace, much to her frustration, became obstructive. When she raised the idea of making a morale-boosting trip to see the British troops in Bosnia, it was blocked because Prince Charles was due to make a similar trip. She was also informed that a visit to Ireland would be inappropriate, while at the memorial service for the two children killed by the IRA's bomb blast at Warrington, Charles, not Diana, was chosen to represent the Queen. Typically, she turned the situation on its head by first calling, and then visiting the devastated parents at home.

A part of the reason for this and similar blocking moves lay with her husband's office which, under the express direction of his private secretary, Commander Richard Aylard, was planning its own PR offensive. Aylard believed that this would redress the balance and portray the Prince in a good light, re-establishing his popularity with media and public alike. With hindsight, Aylard's decision to offer the respected broadcaster Jonathan Dimbleby 'unprecedented access' to the Prince for a warts-and-all television documentary (with a book billed as an authorized biography to follow) was at best foolhardy. In terms of the Prince's public persona it proved disastrous, and the program (which was broadcast in June 1994) is likely to be remembered for the Prince's painful admission of adultery, and his less than manly complaints about the way his parents raised him. So while Diana triumphed in 1993, basking in the media's praise and the public's adulation, Dimbleby and his television crew (with the help of Charles's entire entourage) set about the business of relaunching the Prince. Dimbleby did approach Diana to ask her if she wanted to take part in the program, which was ostensibly being made to mark the twenty-fifth anniversary of Charles's investiture as Prince of Wales. They lunched together and he was charmed by her, but although she was tempted, those close to her, including me, advised her to steer well clear, assuring her that it would be unlikely to bring her either credit or praise. For once, she took our advice.

By the spring of 1993 Diana was becoming increasingly uneasy with having to live at Kensington Palace, surrounded by police surveillance cameras, and with her estranged husband's mainly disapproving relations as close neighbors. She longed to break free and have a place that she could truly call her own. So when her brother, Earl Spencer, telephoned out of the blue and offered her the use of the Garden House at Althorp, her ancestral home, she was both pleased and excited. I was dispatched to Northampton-shire to investigate security, and found it perfect. It would have given her the privacy she desired. Not overlooked by any other building on the estate and with a small house adjacent to it which could be used for the duty protection officer, the four-bedroomed Garden House suited all her requirements perfectly. Matters reached a stage where she even contacted an interior designer and picked out her colour scheme for the interior. Sadly, after building up her hopes her brother telephoned to say that he was no longer happy about the idea because he was uneasy about the added security presence at Althorp. She was devastated. Unsurprisingly, this disappointment led to a coolness between Diana and her brother for a few months, but it also strengthened in her mind the idea of ridding herself of police protection. 'He [Charles Spencer] has a point. Why would anyone want all the fuss that goes with me?' she asked sadly after hearing the news. 'The fuss' was clearly a less than oblique reference to me and my team of protection officers.

Despite her triumphs and her popularity, this was a difficult period, during which the Princess became dangerously self-absorbed. She chose to throw her weight behind two highly emotive and, to her, personal causes – domestic abuse, and eating disorders. In March 1993 she first visited the Chiswick Family Refuge, run by a charismatic and persuasive Canadian, Sandra Horley. It was a charity to which she would devote considerable time over the coming years. Diana joined in the discussion groups with enthusiasm, at one point declaring, 'Well, ladies, we all know what men can be like, don't we?'

I wanted to disappear as all eyes in the room turned on me, the only male present. It was a 'sister-act' she would repeat time and again to make her point. She was a victim, and her erring estranged husband was to blame.

# Chapter 17

For Diana, her sons always came first, and as the far-reaching implications of the dissolution of her marriage became clearer she began to focus on preparing them both, and William in particular, for what lay ahead. Cynics may say that she was using her eldest son as a pawn, as a means of securing her future status and position, but as someone who witnessed at first hand her close relationship with 'her boys', I can say categorically that this is simply untrue. The Princess believed that the preparation of William, and to a lesser extent, Harry, for their public roles was her primary duty. She told me repeatedly that she truly believed that both her sons should be fully aware of what would be expected of them, but that they should also be allowed to develop fully as young men, open to what life would throw at them. She showered them with love, but she listened to them, respected them, and tried to understand them. She was very tactile, often reaching to hug them, to a point at which William, in particular, would become embarrassed and feign pushing her away.

Meanwhile, it seemed that the whole world was turning against her estranged husband. The Princess harbored a pipedream that Charles would effectively disappear. She genuinely believed that the country would be better off if he, Mrs Parker Bowles and their 'cronies', as she called them, were to decamp from Highgrove to an organic haven in Italy or France, leaving her to groom William for kingship. This was, of course, wishful thinking of the most fantastic kind. The Prince of Wales has prepared himself all his life to ascend the throne, as is his duty. At that moment in time, however, it was the Princess who was in the ascendancy, and there were already mutterings in some circles that Prince Charles should step out of the line of succession and allow William to take the throne on the death of the Queen.

At the end of March 1993 we set off once again for the ski slopes of Lech. Diana was determined that, despite all the emotional heartache of their parents' separation, William and Harry should have every chance to enjoy themselves. The holiday followed the pattern of the previous year, which had ended so dramatically with the Princess learning of her father's death. This time, of course, Prince Charles did not join the party, something that made the entire situation much less tense. It was not long, however, before the entire resort was swarming with press from all around the world. Sadly, the paparazzi were not remotely interested in Diana's wish for a peaceful holiday with her sons. To them she was a cash cow, pure and simple. As far as they were concerned she was outside Britain, on their turf, and she was fair game.

Initially, everything was going well. There was the morning photo call at the ski lift which, although Diana did not like it, she tolerated, but what really irritated her was being followed as she walked around the small shopping area.

'Ken, I want you to keep them away from me,' she hissed as we walked into the Arlberg Hotel, illuminated by flashbulbs. I did my best, but there came a moment when my patience snapped. One photographer simply would not take no for an answer. He was within a few feet of the royal party, and the Princess became very upset at what she saw as a gross intrusion. Her reaction was affecting the boys, too, and the situation was in danger of getting out of hand. The pushy photographer told me he wanted an interview with William. I told him to move. He said that this was not my country and that I had no jurisdiction as a policeman in Austria. I asked him where he was from. 'Italy,' he replied.

'Well, it's not your country either. Now just back off!' I thundered. I was rapidly losing my patience and continued to tell him in no uncertain terms to move away. He refused and, as more swarms of photographers moved in nearer, he got too close to the Princess for my liking and I took him down with one swift arm movement. Mayhem ensued, especially when another of his pals followed him down on to the snow when he attempted to punch me. William and Harry loved it.

'Do it again, Ken,' William said, beaming all over his tanned face.

I shepherded them all safely inside the Arlberg and away from the problem. Outside reporters were scribbling in their notebooks, photographers were gesticulating, and one appeared to be acting out a Muhammad Ali fight. I've got some bloody explaining to do, I thought.

I reran the incident in my mind. There was no doubt that Diana had been upset; distressed, even. As the paparazzi moved in for the kill she had started to panic, which was why I had to act decisively. At one point she had screamed 'Go away! Go away!' which had astonished her boys who, until then, had found the whole thing quite amusing.

The Princess immediately retired to her suite, and her sons followed her. I was furious. After a short phone call to Colin Trimming, I went to check on Diana. She was distraught and I told her to be calm and that everything would be fine. Leaving her again, I set off to confront some of the press pack, in the hope that I could make them see sense. I singled out a couple of senior newspaper photographers, whom I knew well, the *Daily Mirror*'s Kent Gavin and Arthur Edwards of the *Sun*, and told them uncompromisingly that all bets were off. The message had to get back to the foreign media, and the paparazzi in particular, that unless they played the game I would make it almost impossible for any of them – journalists or photographers, British or foreign – to find the royal party. There were no more such incidents, but in retrospect, the affair seems hauntingly prophetic, given what would happen to the Princess in the days leading up to her death.

Her near-panic as the paparazzi closed in demonstrated that the Princess was on an emotional see-saw throughout the holiday. Her feeelings about Hoare had unsettled her. She was falling out with everyone, left, right and center, seemingly unable to help herself. Even I found it difficult to reason with her. She had always been erratic, but in the past she had invariably pulled back from the brink. What was to happen next showed just how close she had come to the edge. She leapt off it – literally – and seemed not to care about the consequences.

The first I knew about this latest drama was when I was woken at 6 am by the night-duty officer from my team, PC Mark Jawkowski, who was there to provide on-site protection. Basically, that meant that he was acting as a glorified doorman, there in case of emergency, to ensure that there were no intruders. There was a loud knock on the door of my room. Startled awake, I instinctively jumped from my bed, calling 'Come in!' Mark entered, clearly rattled.

'Mark? What's up?' I asked as he stood nervously at the foot of my bed. Growing impatient when he didn't reply at once, I asked him again, 'Is everything okay?'

'The Princess is okay now, sir,' was his response. By now wide awake, I turned to him and said, 'Hang on, Mark, this sounds serious. Let me put a dressing gown on, then tell me exactly what's happened.'

The young officer took a deep breath and began his account in best evidence-giving manner. At about 5.30 am the doorbell had sounded at the front of the Arlberg Hotel, our fortress against the press, who were scattered all around the resort in the less expensive hotels. Mark went to the door and, to his utter horror, there stood the Princess, dressed and wearing a scarf and a hat. She looked him straight in the eye, said 'Good morning' politely, and went straight to her suite.

'Christ, Mark,' I exclaimed, 'how on earth did she get out? Where is she now?'

'In her room,' he replied, sheepishly. I calmed down. The most important point was that she was safe. Now I had to find out what she had been up to, and stop her doing it again. I made Mark a cup of tea in my room, and when he had drunk it told him to go and get some sleep. It wasn't his fault, I assured him, and I would tackle the Princess when she awoke. As he sipped his tea, he gave me a breakdown of his precise movements, for the record. This was not simply an ass-covering exercise, although God alone knows we needed one: 'Princess Evades Police Protection – Gone For Hours' was not a headline that would enhance our career prospects.

'Take me through it from the top, Mark,' I said. 'At 1 am, when I retired, all doors were locked, yes?'

He nodded.

'So when I went to bed you were in place in the lobby to deal with knocks at the door?' He nodded again, then blurted out, 'I promise you, sir, she did not leave through the front door. I haven't a clue how the hell she got out.'

Mark was becoming increasingly heated. 'Sir, she couldn't have done – I had the only set of keys.' Since there was nothing more to be learned I sent him off to bed and told him not to worry, but added a warning 'Don't say anything to anyone about this.'

Thoroughly alarmed, I dressed in an old jacket and some slacks and headed from the room. I knew there was only one way the Princess could possibly have got out – she had bloody well jumped. We were staying on the first floor of the extension to the hotel, and there was a twenty-foot drop from her balcony to the ground, but that was made less by the deeply drifted snow. I went to check. When I reached the point directly beneath her balcony I found a perfect impression of the Princess's body in the deep snow below. From the hole in the snow, footprints led away into the town of Lech itself. 'God, I hope the bloody paparazzi did not see this,' I thought.

Diana was asleep; after being out all night it was hardly surprising, but there was no point in waking her now to confront her about her leap to freedom. I decided to wait and pick my moment.

That moment came some hours later, after she had dressed and breakfasted. I found her in the sitting room of her suite, getting ready for the day ahead. After we had said our 'good mornings', I came to the point. 'Ma'am,' I said calmly, my face a blank. 'It's about last night. What on earth were you thinking?' She flushed scarlet. She had been discovered, and she knew that she had been completely out of order. 'I don't have a problem with you going out, ma'am, you know that, but you have just *got* to tell me. What were you thinking when you jumped off the balcony? Anything could have happened.' She stayed silent. She knew she had done wrong; she knew she had been foolhardy; she knew she had put herself at risk. She also knew that she had placed me in a deeply compromising position, for if something had happened I would have had to take the blame – and live with the guilt. I then told her that I could not stand too many of these disappearances. 'You know that our relationship has to be based on mutual trust. This is a clear abuse of that.'

'Ken, I just needed some air,' she said at last, her speech higher-pitched than usual, still hot with embarrassment. She continued, 'Yes, I did jump from the balcony. I knew it was okay – it was deep, soft snow, and I knew it would be all right.' I pointed out that anything could have happened. She could have landed on a rock and hurt herself badly. 'It was a damned stupid thing to do,' I added. At that point I knew I had said enough. Lecturing Diana about anything was never wise, even when she knew she had done wrong. I decided to change tack.

'Do you want to tell me where you went?' I asked, knowing perfectly well that she wouldn't tell me.

'I know what I am doing,' was her only response to my question. By now I was thoroughly annoyed and replied, 'No, ma'am, I really don't think you do.'

What Diana actually did for some four or five hours that night remains a mystery, but the 'leap of Lech' gives a clear insight into her state of mind at the time – she wanted to be free of the trappings of her position. It was an act of independence, but also one of defiance. Two years later, when I was on a private visit to Lech, Hannes Schneider, the son of the Arlberg's owner, confirmed that she had jumped from the balcony. Hannes, whom I had dubbed 'Herr No Problem', never seemed to sleep. That night, he said, a relation of his had actually seen her walk through the snow and away from the hotel after throwing herself from the balcony.

Diana's leap marked the beginning of the end of my relationship with her. It was the first of a number of key incidents that, in the end, led to my leaving her service. It is understandable, I suppose, that as she began to break away from her former life, and despite the many years of mutual trust and understanding between us, she began to see me, because of my position, as part of the Establishment against which she was rebelling. The leap from the balcony apart, the rift started subtly. At first she began to hide things from me, where before she had always been open with me no matter what she had been doing. Even so, I am convinced that she was not happy with this and that deep down she knew she could trust me as she always had. But the new circle of people she had gathered around her wanted complete control of her, and the power and influence she wielded, for their own reasons. I tried to nip the problem in the bud and repeatedly confronted her about her new-found secretiveness, but she fudged the issue on every occasion.

She had no intention of answering me, and by her silence made my questions pointless. After a few days the entire Lech incident, which had made me seriously reconsider my position as her Police Protection Officer, had seemingly been eradicated from her memory. She knew I was disappointed and she did her best to win me back by launching one of her unique charm offensives. This was a typical Diana tactic. If she had behaved badly or done something wrong and knew it, she would often simply ignore it, and pretend that it had never happened. A few years earlier I would have wiped it out of my mind too, but I was growing concerned.

On our return from Austria Diana proposed a treat for her sons, a day out at Thorpe Park, an amusement park not far from London. We had all been before, so I knew that covering a day there was a fairly simple security operation. All her troubles seemed to vanish as the Princess, William, Harry and I plunged through breathtaking water rides, the two princes squealing with delight as we raced each other down a 30-foot water slide in wobbly rubber boats. Images of her, looking absolutely stunning in black jeans and a black leather jacket, her hair soaking wet from the water rides, appeared in the newspapers the next day. I also appeared beside her in the photographs, both of us dripping wet, laughing and joking. It is one of my favorite images of us together, and one that I cherish.

Diana was in carefree mood. At last liberated from the shackles of her marriage, she was a woman determined to enjoy herself after the years of frustration. Yes, she was still technically married to Prince Charles, but she was free. As Princess of Wales, she always craved normality. She had been to Paris the previous November on the first solo trip there since her youth, but she had been on official business, surrounded by an entourage, and had created a stir wherever she went. Now she was determined to go again, incognito – or as near to that as we could manage. 'I just want to go shopping with a couple of girlfriends. I just want to be normal. Please fix it for me, Ken,' she pleaded. I told her I would do my best, but added that I could not guarantee that she could go in and out of a great city like Paris without being detected.

'But Ken, I just want to be normal,' she said again. Perhaps her rather obviously manipulative pleading was getting to me, for I replied, 'Don't we all, ma'am'. She looked daggers at me, but said nothing more. Relenting slightly, I again promised that I would do my best, and left her to begin the process of setting the trip in hand. Her traveling companions were Lady Palumbo and Lucia Flecha de Lima. Through Hyatt Palumbo, wife of the billionaire property developer Lord (Peter) Palumbo, we had use of a private jet and we flew undetected to Paris on a beautiful May afternoon. I had arranged the hire of a plain Renault Espace people-carrier at Le Bourget airport, and in that we headed straight for Paris's high-fashion quarter, where Lady Palumbo had arranged for Diana to have a private viewing at Chanel, her favorite French couturier. She spent a couple of hours trying on the latest designs before we went on to some other boutiques in the area. The Princess and her friends spent a few thousand pounds, not very difficult to do in places like that (their purchases including an Hermès tie for me!), and we then headed for the Palumbos' award-winning house in the exclusive district of Neuilly, close to the Bois de Boulogne, where we were to stay.

So far, no one had any idea we were there, and I had taken the decision not to ask for help from local police this time for fear of leaks to the press. Next day, however, through no fault of ours, the secret trip was detected. Once again Diana ate a little, drank a little, shopped a little, and, like many other tourists, took in a few sights. Her visit, give or take the money she and her friends had at their disposal, had been as 'normal' as she could have wished. As for me, I thought we had given the press the slip completely; no one from the British media had an inkling that the Princess was even in Paris. Diana, who loved to think that she had hoodwinked the media, was like a bird released from its cage. She was almost skipping along as we approached the chic Marius et Jeanette restaurant. As I followed our party in, my heart sank. There, sitting on his scooter outside the restaurant, was one man and his lens – Jean-Paul Dousset, who at that time worked with the notorious paparazzo Daniel Angelli. The year before, they had together exposed the Duchess of York's love affair with John Bryan with those infamous toe-sucking photographs, shot from cover with a telephoto lens. Luckily Diana did not spot him and so remained oblivious to the fact that her secret trip was suddenly a secret no longer. As his shutter clicked and clicked, I racked my brains to work out how we had been found out. Then I realized that we hadn't. For in the corner of the restaurant sat the actor Gerard Depardieu, one of France's most celebrated sex symbols, and the reason why Dousset had been waiting outside. The photographer had struck double luck, and doubtless could scarcely believe it.

Depardieu recognized the Princess at once, and like the perfect French gentleman he is, came over immediately to stand by her table, talking of her great beauty and of what a privilege it was for France, for Paris and for him personally that she should be there. She was putty in his hands. And we were all putty in the hands of the freelance photographer outside, who must already have been working out exactly how much he was going to make by selling a set of pictures of the world's most famous woman at a secret assignation with France's sexiest movie star. I decided to act immediately.

Without saying anything to Diana other than a mumbled apology I slipped out and confronted Dousset. He looked surprised, but was perfectly courteous. We talked around matters for a few moments and then, knowing that he was not a security threat, I offered him a deal. If he kept a discreet distance so that the Princess did not know he was watching her, I would not interfere with his job. In return, he would not release the pictures until we were safely out of France, so that she would not be mobbed and thus have her short break ruined, and her security put at increased risk. He agreed, and was as good as his word. For the rest of the day Jean-Paul trailed us, but always at a distance and never too close to alert the Princess. True to our deal, he dispatched his pictures only after we had left Paris (and I have to say that his covert photography was very professional). I was happy too. Through my secret deal – for I never told the Princess – I had kept the number of paparazzi to the smallest number possible – one – and Diana was able to enjoy a trouble-free break. Obviously, she would not be too happy when she found out that photographs had been taken, but I reasoned that by the time she discovered what had happened she would be safely back at Kensington Palace, refreshed from her brief interlude in Paris, and my job would have been done.

Not long afterwards, on 12 May, a signed memorandum from Sir Robert Fellowes arrived on Diana's desk giving her official sanction for the next stage of her solo international career – a trip to Zimbabwe. The last line read simply, 'Her Majesty would be quite content with such a visit taking place.' The Princess was delighted. She knew that the Palace's hands were tied, for if they thwarted her she would leak the story to a friendly journalist, leaving the Palace looking, at best, petty, and at worst, spiteful and vindictive. The Queen, however, wanted a favor in return, and asked Diana and Charles to put on a public show of unity to honor World War II veterans, to which she agreed with alacrity. Outwardly, as she and her husband arrived together at Liverpool's Anglican Cathedral to mark the fiftieth anniversary of the Allied victory in the Battle of the Atlantic, the Princess was in an excellent mood. Prince Charles, at first a little apprehensive, found his estranged wife charming company and soon relaxed. Watching them smiling and laughing together in the blustery wind and rain, some onlookers found it difficult to understand why they had separated, and a number of misguided reporters even wondered in print whether their appearance together marked the start of a reconciliation. Nor could Diana resist the chance to show her husband what he was missing. One veteran of the battle, George Stansfield, dared to put this to the Prince. 'You both look wonderful. It is so nice to see you together again,' he said.

Charles made one of his flippant, off-the-cuff replies, which seemed to me to speak volumes about the true nature of the relationship. 'It's all done with mirrors,' he said, without looking up at his wife, who was standing a few feet away. His response was perfectly truthful. Deep animosity and mistrust governed their relationship, and on that day they were simply following the Queen's orders in a public show which, like a trick with mirrors, was really only an illusion. Diana put on a perfect performance for the crowds, but she did so for her mother-in-law, thus letting the Queen know that if Diana got what she wanted, she was happy to repay the favor.

In general, 1993 was still going well for Diana, but she was brought down to earth with the news of the death of my colleague and friend, and her former police protection officer, Chief Inspector Graham Smith. She broke down in tears when I told her the news even though it had not been unexpected. A few days earlier we had smuggled the desperately ill Graham from the Royal Marsden Hospital and taken him to dine at San Lorenzo. Skeletally thin, he was hardly recognizable, but he still maintained his sense of humor to the end, and we spent hours talking over old times. All three of us knew that it would be our last meeting, but nothing was said and it proved to be an evening of joy. At the funeral the Princess was distraught. She hugged Graham's widow, Eunice, and consoled his children, Emma and Alexander. He was in his mid-fifties.

A few weeks later, Diana was back on her official duty abroad, her personal campaign trail, more determined than ever to make her mark. It was a scorching July day when we touched down in Harare, the capital of Zimbabwe, and she embarked on what I believe to be the highest point of her royal career. Before agreeing to go she had not only sought clearance from the Queen, but also from Princess Anne. Until then she had shied away from African tours because, in royal terms, the continent was regarded as Anne's territory. Although both the Palace and the British High Commission in Harare had ruled that this was to be a low-key visit, it was in effect a major set-piece tour that followed the pattern of all previous official visits made by the Waleses together prior to the separation. The only difference was that Prince Charles was not included, and thus Diana had the speaking part.

After claims that her trips were a waste of taxpayers' money, Diana had decided to fly out Economy class, although British Airways did ensure that she was 'in the bubble' (on the upper deck of the 747) and that she had three seats to herself so that she could stretch out and sleep. With Patrick Jephson, her sister Lady Sarah McCorquodale as lady-in-waiting, Geoff Crawford, who had replaced Dickie Arbiter as her press secretary, and me heading up security, Diana had what she called her 'A team' to support her. In her desire to become a roving ambassador, she was helped by the fact that many heads of state in foreign countries were only too delighted to accommodate her. Robert Mugabe, President of Zimbabwe, was completely smitten by her. He had not addressed a press conference to the Western media for years, but after spending half an hour with Diana seemed positively anxious to share the experience with the traveling British press corps. 'She brings a little light into your life, naturally you feel elated,' he told the astonished journalists who had gathered outside Government House. Diana later confided to me that she had found him a 'frightening little man' who had not stopped sweating throughout their meeting, adding with a mischievous smile, in typical Diana fashion, 'It *was* rather hot, Ken.' The Princess had been steered away from political controversy by Foreign Office advisers, particularly the issue of land acquisition that was to erupt so bloodily a few years later. Instead she focused on the work of three charities, the International Red Cross, Help the Aged and the Leprosy Mission, of all of which she was patron. She even avoided the controversial subject of AIDS.

Initially, when the trip began the press were more interested in the Spencer sisters' reaction to the marriage of their former stepmother, Raine, Countess Spencer, to a French count. 'As far as I am concerned that woman is ex. She is no longer my stepmother,' Diana said, and then proceeded to giggle with her sister Sarah over newspaper photographs of Raine in her wedding dress. This bitter feud with Raine would end before Diana's death and the two women would become close, united by their mutual love of, and respect for, Diana's late father, Johnny Spencer. That aside, the Princess's excitement about the job in hand rubbed off on the rest of the team. She led by example, and our sense of kinship and our morale were high. In many respects she was the perfect ambassador for her causes, prepared to endure all that the Third World had to offer, focused on what she was there to achieve. Nevertheless, she did have her off moments, although they were usually over fairly quickly.

One evening, during a particularly overcrowded reception in Harare, she became increasingly frustrated as it seemed that the entire population of Zimbabwe had turned up to shake her hand. It irritated her, too, that the ratpack had managed to buy tickets for the event, and in particular that her sister, Lady Sarah, was having a sneaky cigarette with them. By the time I freed her from the mêlée she was fuming, particularly at the unfortunate Patrick Jephson, who bore the brunt of her anger. 'I'm very unhappy,' she told him, loudly enough for the High Commissioner and his wife to hear. And with that she retired.

Patrick was distraught. Had all his planning gone awry? What would the Princess's mood be like in the morning? Listening to him airing his worries, I decided that the poor man needed a drink. There was another big day ahead of us all tomorrow, and he needed to wind down if he was going to get a wink of sleep. Diana, as Patrick had predicted, was in a foul mood with all of us, including Lady Sarah, the following day. During these moments of schoolgirl petulance there was nothing one could do but meet her head on. That evening, at my suggestion, after the official engagements for the day were over and the Princess had gone to bed, the entire royal party gathered downstairs in the High Commission around the grand piano. After I had led an enthusiastic sing-song Diana descended the stairs, ostensibly to complain about the noise. In reality she was feeling left out. Within a few minutes she was joining in with the rest of us, and the tension that had threatened to spoil the tour immediately disappeared.

My enduring memory of the visit is an almost biblical scene. The Princess flew deep into the African bush, to the Mazerera Red Cross feeding center. There, standing by a huge iron cooking pot she served the tiny children from the ancient Karanga tribe one by one. I watched one hungry little boy hold up his bowl to this beautiful lady. Four-year-old Tsungai Hove had walked seven miles through the heat and dust to the feeding center. As his turn came to collect his only daily meal he boldly pushed the bowl towards her like an African Oliver Twist. Diana looked down and smiled at him, and the shy smile he gave her in return was almost heart-rending. She relished the part she was playing, ladling huge portions of bean stew from the cooking pot into the bowls of the patient children. The press lapped up the photo opportunity and one British newspaper ran the headline the next day, 'Dinner Lady – Diana serves up royal treat for hungry children.'

Yet the experience had troubled the Princess. She was close to tears as we flew back to Harare, because she knew that she was returning to comfort and plenty, while these poor, hungry children faced a trek of many miles back to their mud-hut homes in the drought-ridden countryside. Those who believe that Diana's work was nothing more than a series of photo opportunities in glamorous locations around the world should have seen this drained, exhausted woman sitting in the back of a helicopter that day and heard her speak of the heartbreaking scenes she had just witnessed.

# Chapter 18

A FTER SHE SEPARATED FROM HER HUSBAND, Diana's fascination with Oliver Hoare intensified. She had made him the center of her world, and in return she demanded his complete attention. Those of us close to her found that although she could still be great fun, her mood swings became more dramatic, and accusations of treachery against members of her inner circle more frequent and ferocious. She was particularly upset when press reports began to circulate hinting at an association with Hoare. I had warned her that it was inevitable that the story would leak out. The frequency of their meetings – as well as the secrecy, which would always rouse the suspicions of any lurking journalist or photographer lucky enough to stumble over one of their assignations – meant that it could not be very long before somebody blew the lid off the story.

I did not think that Hoare was good for the Princess, and tried gently to persuade her at least to be more cautious. I also rather solemnly reminded her that there was his wife to consider. This was not a popular remark to make. The Princess hated being reminded that Hoare was married and, worse, that she herself had initially gone out of her way to befriend his wife.

As her frustration intensified, so Diana's demands increased. Lonely and confused, she began phoning the Hoares' house in Chelsea, making several hundred telephone calls but immediately putting down the phone if Diane answered. For Diane Hoare, a strong and proud woman, being plagued by nuisance calls from Diana was the final straw. In October 1993 she decided to contact the police.

Detectives quickly traced the calls to private numbers inside Kensington Palace. At this point I was called in by Bob Marsh, the then Commander of Royalty Protection, who, convinced that the calls were being made by a disgruntled member of her staff, asked me if I could shed any light on who that person might be. At first, I thought he was not serious, and asked him whether he honestly believed this story. He said that he did and that he intended to inform the Commissioner accordingly. I asked him why he thought a member of the Prince and Princess of Wales's household would do such a thing, but pulled myself up when I realized that he knew nothing about Diana's friendship with Hoare. I felt it my duty to break my golden rule and tell him about Diana and Hoare. He was shocked when I told him that he need look no further for a culprit than the Princess herself. I felt dreadful, as though I had betrayed her. Equally, though, I could not let some innocent member of Diana's staff come under suspicion, nor could I let my service and department suffer the consequences of being led into pursuing such innocents – public ridicule – when the truth eventually came out.

The *News of the World* broke the story, which led to the journalist, Gary Jones, scooping the coveted Reporter of the Year award. Faced with extremely bad publicity – for even the public, who adored her, drew the line at her harassing the wife of a man with whom she was infatuated – Diana brooded over what she saw as the unfairness of her persecution by the media. Not once did she show any remorse, nor did she seem to think that she had done anything wrong. She simply did her best to distance herself from the allegations. She admitted having made some calls to the Hoare house, but insisted that she had not been responsible for the majority. This, of course, like the disgruntled-member-of-staff story, was also not true. The police traced at least 400 nuisance calls to her, and might easily have charged her. She knew, however, as I did, that it was never going to get that far. Diane Hoare had made her point, and the Princess backed off. Her friendship with Oliver Hoare cooled and, before long, was over. By then, however, I had left her service.

What really troubled me about her obsession with Hoare was that it created suspicion in Diana's mind that I, and the police in general, impinged upon her freedom. This, I am sure led to her decision to do without police protection – a decision which, I truly believe, resulted in her death.

Mickey and Minnie, Disney's King and Queen, were there to greet us on the fifth floor of the Grand Floridian Beach Resort when we arrived on that afternoon. Harry's face lit up. Not that he was interested in being cuddled by people dressed as two giant cartoon characters – he wanted to get to the rides. Diana was thrilled too, but for different reasons. Her sons, instead of being at Balmoral with their father, as they usually were in August, were free; free to do what other children did on holiday.

My reconnaissance some weeks earlier had proved invaluable. I advised Diana in my briefing memo that the fact that Disney is spread over 43 square miles was to our advantage in our habitual battle to outwit the media because Disney, unlike any other theme park, has a VIP package which uses reserved routes to rides and attractions, along a predetermined course. A network of restricted paths and tunnels, not accessible to the public, enabled special guests literally to pop up at the front of queues and go straight on the ride without anyone elsewhere in the park knowing which attraction they were on. Moreover, conscious of Diana's fear of being criticized for using her royal status to secure star treatment, my memo, dated 2 August 1993, reassured her because I had recommended the VIP package for security reasons: 'At this time of the year up to 1 million people could be using the complex. Many rides and attractions will have queues of 2 to 3 hours' waiting. The VIP method is not queue-jumping, and will not be seen by others so to be.' The note was returned with a huge tick from her pen through that section.

Something was nagging me about this trip, however. It came at a time when the Princess, understandably, wanted to rid herself of the trappings of royalty. As a result, she was inevitably beginning to regard her police protection as another constant reminder that although she was now distanced from the royal family because of her separation from Prince Charles, she was still enveloped by the system. The trip also took place at a critical point in her uncompromising propaganda war against her husband. With her usual sure instinct for these things, she knew that photographs of her and the boys enjoying the sort of holiday experienced by millions of ordinary people would be seen as a refreshing change, while Charles would once again be unfairly portrayed as a dreary, out-of-touch, and above all absent father. It was too good a photo opportunity for Diana to miss.

[234]

From the moment Sid Bass, a senior Disney executive, had invited her and the boys, assuring them of a minimum of fuss, I had felt that she was acting strangely about this trip. I sensed that she was not being completely straight with me. As I have said, it is standard protection practice, and essential for security, to carry out a reconnaissance ahead of any visit, official or private, planned by members of the royal family. As well as the two-day stopover at Disney's Florida complex in Orlando, she proposed to spend the rest of the week at the family holiday home of her friend Kate Menzies at Lyford Cay in the Bahamas, a short flight from Florida. As I was preparing to leave on the reconnaissance, however, the Princess told me out of the blue that she did not think that it was necessary. I was a little taken aback; she knew the rules as well as I did.

'Ken, I really don't think there is any need for you to go and check this one. You must stop wasting the taxpayers' money,' she said.

I looked at her quizzically, before answering, 'Ma'am, with the greatest respect, you know the police procedures. The security arrangements for any visit made by you and your sons is my call.' Then I added, only half jokingly, 'And since when have you been worried about spending taxpayers' money?'

In retrospect, this was perhaps a little blunt, or even disrespectful, but we were going through one of our difficult periods, and I was not in the mood to be told how to do my job.

Diana did not challenge my decision again, but I was so perturbed that I asked her directly if she was keeping something from me. Again she refused to talk about it, but intuition told me that something was up. Although she wanted her sons to have a good holiday, I suspected that she was planning to use this trip with her sons to hit back at the Prince, as the state of their relationship continued to deteriorate, fuelled by a concerted PR offensive in the press. That was beyond my remit, however, and there was in any case very little I could do to stop her pursuing that ultimately self-destructive war except – as usual – advise caution.

On the advance security review at Orlando one of my first tasks was to address senior Disney security managers, so that between us we could ensure that Diana and her sons would be safe during their stay. Most of the professionals employed by Disney to police their resort were former state security officers or FBI agents. They were great guys – utterly professional, and convinced that if they could deal with the visit of a US President and Michael Jackson, then looking after 'Lady Di', as they called her, would be 'a piece of cake'. I was not so sure, however.

Diana's uncharacteristic attitude to the reconnaissance puzzled me, and I still had that nagging feeling of doubt about her motives. Although she had assured me that, apart from her and the boys, only I knew about the private holiday, I had a hunch that she had released the information about her trip to the British press via a sympathetic reporter. I therefore asked one of Disney's senior security chiefs if it would be possible to run a name check through the company's computer. Within seconds the name Richard Kay flashed up on the screen. The *Daily Mail* journalist was booked to arrive at the Grand Floridian on exactly the same day as Diana; even more significantly, the booking had been made on the very day that Diana had told me of her wish to go to Florida. My hunch had proved correct, and I now understood why Diana had been acting so strangely. It was clear that she had personally tipped Kay off, and I was reasonably certain that he would have passed on the information, at her behest, to the rest of the royal ratpack. She had wanted to stop my advance security check because she was worried that I might discover what she was planning. She had been right to be worried, but at least I now knew what I was dealing with.

Despite my disappointment at this sly behavior I still had a job to do. Next day, confident that everything was under control at Disney, I flew to Nassau in the Bahamas to reconnoiter the second phase of the proposed holiday. I was met by Sergeant Glen Roy of the Bahamas Police Department, who drove me to Lyford Cay to check the arrangements at 'Casuarina Beach', the house belonging to the Menzies family where the Princess and her party were to stay. It turned out to be set in a development that afforded a great deal of privacy, being part of a huge luxury complex, privately policed and spotlessly maintained. The house itself had a magnificent swimming pool with the beach less than fifty yards away and there was an added bonus at that time of the year, for despite the temperatures nudging 95°F, this was low season, with very few people around.

Diana would be accompanied by her girlfriends Kate Menzies and Catherine Soames, and otherwise by only one member of staff, the boys' nanny, Olga Powell. William was joined by a schoolfriend, Andrew Charlton, and Harry had Catherine's equally impish son, also Harry, as a playmate. My team consisted of Trevor Bettles, 'Jack' Tarr, Dave Sharp and night-duty officer PC Knights.

It soon became abundantly clear, however, that, given the size of the party, there would not be enough room in the house for the entire protection team, so I decided to try to rent a nearby villa. On the following day I was put in touch with an American named Tom Wyman, who was happy to rent out his house, with its exclusive beach frontage, and which just happened to be about twice the size of Diana's holiday accommodation, for the reduced, off-season price of $5,000 (£3,300) for the week.

Disney had arranged everything perfectly and after our first foray into the Magic Kingdom on the day we arrived the boys were already alight with excitement. Better still, apart from Disney's own photographer there was not a cameraman in sight. I sensed, however, that the Princess was a little edgy.

Next morning, we set off on an incredibly full program, determined to pack as much in as possible. As we crisscrossed Disney World underground or on the restricted paths, going from ride to ride, it became clear that the media had already arrived *en masse*. Some had even booked into our hotel, but Disney's security proved to be extremely effective at keeping them away. Somehow, however, they got word that Diana and her sons were heading for MGM's *Indiana Jones Stunt Spectacular* (the two princes were obsessed with the phenomenally successful movie, starring Harrison Ford), and several Fleet Street photographers had already positioned themselves inside the auditorium.

With Diana and the boys safely settled in their seats, the show got under way. Behind us in the back row, I could hear a commotion as Disney security officers, who had decided to eject anyone they thought looked like a member of the press, set about their task with a will. Most of the press men simply left, but one of the photographers, Frank Barrett, a spirited individual from the *Daily Star*, refused to leave and started spouting something about press freedom in his loud cockney twang.

'There is no such thing here, sir. This is the Magic Kingdom and we have our own laws and rules,' one of the officers said as he hustled Barrett out of the auditorium. The offending cameraman was then 'arrested' and taken to a Disney detention center, where he was threatened with 'deportation from the Magic Kingdom', until I personally intervened on his behalf.

With this kind of backup, there was no need to negotiate with the press or hold daily briefings, because we could do exactly what we wanted without them knowing. William and Harry were clearly having the best fun of their lives, which certainly lightened the Princess's mood, and the sense of developing tension seemed to evaporate.

Deep down, however, I was still unhappy about Diana's decision to tip off the media about the visit. Yet much to her private irritation, the VIP system of driving along the restricted routes, or walking along the labyrinth of underground walkways, meant that for most of the time we were out of sight. So far not one photograph had appeared in the press. Some journalists had even resorted to placing an advertisement in the local newspaper, asking any tourist who had taken a photograph of the Princess and her sons to call them. So far so good – except that, mysteriously the press kept arriving in roughly the right place, albeit usually a few minutes too late. But whatever her motives (which, to be fair, were above all to ensure that her sons had a terrific holiday), William and Harry were in their element. That in turn could be relied upon to make their mother happy. I returned to my suite that evening convinced that the tide was turning, and that in a few days Diana would be her usual fun-loving self.

My hopes were to be dashed, however, when she appeared next morning in the foulest of moods. Not even her sons' happiness could shake her out of it. She had taken another call from her lawyer, which had driven home to her the fact that, even in the Florida sunshine, she could not escape the pressures arising from her separation from Prince Charles. From her fulminating it was clear that she clearly wanted to strike back at her husband, but I sensed that the security operation had been too good for her to have achieved the PR coup she had tried secretly to orchestrate. Spoiling for a fight, she lashed out at the people nearest to her, and the strain was beginning to tell on Katie and Catherine.

My heart sank further when, prior to our departure for Nassau that day, I received information that the media were aware of our destination. At the very least, it meant that I had drastically to rethink my security plans. I immediately redeployed Dave Sharp to travel ahead of us and establish a daily patrol around Lyford Cay. It proved a politic move. Dave, with the help of a private security company employed by the property owners, detained two men who claimed to be 'looking for the royal party', having read about the Princess's impending arrival in a local newspaper. I also increased the night mobile patrols by the Bahamas police, and had them maintain a daily shoreside patrol to prevent unauthorized landings.

Despite the arrest of the two trespassers, I was confident that the Princess would be safe, and told her so. I also reminded her that I had rented another house near by to afford her and her friends greater privacy, and that I had engaged night patrols and a local police presence outside. Last, I explained that while this was not a perfect security arrangement, I was prepared to compromise, and for this she seemed genuinely grateful. My careful arrangements were to backfire, however. Within a few hours of arriving William and Harry appeared at the 'police house', and before long had made it obvious to their mother that they much preferred our villa and being with us on the beach. It was perfectly understandable – after all, what young boy wants to be holed up with three thirty-something women, and their own nanny, when they could be messing around on the beach away from the parental eye? – but it was hardly tactful. Unwittingly, they had placed me in a difficult position. Diana, who was, I think, looking for an excuse to criticize me, was livid. She found it unbelievable that my accommodation might be superior to hers, and lashed out accordingly, wanting to know how much it cost, and who was footing the bill.

'Ken, this cannot be right,' she raged. 'Who is paying for this?'

Equally angry, I hit back. 'Where do you think the money is coming from, ma'am? The Metropolitan Police Force, of course.'

'So I was right. The taxpayer is having to pay for you again, Ken. It's all too much.'

'With the greatest respect, ma'am, we have already covered this,' I replied, doing my best not to lose my temper. I had been on duty for fourteen days without a break, and in the circumstances I thought it best to step back from the situation and hope that this would lessen the tension. Still seething, I left, before I said something I might have regretted.

The dialogue between us was waning fast. For me, it had reached a point where talking to the Princess was really a question of stating the bare essentials, and stopping at that. As strange as it may seem now, I think that a part of the problem was that Diana had not been discovered by the chasing press (for which I was to some extent responsible); she was spoiling for a high-profile confrontation with the press, but perhaps more significantly she was also desperate for the publicity.

On one occasion when the press were bobbing about aimlessly offshore in their chartered boat, hoping to get a photograph of Diana or the princes, she actually walked outside the house and began striding up and down the beach looking out to sea. Unfortunately, the press had focused on our large 'police house', and because I was sitting outside it with Dave Sharp, they assumed that it must be where the Princess was staying. Even more unfortunately, the two boys then came over and rushed on to the beach and into the water for a swim, which was all the confirmation the media needed. Pictures of our 'police house' were published in all the British national newspapers with captions saying that it was Diana's 'holiday home in paradise' (something which, inevitably, led to me having to justify the cost to senior management in my department).

Out on their boat the hacks took a few pictures of the boys. I contacted the local police chief and took a launch out to the press boat, the aptly named *No Limit*, to ask them to move away and leave Diana and her party in peace. It was a very light-hearted affair. After a few jokey comments I said that since they had got their photographs, they could move on, and perhaps go fishing. They agreed. I made one mistake, however, while talking to Arthur Edwards, the *Sun*'s royal photographer. After years following Diana around the world Arthur, a perceptive man, knew instinctively that something was wrong, probably from my demeanor.

'How's Ma'am?' he asked. It was wrong of me to do so, but I was still frustrated at Diana's behavior towards me. In reply, I shrugged my shoulders and gave a rueful grin, as though to suggest that she needed a good talking to. It was harmless enough, but it was a moment that came back to haunt me. After Diana had returned to Britain, she got wind of what had happened and suggested that I had spoken indiscreetly to a member of the press. Naturally, this led to another sticky conversation between the Princess and me.

By the end of the holiday storm clouds were gathering both literally and metaphorically. The Princess had not had a good time, and she was at odds with everyone. It was clear that she was finding the pressure arising from her separation and her new life difficult to cope with, even on holiday with friends. She was behaving increasingly erratically, and before we left for the flight back to

Britain she made one last concerted effort to be photographed, which for security reasons I thwarted. She was not pleased.

'I'll do what I want, Ken. I think it's so unfair that I can't do what I want. I just want to be normal. God! – *nobody* understands me,' she said petulantly. After years of operating on her wavelength, I was now beginning to think that perhaps she had a point and that no one did understand her – not even her.

As for me, I now suspected her motives, and felt that I no longer understood what she was trying to achieve. I seriously doubted whether she knew, either. There was no question now that it was only a matter of time before we parted company. As sad as I was at the thought of leaving her service, if the Princess no longer felt that she could be completely open and honest with me in my professional capacity, I could not offer her the level of protection on which my department prides itself. I think that Diana also had mixed feelings about the course she was following, but deep down she believed that if she was to break free of the trappings of royalty that so irked and hampered her, then she would have to rescind her police protection. It was a high-risk strategy.

The closing chapter in my time as the Princess's protection officer was marred by the sneak-pictures row, in which she was photographed by a concealed camera while working out at LA Fitness, the West London gym she attended. The Princess had talked to me about the possibility of photographs having been illicitly taken of her in the gym six months previously, in May 1993, but had refused to tell me why she thought this. In early November, the *Sunday Mirror* and then the *Daily Mirror* carried an exclusive showing photographs of Diana, wearing a leotard, exercising at the gym. She acted swiftly, bringing a successful action against the paper for invasion of privacy. It seemed to be a clear-cut case, and the hypocritical chorus of disapproval aimed at the *Mirror* by rival newspapers was deafening. The row over the pictures made front-page news because it was the first time that the Princess had taken legal action against a newspaper. It perturbed me, however, raising serious questions in my mind about possible collusion between Diana and the gym's owner, Bryce Taylor. I remain convinced that she had invented an elaborate sting to ensnare a newspaper and then milk the publicity – and the public's sympathy – for all they were worth.

When the matter went to law I offered to make a statement, but since this would have reflected my concern, my offer was declined. My evidence would have been of little help to Diana if she had taken the case to court; indeed, it might have caused the action to backfire on her.

In the event injunctions were granted preventing further pictures being published, and the case was brought against the paper and Taylor. In the end Diana settled out of court, receiving an apology, a sum by way of damages paid to a charity nominated by her, and the negatives and prints of the photographs.

Although Diana claimed victory in the 'peeping Tom pictures' furore, if anything Bryce Taylor was the only real winner. He reportedly received $375,000 (£250,000) as part of an agreement struck in secret between the two sides to prevent the embarrassment of a royal court case. Although the Princess was spared a courtroom appearance – which might have proved extremely embarrassing – and had her costs met, only Taylor and a couple of charities had truly benefited. Diana, as I knew only too well, escaped an embarrassing (and potentially very costly) legal battle in which she was, to my mind, by no means a wholly innocent party.

My combative stance over Diana's legal fight effectively sealed my fate. On a beautiful, typically English autumn day, I made my decision to go. It was a perfect day for a mother to watch her son competing in a soccer match. Sadly, the stress of the Disney trip and the holiday in the Bahamas meant that Diana and I were going through one of our silent periods – formal greetings, a few questions, brief but polite answers, plenty of 'Yes, ma'ams'. She was clearly upset with me and, irritated myself, I was not going to show that I cared one way or the other about her apparent displeasure. Her behavior towards me before, during and after the holiday, still rankled. Worse still, her refusal to co-operate and to be totally open with me had left me decidedly uncomfortable about my position, something made worse, to my mind, by the growing influence of Oliver Hoare and a number of other advisers and hangers-on.

On the morning of William's soccer match Diana told me that she wanted to drive the car. She was in a difficult and petulant mood, ready to snap at anything I said – even by her standards, I knew I was in for a rough ride. At times like this it was best to say nothing, or at least to confine oneself to basic replies. Somewhat pompously, I reminded her to do her best to stick to the speed limit, and with that we set off for her son's Surrey-based prep school, where she was due to watch Prince William playing in the game. When we arrived, however, her vindictive mood persisted. Even William did not escape, and came in for some admittedly light-hearted criticism from his mother, which must have embarrassed him in front of his schoolfellows.

Her behavior struck me as unnecessary as well as unkind, and I felt for William. We drove back along the motorway to London in the mid-afternoon sunshine. Diana was still spoiling for a fight and I, tired by now of buttoning my lip, was more than ready to give her one.

An embarrassing silence reigned as we drove along Kensington High Street, approaching Kensington Palace. Suddenly Diana veered over to the side of the road and slammed on the brakes, declaring that she wanted to go shopping for CDs. The only problem was that she had decided to park on a double yellow line. She switched off the engine, opened her door and started to get out. I broke the silence. 'Ma'am, you are illegally parked. You can't park here. You know that it's against the law.' She turned and looked daggers at me. 'You're a policeman, aren't you? You sort it out,' she ordered. This was the last straw. I was not having her tell me to help her break the law, no matter how petty the offence. 'Ma'am, with the greatest respect, you know I will not allow that. If you park here and they tow the car away, it will be on your head.'

Now she was furious. Letting out a deep sigh of frustration, she got back in her seat and slammed the door, before racing off along the busy street in search of a parking space. I suggested that we park in Kensington Palace Gardens, and told her that I would inform the police officer on duty opposite the Israeli Embassy. That too she ignored. I tried again, suggesting that we return to Kensington Palace, only a few hundred yards away, and then walk to Tower Records together. Again, no answer. Then, right on cue, tears began to well up in those bright blue eyes, though more out of frustration than emotion, I felt. Seconds later, she pulled up at the palace, jumped out of the car and ran back towards the high street, declaring over her shoulder that she was going shopping.

'That is *it*,' I said out loud. I knew there and then that this was the end. It seemed ridiculous that a relationship that had lasted so many years was to end in a row over illegal parking, but there was no going back now. Still sitting in the car, I composed my letter of resignation in my head and began to evaluate my options. Yet even the prospect of leaving Royalty Protection and returning to uniform did not worry me. After the antics of the Princess over the last few weeks, I honestly thought that anything would be better than this ridiculous existence. Egos aside, I knew that, professionally, I had no option – she had made my job impossible, and consequently was jeopardizing her own security.

I did not chase after the Princess, because I knew from years of experience that it would not be long before she returned to the car. She had no money with her – something quite common among royalty. She would need cash to pay for whatever she bought. Sure enough, she was back within minutes, asking me for money to pay for the handful of CDs she had chosen. I dutifully handed some over and went with her to the shop to pay. We then returned to Kensington Palace. Once at her apartment, I turned and calmly broke the news to her. 'Ma'am, I have decided to resign as your personal protection officer. I will be speaking to Colin this afternoon and will be asking to be switched to other duties as soon as possible.' My voice sounded curiously cold and remote to me, but the Princess said nothing. She stepped out of the car and walked, head bowed, into Kensington Palace. She did not look back.

I am not sure whether the Princess was shocked, or had been expecting me to resign. I honestly believe that she wanted me to quit, but did not have the strength at that time to ask for my resignation. When I told Colin Trimming, however, he was not convinced I was doing the right thing. He thought that the tension between the Princess and me was a passing phase, one of our cold-war periods that would blow over. But I assured him that I had had enough, and asked him to back my decision. Next day I went to see the Commander, handed in my formal resignation and asked for a transfer. He asked me to stay on for a few more weeks, but I insisted that this was impossible given the deterioration in my relationship with the Princess.

News of my departure hit the press the next day, leaked to the *Daily Mail*; the *Sun* and the *Daily Express* also got the tip. One headline read, 'Diana Loses Her Top Cop', but I was treated fairly by the newspapers. The journalists I had worked alongside for years knew me, and were shrewd enough not to swallow the official line completely. The reports said that I was much more than her policeman, and interpreted my departure as a decisive moment in the Princess's story. She had lost, they wrote, not only a protection officer, but also a friend – who now, they asked, was left for her to trust?

There was a brief flurry of publicity, but I answered no calls and made no comments. I was told to take some leave while the Commander arranged a new role for me inside the squad, but I asked for the matter to be resolved as quickly as possible. As a result I was offered a position in charge of visiting foreign royalty and VIPs, and immediately accepted it. Almost at once the tension lifted, and I knew that I had done the right thing.

A few days later, once the dust had settled, I received a call from Colin Trimming. He told me that the Princess had asked to see me because she wanted to give me something. I declined. Colin said that it was my choice and that naturally I did not have to go, but he added that my seeing her would make life easier for everyone in the department, including my team of protection officers, who had been left to pick up the pieces after my sudden departure. I told him that I accepted what he said, but added with, I'm ashamed to say, rather childish gracelessness, that I simply did not want one of her personalized carriage clocks. Ever the diplomat, he left me to ponder my decision. He knew me as a friend as well as a colleague, and realized that this was neither the time nor the place to push the issue. I was still furious, and my anger was in danger of turning to bitterness.

In the end I relented. A couple of days later I went to the Princess's apartment for the formal handover of the carriage clock, personalized with her monogram, a 'D' surmounted by a coronet. Although it would have been bad manners to have refused this audience, I would have preferred to have been anywhere else but with her. Our relationship, once so strong, was now at an end, and both of us knew it.

I could not forget how close we had become, and perhaps I should have made a greater effort to heal the rift between us. At that time, however, I felt she was determined on a course that might end with her destroying herself, although she seemed unable to understand that. Whatever I said or did not say during this meeting would make no difference at all. Few words were spoken, and the Princess could hardly look me in the eye, a sure sign that she was feeling embarrassed or guilty, or was hiding something.

I knew that she felt isolated, alone and concerned for her future, and that a part of her wanted to ask me to come back.

'You're not happy, are you, Ken?' she asked, discarding the forced civility of the meeting.

'No, ma'am, I most certainly am not,' I said. 'But most of all, ma'am, I am very concerned for your security.'

'Oh, I am okay, Ken,' she said. She seemed uncertain whether to remain serious or lapse into her usual giggling manner.

'Yes, ma'am, you on your own are fine. But it is the position others are placing you in that worries me. These people will not protect you, ma'am – they are only interested in protecting themselves. You know it, and I know it.'

She listened, but said nothing. I am sure now that, deep down, she agreed with what I was saying, but she did not want to admit that I might be right. It was clear to her that I had no intention of returning, and, after my outburst, she was not going to ask me. She did not want to discuss her tangled love life, either, and changed the subject with sublime dexterity. I smiled to myself. She had learned many skills in the time that I had known her, and escaping from potentially embarrassing situations was one of them. She then rather formally thanked me for my loyal service and wished me good luck in my career and my future. I thanked her in return, probably a little too brusquely, turned and walked out of her Kensington Palace apartment for the last time. I did not look back.

Our paths crossed again a few days later, however, something that ultimately led to my receiving a furious letter from the Princess over my decision to sue the *Sun*. I had decided to take action against the newspaper after it sensationalized a chance meeting that I had with the Princess in a London street. Under the headline 'Di's Secret Meeting With Cop Pal – Chat in Quiet Lane', the offending article went on to claim that the Princess had arranged a clandestine get-together with me. Describing me as her 'emotional stalwart', the reporter wrongly alleged that this had been an arranged meeting, and that she had wanted to meet me after anti-Diana courtiers had forced me out. None of the allegations were true and, concerned that senior officers might think that I had abused my position by meeting the Princess on duty time, I decided to act independently to quash the *Sun*'s claims.

What had happened was this. I had been driving with a member of the Royalty and Diplomatic Protection squad, Sergeant Ian

Huggett. He did not know where a number of the embassies were, and I had taken him on a tour of them. As we turned into Cadogan Place, Knightsbridge, Ian saw Diana's black Audi coming towards us. It would have been extremely rude if I had not stopped to speak to her, especially after the animosity that had surrounded my departure. As we drew alongside each other we both stopped our cars and wound down our windows. I asked her how she was. Then, since we were blocking the road, I asked Ian to pull the car over and park. I got out and walked back a few yards to the Princess's car and leant in through the driver's window to talk to her. Again I asked her how she was, and she smiled and said that she was fine. The strain that had clouded our last meeting had evaporated. Just then, however, I noticed two photographers approaching on foot, and told her that I thought they were following her. 'I know, Ken, I can't shake them off,' she said.

'It's best if you drive off, ma'am,' I replied. She smiled and, with a wave, pulled out and disappeared into the traffic.

It was to be our last meeting. When the article and photograph appeared in the *Sun* on 25 November, without Diana's knowledge, I contacted the Police Federation, who instructed solicitors to pursue the matter on my behalf. A few months later, while still waiting for the case to come to court, I received a furious letter from the Princess, who was upset that I had taken legal action against the newspaper without consulting her first. She added that I had disappointed her, and that she now feared a subpoena forcing her to give evidence. It was, of course, an overreaction on her part, and in the event the newspaper settled out of court.

In the strange and sometimes incomprehensible world of royalty, there is little point in trying to link experience with reality, for, like the past, that world really is a foreign country – they do things differently there. As I look back on the years I spent alongside the Princess, I realize, too, that there is no point in bitterness at how they ended, because what happened was inevitable. Indeed, what is surprising, in two individuals both with strong characters, is that our 'partnership' lasted as long as it did. Diana demanded so much attention that at times I felt almost stifled. Yet I gave it fully and without question because I believed in her. It is a measure of her extraordinary personality that she could inspire that belief in people and, far more often than not, live up to it.

She was a truly inspirational woman who had the ability to change things for the better. She knew how to lift people from the grayness of normality and make them feel truly special. She did the same with me. Inevitably, when you live and work at such close proximity tempers will flare. I may have been wrong to react in the way I did, and perhaps I too behaved petulantly. Even so, I believe that my leaving her had to happen at some time, and that it was probably appropriate that it happened when it did, as her new life was unfolding before her.

On 4 December 1993, the award-winning columnist of the *Daily Mail*, Lynda Lee-Potter, wrote a rather flattering piece assessing the impact of my departure upon the Princess. Knowing Diana's almost obsessive daily dependence on that newspaper, she would have undoubtedly have read it.

'The departure of her personal bodyguard, Detective Inspector Ken Wharfe, was cataclysmic because he was loyal, shrewd, respectful, good fun and above all full of common sense. He more than anybody kept her in touch with reality and the truth.'

# Chapter 19

I T WAS AN UNUSUALLY OPPRESSIVE NIGHT, as though the day's
heat had never really dissipated. In my weekend cottage in
Dorset, I lay in my bed on the verge of sleep, restless in the
warmth and airlessness. For some reason Diana was on my mind. I
had been following the unedifying events of her extended summer
holiday with increasing concern. The newspapers had been packed
with stories and pictures of the Princess and the new man in her
life, Dodi Fayed, on holiday together off Sardinia's Emerald Coast
aboard the yacht *Jonikal*, owned by Dodi's father, Mohamed
Fayed.

At about 4 am, the night was suddenly broken by the sound of my
pager. Still only half asleep, I fumbled around in the dark, to find
that it was vibrating. What on earth was going on? Was Buckingham
Palace under siege, or something? The pager message demanded
that I contact, urgently, Chief Superintendent Dai Davies of the
Royalty and Diplomatic Protection Department. There was no
telephone in my cottage (for the express reason that this was my
retreat, a place free from contact), so I hurriedly threw on some old
clothes and walked up to the telephone box a few minutes up the
road. The sky was already lightening with the early dawn, and the
light in the box seemed pale and feeble. I called Dai, and was put
through immediately.

'I am afraid I've got some bad news for you,' he said, without
preamble. His voice sounded strained, although that didn't register
on me until later.

Jokingly, I replied, 'Well, Dai, I didn't expect it to be good news
at this time of the morning.'

He then told me that the Princess of Wales had been killed in a road accident in Paris. Just that. Stunned, I said nothing. Dai continued, 'I'd like you to return to London as soon as you can in order to help co-ordinate the funeral arrangements.'

Shocked almost beyond speech, I agreed. Then I replaced the receiver and returned home.

There have been times since I left Diana's side when I have questioned whether I was right to resign. This awful moment was the most poignant, however. Diana, whom I had guarded for so many years, had fought for life through terrible pain, and now lay dead in a Paris hospital. Over and over, I kept thinking, How on earth could this have happened? And even as I thought, her tragic death, like so much of her remarkable life, was unfolding before the world on television.

I sat in silence for a minute as memories of the good times I had shared with the Princess flashed through my mind. Dawn was breaking, and in that first silence of morning before the birds begin to greet the day I could almost hear her laugh. My thoughts returned to my youth and the assassination of President Kennedy. People used to talk about where they had been when they heard that he had been killed, something that they would never forget. Now, I thought, the same would be true of the death of the Princess. This time, however, there was no assassin. My mind would not switch off. It kept returning to the same questions: Could anything have been done to save her? Who was to blame?

Some versions of Diana's life written after her death are based on ignorance or bitterness, or both. Yet if there is one account that has compelled me to put pen to paper, it is Trevor Rees-Jones's *The Bodyguard's Story*, subtitled *Diana, the Crash and the Sole Survivor*. For the record, I had complete charge of the Princess's protection for nearly six years while Rees-Jones – who, though terribly injured, was the sole survivor of the Paris crash – was at her side for a matter of weeks. So, on behalf of all the professional men and women of the Royalty and Diplomatic Protection Department of the Metropolitan Police Force, let me say that neither Rees-Jones nor any of the other bodyguards who attended Diana in the months preceding her death were members of our department. Rees-Jones was a former soldier who had not received the training necessary to protect a member of the royal family. And I know perfectly well that if any Scotland Yard

Protection officer had been in Paris with her, then Diana would never have got into a car controlled by a drunk driver and she would be alive today. Not only experience, but common sense, show this to be so.

When Diana elected to refuse the Queen's offer to keep her round-the-clock Scotland Yard protection in place, she inadvertently set off the chain of events that led to her death. Diana, like most of the royal family, accepted her police protection officers as a fact of life – we were part of the scenery. She had little idea of the years of training and experience required to do the job effectively.

In the years that have followed her death I have studied the official reports of what happened in the days and hours leading up to the accident. With increasing irritation, not to say incredulity, I have listened to the conspiracy theories promoted by Mohamed Fayed and his advisers and supporters. My view, based on decades of police experience, and in particular of high-profile protection duties, is that Diana's death was a tragic accident that could and should have been avoided. Her death, and those of two other people, were caused, not by a conspiracy to remove her as an embarrassment to the royal family and the British Establishment, but by a tragic mix of high spirits, over-confidence, and human error.

There are several irrefutable facts. It is clear from the findings of the various official reports that the driver, Henri Paul, had drunk far more than was either legal or sensible, while Dodi Fayed's erratic behavior, as well as the heightened tension caused by the chasing paparazzi, also contributed to the crash. Yet what amazed me in the aftermath of the accident was that no one properly questioned the role of the Princess's protection team in Paris. If Scotland Yard had been responsible for the Princess's safety that night, rather than the Fayed team, and an accident had still occurred, then there would have been an immediate and full-scale inquiry into how and why the protection failed. Officers involved would have been subjected to rigorous questioning about their actions, and required to justify every action they took preceding the crash. Any perceived failure on their part would have had catastrophic consequences for their careers, up to and including legal – and possibly criminal – proceedings against them.

To reach an intelligent assessment of why the Princess of Wales died, it is inevitable that the role of Rees-Jones has to be examined. The former soldier had been engaged by Mohamed Fayed to protect the Princess and his son. Had the bodyguard been trained by the Metropolitan Police, it would have been his duty to say no to his nominal employer, Dodi Fayed, if he believed the latter's actions, or anyone else's, compromised the safety of his principals. Furthermore, if, as he suggests, Dodi Fayed, ordered Henri Paul to drive too fast, Rees-Jones should have countermanded those instructions and ordered Paul to slow down.

The events leading up to the crash in the Alma tunnel are worth dissecting forensically because they expose the sequence of errors that cost Diana her life. To understand the seriousness of those errors, they have to be placed in context. On 30 August, after being spotted by two photographers, Roberto Frezza and Salvo La Fata, who were speeding along the coast in a rubber dinghy, Dodi and Diana decided to cut short their Sardinian cruise. After refusing to pose, they were apparently subjected to foul-mouthed abuse from the photographers, which upset the Princess. Dodi then made a sudden decision to escape the area and ordered his bodyguards to make arrangements to fly to Paris. A few hours later, he, the Princess and his security team boarded a Harrods Gulfstream jet at Olbia airport, in northern Sardinia, and flew to Paris. The party knew for certain before they left at 1.45 pm that the paparazzi would be waiting for them on arrival at Le Bourget airport. Ninety minutes later they were met there by the deputy head of security for the Ritz Hotel, Paris (another Fayed establishment), forty-one-year-old Henri Paul. By this stage, the security team of Rees-Jones and his partner Kes Wingfield had already made their first serious error. Instead of focusing on the physical safety of Dodi and Diana, they appear to have made protecting the couple from the press their top priority. They could not have been more wrong. The paparazzi, after all, were firing flashguns, not bullets.

A romantic night in Paris was apparently all part of Dodi Fayed's grand plan. According to his father, there was a $300,000 (£200,000) diamond engagement ring awaiting collection at the Paris jeweler, Repossi, in the Place Vendôme, for Dodi was allegedly intending to ask the Princess to marry him. He had also made plans for the two of them to visit the villa in western Paris formerly owned by the Duke of Windsor, which his father had bought some years earlier. (Ironically, the Duke of Windsor, once, briefly, King Edward VIII until his abdication in 1936, had been Prince Charles's great-uncle.)

As the Gulfstream touched down at Le Bourget Diana could see from the window by her seat that the paparazzi lay in wait. Rees-Jones led the Princess down the steps, followed by the rest of the party. They left the airport by car, and on this occasion the security planning was right. Someone had arranged for the party to be escorted to the *autoroute* by French police motorcycle outriders. Within minutes, however, the paparazzi, all on motorcycles themselves, were racing behind them.

As the car carrying Diana and Dodi headed for Paris, pursued by the paparazzi, the driver, Philippe Dourneau, kept a cool head. Sensibly, he refused to try to outpace the motorbikes haring after them, with the result that the photographers' chase was over in minutes. The paparazzi soon had the pictures of the couple they wanted, and peeled off to have them processed and sent off. With their mission complete, there was no need for them to continue in a potentially dangerous pursuit.

A few minutes later, at around four o'clock, the car pulled into the entrance of the Duke of Windsor's former villa. The couple wandered around the gardens, and sat and talked on a bench for a while, before taking the first of several fateful decisions. Rather than stay in the villa, which would have made good sense from a security point of view, they called on the security team to make arrangements for them to go to the Ritz. Diana, it appears, wanted to go shopping for presents for Harry's birthday. As the Princess arrived at the hotel a photographer startled her as he leapt out to take her picture, which both alarmed and upset her. Once inside, she and Dodi retired to the opulent Imperial Suite to freshen up, after which Diana went to the hairdresser and Dodi made some telephone calls.

The Princess later telephoned her sons who were staying at Balmoral with their father and grandparents, and then made a further call to *Daily Mail* reporter Richard Kay, in which she apparently told him how much she was looking forward to spending a few days with William and Harry before they returned to school early in September. She also told him that she was again planning to quit public life, this time for good. Richard later wrote that Diana had sounded happier than he had ever known her, and added that he believed it possible that one day Dodi Fayed and the Princess would marry.

Outside the hotel, the small crowd of paparazzi stood around waiting for the couple's next move. The bodyguards had apparently gone for something to eat, but returned in due course. To add to the confusion, Dodi now decided that he wanted to return to his apartment on the Champs-Élysées so that he could change for dinner. They left the hotel by a rear entrance, with Dodi and Diana in one car and Rees-Jones and his partner, Wingfield, following in a Range Rover. If tried and tested security procedures had been followed, however, one of them should have been in the car with the Princess and Dodi.

A scuffle with photographers took place outside as Diana left the building. Emotions were running high on both sides – the photographers desperate to secure yet more lucrative pictures, and Diana and Dodi anxious that they should be left in peace – but on Dodi's instructions they continued on this unnecessary tour of Paris, knowing that the paparazzi were still hungry for pictures. At this point, if I had been with Diana, I would have intervened and seriously questioned the sense of what they were doing. Yet it appears that no one had considered the easiest and most sensible course – staying at the Ritz for the night until the almost manic mood among the paparazzi had subsided.

To be fair, Rees-Jones and Wingfield were hampered in what they could or could not do by the fact that they were effectively paid employees of the people they were guarding. As I have said before, Scotland Yard police protection officers answer to their senior officers, not their principals. It is an important distinction, for it allows them, if the situation in their view demands it, to ignore or overrule their principals' decisions. That said, however, there was nothing to stop one of them telephoning the local *gendarmerie* on their own initiative to ask for backup assistance, without necessarily even informing Dodi or Diana.

Diana was clearly in a highly charged emotional state that night. According to most accounts, she was behaving irrationally and at times almost hysterically, her mood alternating between excitement and near panic. It was a situation that I had faced with her on many occasions and at such times I had to use every ounce of diplomacy I possessed. It was not easy, but with patience she could be persuaded to calm down. Dodi, by all accounts a kind and gentle man, was both desperate to please his new love, and concerned for her.

According to his father's version of events, Dodi had other things on his mind that may explain why he too was acting irrationally. What is clear, however, is that he was losing perspective, with the result that, perhaps in a misguided bid to impress the Princess, he was making rash and ill-conceived decisions.

For Rees-Jones and Wingfield the combination of these two factors – the Princess's mood swings and Dodi's constantly changing decisions – must have made their job even more difficult. In such circumstances firm direction and a cool head were needed.

It was then that the bodyguards needed to take control but, lacking both experience and, as employees, authority, they continued to follow Dodi Fayed's lead. He, for whatever reason, was shuttling the Princess around Paris, ending this tour with a visit to the Benoit bistro on the rue Saint-Martin, where it has been said he hoped to propose. As they approached the Benoit, however, they saw that it had been staked out by a battery of photographers, who had been tipped off about the couple's movements. Although in my experience a press presence would normally never have deterred her, they gave up on the bistro and returned to the Ritz, where they were again confronted by paparazzi. Once inside the couple settled down for dinner at L'Espadon, the hotel's Michelin two-star restaurant, but had no sooner started their meal than they abandoned it, fearing that someone inside was about to take pictures of them, a clear indication of the paranoia that had enveloped them both. They returned to their suite, where they continued their dinner alone.

Then came the fatal error. During the meal Dodi ordered his security team to make arrangements for him and Diana to return to his apartment. He ruled that his regular chauffeur, Philippe Dourneau, who had driven so coolly and sensibly earlier in the day when the paparazzi had given chase, should drive the Range Rover away from the hotel on some kind of decoy run, in the hopes that the photographers would follow it. When they were ready Diana and Dodi would leave from the back entrance in a leased Mercedes driven by Henri Paul, who, although off duty by now, would be called back. Apparently, both Rees-Jones and Wingfield thought that this plan was a bad one, telling Dodi that it was wrong to separate the vehicles, something which, in their view, ran contrary to their training and to other guidelines on the safety of their principals.

They were overruled by Dodi, however. Rees-Jones and Wingfield seem to have been persuaded to focus on evading the photographers, rather than on providing security.

I have referred in this book to several occasions when I was required to negotiate photo opportunities that had involved scores of journalists and photographers. As a result of these arrangements, security was strengthened. I am convinced that had there been similar communication between the bodyguards and the media outside the Ritz, then they could have arranged a properly controlled and timed departure. Instead, they committed a grave error of judgment, in my opinion, by continuing with the game of 'beat the paparazzi', a game they lost.

Dodi was courting disaster. His decision to keep ferrying the Princess around Paris was simply agitating the paparazzi, who actually needed guidance – as strange as that may sound – if order was to be maintained. During publicized events, both royal and government, official media representatives brief and advise the assembled media. These briefings are essential to both sides. Had a statement been issued to the media that night, explaining that Dodi and the Princess were tired after a long day and had decided to stay overnight at the Ritz, most of the press would have simply given up the chase and left the area, if only for a few hours.

Rees-Jones's lack of understanding of the paparazzi is crucial. He appears to be reverting to his army days when he describes the press as 'the enemy' and refers to the photographers as if they are 'snipers', comparing their long lenses with rifle barrels. In adopting this attitude, he failed to appreciate the situation he faced.

There were a number of other factors that contributed to the failures in security. Rees-Jones claims that Henri Paul 'turned out to be drunk' when he appeared in answer to Dodi's summons. In fact, Henri Paul was so intoxicated that any protection officer should have known immediately that he was incapable of driving a car, and acted decisively as a result. The autopsy showed that Paul's blood/alcohol count was more than twice the legal limit for drivers, and his blood also showed traces of other prescribed drugs that would have affected his ability to drive.

Rees-Jones states in his book that Ben Murrell, one of Fayed's British security men posted to the Windsor villa, had noticed while chatting with Henri Paul that day that he 'smelt as if he had had a very good lunch'. Significantly, in addition to Murrell's comments, Wingfield and Rees-Jones sat in the bar of the Ritz around at 10 pm with Paul, and watched him drink, although Paul apparently told the two bodyguards he was drinking pineapple juice. He ordered a pastis, a very strong liquor with a pungent and easily detectable aniseed smell. It is usually drunk mixed with water, which turns the liquid cloudy, producing a color similar to that of a pineapple juice. I am convinced, however, that if two Scotland Yard protection officers had been sitting alongside Paul, they would have detected immediately that he was drinking alcohol.

Why didn't the bodyguards stop Henri Paul from driving, or, if that failed, prevent the principals from traveling with him? The answer, I think, lies in the employees/employer relationship between them and Dodi Fayed. They had no opportunities for negotiation, or even to offer suggestions, and least of all for a show of initiative. By contrast, Henri Paul was a senior man in the Fayed organization in Paris. Under these circumstances, even knowing that something was wrong, the bodyguards may have been prepared to sit tight and say nothing, rather than advise Dodi and the Princess of their doubts about Henri Paul's fitness to drive.

It is possible that Henri Paul had an extraordinary capacity to consume alcohol and conceal its effects. That said, however, one glaring action by Paul should have alerted Rees-Jones to the state of the driver. As the Mercedes pulled away, Paul is said by some sources to have leant out of the window and issued a 'catch-us-if-you-can' challenge to the waiting paparazzi. It was not the act of a sober, cool-headed driver, and it acted upon the photographers like a red rag to a bull.

It was said at the time that Henri Paul had been trained as a chauffeur by Mercedes and had attended an evasive anti-hijack driving course. Yet his erratic driving on the way to Dodi's apartment was not in line with the skills and the ability to remain calm in difficult situations, that I have come to expect in a chauffeur trained to such high standards and which Philippe Dourneau had demonstrated so well earlier that day.

According to Rees-Jones, at the crucial moment, when those expert driving skills were most needed, Paul failed to recognize that he was in charge of a high-powered Mercedes automatic. In his book, Rees-Jones states that Henri Paul 'throws the gear into neutral', believing it to be a manually operated gearbox, which causes the Mercedes to free-wheel at more than 110 kph (over 60 mph) into the unforgiving concrete pillar in the Alma tunnel.

It is clear that the bodyguard was not comfortable with the way Paul was driving just prior to the accident, for he apparently tried to put on his seat belt, pulling it partly across his chest, but failed to buckle it in time (what saved his life was the air bag). What concerns me, however, is that as the bodyguard he should have instructed all of the passengers – including the driver – to fasten their seat belts before they left the Ritz. When I worked with the Princess, she would automatically fasten her belt the moment she got into the car, whether as driver or passenger. Yet she was not wearing one at the time of the crash. I can only assume that Rees-Jones did not feel comfortable in addressing matters with Dodi Fayed that might have been controversial, even confrontational.

One statement in Rees-Jones's book seems to epitomize his layman's approach to security, and perhaps allows us an insight into why and where he went wrong. His claim to be a 'good bloke in a fight' raises serious questions about his suitability for the job he was tasked with. The ability to acquit oneself well in a brawl is, unequivocally, not qualification enough to protect someone like Diana. In fact, the last thing a protection officer should be involved in is a fight. The primary role of a protection officer is to use his or her intelligence, contacts and instincts to avoid the principal becoming embroiled in any dangerous situation; essentially, to keep their charge out of harm's way by avoiding confrontation. Except during an actual attack, aggressive action is the last option, and must only be used when all other courses of action have been tried and exhausted. In my protection career I used such physical tactics only very occasionally, and then only as a last resort.

The basic key to good protection is preparation. When Rees-Jones first heard of his appointment to guard Diana in France, instead of informally contacting Scotland Yard for a briefing or off-the-record advice, he simply reflects that it is going to be 'a hell of an interesting trip to be on'. Again, there is no suggestion in his book that he or Wingfield carried out reconnaissances before escorting Dodi and Diana to any destination in Paris, something that would, for instance, have saved them a good deal of trouble at the Benoit bistro.

I suspect, too, that the bodyguard was somewhat overawed by the Princess – as many people were – and in his book he recalls that he wanted to do things to please her, and mentions how attractive he found her. As I have said often before, however, if your job is to guard someone, you have to be able to talk to that person honestly. You cannot, for their safety's sake, be in awe of them. A protection officer's most crucial skill is not strength or the ability to fire a gun, but communication. You need to have the confidence and the strength of purpose to say no to your principal. Rees-Jones and Wingfield should have questioned the necessity to leave the Ritz and return to Dodi's apartment. And if, as Rees-Jones repeatedly states, his primary concern was the presence of the paparazzi, he should have told the Princess and Dodi that, in the absence of local police help, they should stay at the hotel and leave in the morning at daybreak. If Dodi had remained adamant about returning to the apartment, Rees-Jones should then have insisted that, in order to put this plan into operation, he needed local police assistance. I am entirely confident that had such a request been made to the senior police officer on duty, it would have been met with alacrity. Having worked in Paris with the Princess myself, I know that the French authorities would have taken the situation very seriously, and offered every assistance they could. Gendarmes would have arrived to control the waiting press, and the journey from the hotel to the apartment would then have been made under police escort. They would have dictated the route and a safe speed for the journey, while any pursuing photographers would have been held back at a safe distance. There would have been no accident.

Some readers may think that I have judged Rees-Jones too harshly. I have nothing against him personally, and am genuinely sorry that he had to endure such pain and mental suffering in the years after the crash, as well as having to live with the physical effects of his injuries. My assessment of what he did and, perhaps more importantly, what he did not do, is based on my professional experience, as well as my detailed knowledge of the woman whom I protected for years. Diana was used to security being done competently, quietly and without fuss by Scotland Yard. It must have seemed very simple to her, and virtually invisible. She would have been quite unaware that private security guards like Trevor Rees-Jones were not capable of giving her the total security blanket that Scotland Yard had done. Nor would Fayed, who hired Rees-Jones, have had the experience of dealing with the massed paparazzi that Diana engendered. In my opinion, they were all completely out of their depths.

One of the more depressing aspects of the aftermath of the Princess's death is the proliferation of conspiracy theories, most saying that she was murdered by some agency or other, for one nefarious purpose or another. Yet her death is not comparable to the assassination of John F. Kennedy. There were no bullets, just a drunken driver, a bodyguard who was inexperienced in protecting such a high-profile principal, and an over-zealous boyfriend trying to impress. Like so many thousands of others each year, the Princess of Wales died in a mundane road accident.

Mohamed Fayed, his then press spokesman, the former BBC correspondent Michael Cole, and his chief security officer, former Scotland Yard Detective Chief Superintendent John McNamara, have all supported the view that Dodi and Diana were assassinated as part of a conspiracy involving US and British intelligence agencies.

Essentially, Fayed's conspiracy theory rests on a claim that the British Establishment was unhappy that the mother of a future heir to the throne was planning to marry into the Fayed family (and, in some versions, that she was expecting Dodi's child) because they are Arabs and Muslims.

He also claims that the US Central Intelligence Agency was electronically eavesdropping on the Princess and Dodi; and that both the CIA and MI6 (the British intelligence and espionage agency) had agents in Paris on the night of the crash, and that both agencies were working together monitoring the movements of the couple in preparation for an assassination. He states that the driver of the Mercedes, his own deputy head of security at the Paris Ritz, Henri Paul, was an MI6 agent and that he was used as a disposable 'pawn' in this plot, and had been ordered to take the river route via the Alma tunnel on the night of the crash rather than the direct route by the Champs-Élysées.

The crux of the conspiracy, he says, centers on an elaborate assassination of the Princess involving a white Fiat Uno car, which was never found. The Fiat was used to slow the speeding Mercedes, thereby enabling the passenger on a motorcycle that overtook the Princess's car (both rider and passenger being secret agents) to fire a flashgun or similar high-intensity light in the face of Henri Paul in order to blind him momentarily, forcing him to lose control and crash.

Other issues raised by Fayed's spokesman, Cole, include a belief that the blood samples supposedly from Henri Paul, which show that he was excessively over the prescribed legal alcohol limit for drivers, were not in fact his. He claimed, too, that Diana's body was embalmed, contrary to French law, apparently as part of a conspiracy to cover up her alleged pregnancy. Fayed maintains that his son, Dodi, told him that the Princess was pregnant some hours before the crash.

In my professional opinion there is no evidence to support this conspiracy theory or any part of it; it is pure speculation. Even if Fayed's claims that Diana was pregnant and about to wed his son were true, it is impossible to believe that the Queen, Prince Philip and the British government, among others, were prepared to murder four innocent people in order to remove the most popular and high-profile member of the royal family. Nevertheless, this needs to be seen in perspective. The royal family has undergone a metamorphosis, and is no longer locked in a royal timewarp. In her fifty years on the throne, the Queen has acknowledged change and reacted to it, even within her family. Her own sister, Princess Margaret, married a commoner and became the first senior member of the royal family to divorce. Of the Queen's own four children, three have divorced; all three married commoners, and the Prince of Wales currently maintains a liaison with a divorcée and another commoner, Camilla Parker Bowles. I have to say that, in my experience of working with the royal family for the past sixteen years, if the Queen, or any other member of the royal family, believed that Diana was in love with Dodi Fayed and wished to marry him and have his child, then she would have given the union her blessing.

A conspiracy is a secret plan, involving more than one person, to commit a crime or to do harm to another person. In this case, as I have outlined, it is Mohamed Fayed's belief that the conspiracy involved the secret services from both Britain and America working in collusion. The argument is deeply flawed, and one has only to look at the likely method of execution to see that. To stage a crash in a tunnel at night with a guarantee of killing all four people in the car would be impossible; evidenced by the fact that Rees-Jones lived and that Diana survived the crash, if only for a few hours. What should also be factored in is that if Diana and Dodi had been wearing seat belts, both would almost certainly have survived. The theory is completely untenable, especially given that neither the CIA nor MI6 (if indeed they were monitoring the situation at all) would have had any information about the impromptu movements of Dodi and Diana, and therefore no time in which to set the mechanics of the assassination in operation. Moreover, I have made no mention of the thousands of variables – such as traffic, weather, road conditions, and the random presence of witnesses – that would have made such an assassination attempt completely unworkable. No intelligence agency in the world would have given such a plan even half a glance.

The death of Diana, Princess of Wales, was not a murder by conspiracy, but a tragic accident that could, and should, have been avoided.

Yet what is done, is done, and no amount of rehashing the might-have-beens will ever undo the results of that terrible crash. The reverberations of her death traveled around the world, touching millions of lives, just as she had touched them when she was alive. I just hope that people will remember her as she was at her best, a warm-hearted and fun-loving woman who, as she wished, really did make a difference.

It is probably a vain hope, but I owe it to her.

# Postscript
## to the paperback edition

THE PUBLICATION OF THIS MEMOIR in August 2002 helped to trigger six months of relentless newspaper stories about the Princess; indeed, at times it seemed almost as if she were still alive. One man emerged at the centre of this storm – her former butler, Paul Burrell. Since Burrell was awaiting his trial on theft charges when this book was published, I was advised for legal reasons not to include anything about him.

Now is perhaps a good opportunity to set the record straight about Paul Burrell and what I saw of the nature of his relationship with the Princess during my time with her. In the aftermath of her death, he emerged as her 'rock', and was widely seen as such by both the media and the public. Immediately after the accident he was flown out to Paris to 'dress the dead Princess', and reports began to appear in the national press about the state of his health and the impact her death was having upon him.

I had known Paul for a number of years, and had watched him rise in Diana's household. To understand how he came to hold such a high place, however, it is necessary to go back to the days immediately before Diana's official separation from her husband, which proved to be a watershed for everyone who worked for the Prince and Princess, since the single Wales household would now become two. When I first knew Burrell he was an under-butler at Highgrove, effectively number two to the senior butler, Harold Brown, who was based at Kensington Palace. Harold, who would himself achieve notoriety after his trial for alleged theft of Diana's property also collapsed just weeks after Burrell's, chose to stay on the Princess's staff at Kensington Palace when she and Prince Charles officially separated in November 1992. It was D-day for the Wales household, each of whose members had to decide which master they would serve. As a result, Burrell was left in limbo; Diana, after all did not need two butlers, and Prince Charles had made it clear that he had no intention of offering Burrell a job within his household which, after the separation, would be based at St James's Palace and at Highgrove. Torn, Burrell seemed to adopt a 'sitting-on-the-fence' policy. He enjoyed living at Highgrove, where he and his wife, Maria, were happily ensconced in a grace-and-favor cottage; equally, like any royal servant, he wanted to be close to the source of power, and the Princess was undoubtedly winning the battle for the hearts and minds of the press and the public. Prince Charles, however, appeared not to want to employ him, possibly because he knew Burrell was close to Diana, and he did not want anyone who might turn out to be a spy on his payroll, reporting his every move back to her.

Burrell's rise had not been without incident. After joining the Queen's staff as a footman at Buckingham Palace, in the early 1980s he was caught up in an incident involving crew members of the Royal Yacht *Britannia*. His name came to the attention of military police after they had arrested eleven Royal Navy sailors in a swoop on *Britannia* in 1981 (the Royal Yacht was a naval vessel). The case hit the headlines in the *News of the World*, the Sunday tabloid having always reveled in the more salacious side of royal life. Nine of the servicemen were jailed for homosexuality, illegal in the armed forces at the time. Burrell was cleared of any involvement in the case. Some three years later he married Maria, who was also a royal servant, and then applied for and secured a position working for the Prince and Princess of Wales.

When I came to know Burrell some years later, he struck me as being the archetypal kind of royal servant. He knew exactly how best to flatter the Princess and, if necessary, to win her over. He seemed always to be the first to pay her a compliment about, say, her hair, or a new outfit, and the last person at night to tell her what a fantastic job she was doing. Like many famous people, Diana could be extremely insecure at times, and craved such praise even when it came from a low-ranking servant.

I knew that some of the Waleses' staff were wary of Burrell, but to be fair, the period immediately before and after the separation was a difficult time for anybody associated with the Prince and Princess. Albeit without the torture, bloodletting and executions, the process of splitting the households became a kind of Spanish Inquisition. Naturally worried for their positions, some people began to whisper against others, hoping thereby to protect their own job, or to win a new and more favorable one. Once tarnished, especially in Diana's eyes, and regardless of whether any allegations were true or not, a person was out. The Princess's affable, utterly professional chauffeur, Simon Solari, was a constant source of irritation to some of those involved in the infighting, as was I. Undoubtedly there were those who wanted us out, envious of the relationship we both had with the Princess, which was built on professionalism and mutual trust. The static role of some household servants was at odds with the freedom and contact with the Princess that I and some others enjoyed. Since I was employed by the police, my position was, luckily, beyond the reach of any enemy within her household – doubtless a source of frustration to those who wanted me gone.

Simon, however, was a different matter. He was on the payroll, and it was known that he was wavering about whether he should stay with Diana, or go in the aftermath of the separation. As soon as the poison was planted, after someone had told Diana of his indecision, her attitude towards him changed. She began to wonder if her driver – the man who knew her movements – could be trusted. As it happened, it was this paranoia in the Princess that made Simon's decision to leave her side much easier. There was no reason why he should be subjected to her mistrust, and in consequence he decided to take a post as a valet on Prince Charles's staff.

The irrepressible Mervyn Wycherley, Diana's charismatic chef, was another victim of the prevailing paranoia. Muscular, flamboyant, and extremely witty, Mervyn was devoted to the Princess, and she was fond of him in return. Much more than the man who prepared her food (exquisitely, too, I might add), he became a close friend whose loyalty to her was unquestioned. There were some, however, who wanted to break that intimacy, seeing it as a threat to their own positions.

After the separation and the first round of resignations and moves, Harold Brown was yet another casualty, after Diana had made it clear that she wanted to promote Burrell as her butler and could not justify having two; Brown was rescued by Princess

Margaret, who appointed him as her butler. The irony of this was that it was Harold who had persuaded Diana to take Burrell on at Kensington Palace as under-butler – his number two, in other words – something that backfired on him when, some time later, the decision to save the cost of employing two butlers came to be taken. Mervyn went next, his position thoroughly undermined until he could no longer do his job with any confidence. By the time the two separate establishments had been set up, the Princess presided over a household that had Paul Burrell at its head.

It is fair to say that the Princess liked Burrell, but she had also been fond of many other members of her personal staff, like Mervyn and Simon and George Smith, the former Welsh Guardsman who worked as a butler's assistant. For my part, I have to admit that I did not like the newly appointed butler, although I couldn't really have said why not.

Whatever her liking for Burrell, however, Diana's trust in him was severely dented one day when, as she told me, she caught him searching, without her permission, through papers on her desk. It was a curious incident, although not without its funny side. I had accompanied the Princess to her daily early-morning workout at the gym, and we had returned to Kensington Palace at some time after 8.30, since we were due to go out again at 9.30. We separated on our arrival, Diana to shower and change, and I to check something in my office. Not long afterwards I heard a curious noise. It sounded like people laughing, or crying, or even arguing, and I set off to find out what the commotion was about. At the foot of the staircase, I came across the most extraordinary sight. Paul Burrell was crouched down on the carpet, holding the Princess's ankles and begging for forgiveness.

I asked Diana what had happened, and she replied that on entering her sitting room she had found Burrell going through some papers on her desk, among which there were some personal letters. Understandably furious, she had ordered him from the room, and had left it herself a few moments later. At the foot of the stairs, however, Burrell approached her again, but as she began to ask him about what he had been doing at her desk he suddenly dropped to his knees, grabbed hold of her ankles with his hands and began kissing her feet, pleading to be forgiven. Diana, although still extremely displeased, had begun to laugh, and it was the sound of her laughter, coupled with Burrell's pleas, that had prompted me to investigate. I could scarcely believe my eyes when I came across this bizarre spectacle.

'What on earth are you doing?' I said to the now prostrate butler, although it was difficult to sound too stern, given that the Princess was by now desperately trying to stifle her laughter.

'What do you think you are doing?' I repeated. Getting little comprehensible response, I asked Diana if she wanted to take the matter further, and in the presence of Burrell stated that, if he had indeed been going through the Princess's papers, then his behavior was unforgivably disloyal, quite apart from being deeply unprofessional. Burrell seemed unable to explain his actions and was crying pathetically. I questioned him again, but received no coherent answer. By now I realized that we were in danger of being late for the Princess's next appointment, so telling Burrell to grow up, I ordered him to get up off the carpet and make himself scarce. Thus dismissed, he scurried off towards the butler's pantry, and we made ready to leave the palace.

In the car, Diana again explained what had happened – as she saw it, at least – adding that she simply could not tolerate anyone, and especially not a servant in an important position, whom she suspected of poking around in her private affairs. I agreed that if Burrell had indeed been going through her papers, as she alleged, then it was wholly unacceptable. For days Diana remained furious, and it required all Burrell's powers to win back her favor. He was 'out', as she termed it, for several weeks after that.

The incident became common knowledge among the Princess's staff. So it came as no surprise to me, following the collapse of his trial in November 2002, and after he had sold his story to the *Daily Mirror*, when the foot-kissing incident appeared in its rival tabloid, the *Sun*. The piece went on to discuss one of Burrell's claims that had been debated at his trial:

'One palace aide said: "Paul was not the rock that he made out to be. Yes, he was close to the Princess – but there was a time when she was going to sack him. It was well known within royal circles that Diana wanted to get rid of him . . . The Princess had wanted to sack him after she believed he was reading her personal correspondence. She allowed him to stay but did not speak to him for quite a while."' The paper also quoted the late Queen Mother's trusted servant, Billy Tallon, as having told friends that the Princess would have sacked Burrell had she not been killed in the Paris car crash in 1997.

'The former servant, nicknamed "Backstairs Billy" by royals, said: "He [Burrell] would have been out by that Christmas."' The *Sun* also alleged that Burrell had become so concerned that he might be sacked by the Princess that he 'CONTACTED a New York agency which specializes in hiring staff for Hollywood's top stars; and PLEADED with the head of personnel at Buckingham Palace to be moved to a new royal post.'

What is undoubtedly true is that Burrell is not the only person to have been called a 'rock' by the Princess. She was very much a 'hands-on' employer, and from time to time certain people were in favor, although no one member of staff was singled out for favoritism. As I have said, it is fair to say that Burrell was liked by the Princess, but so were many other members of her personal staff. As Diana's mother, Frances Shand Kydd, said in evidence at the Old Bailey during Burrell's trial, her daughter had many 'rocks', among them Frances herself, despite an estrangement during the last months of Diana's life. She called me her rock, she called Mervyn and Simon rocks, she called her secretary, Victoria Mendham, her rock. It was an expression that she used frequently to acknowledge the dedication of her small but loyal team.

Certainly Paul Burrell was one of these people, although there were times of isolation from her favor, as periodically happened to all of us. Yet while others tended to be unconcerned by these occasional falls from grace, Burrell always seemed to be preoccupied with being popular with his patron; indeed, in my opinion it became an obsession, one that, according to his version of events, led him to believe that he was the only person whom Diana could trust, apparently to the exclusion of her own family. This was a surprise to me, for what I witnessed told a very different story.

Although Burrell was not involved, I once had to deal with suspicions of impropriety among staff, something which, given the disappearance of valuable or significant items since her death, has some relevance. During her affair with James Hewitt, Diana discovered that some earrings he had sent her as a present had simply not arrived – or not with her, at least. James had foolishly sent them in the post, in a package marked 'Personal' and addressed to her, for some reason believing that she opened her mail herself (in fact, her mail – and there was a great deal of it even then – was opened by the staff in her office). Intended as a surprise, the package and its contents went missing, so that when, some time later, James, slightly surprised not to have been thanked for his generosity, asked the Princess if she had liked the earrings, she stormed around the office demanding to know what had happened to the package.

Everybody on the staff denied any knowledge of ever having seen the package, which annoyed the Princess even more. By now thoroughly enraged, she called me into her study, explained what had happened, and asked me if I could investigate the matter privately and, above all, discreetly. She stressed that, given the delicacy of the matter, she did not want it to go any further; equally, however, she wanted her precious present delivered to her as soon as possible.

Deciding that there was only one way to handle this without causing a major stir, I interviewed all of Diana's personal staff and told them of her displeasure, and the reason for it. I explained, omitting the details of the sender and of the missing items (after all, the thief would know well enough), that the Princess knew what was in the package and when it had been sent, and wanted its contents returned immediately. I therefore arranged an amnesty: if the guilty person returned the stolen property to my desk by nine o'clock the next morning, then the matter would be dropped. But, I stressed, if it was not returned then I, as a police officer, would be duty bound to pursue the matter, and to ask another police officer to question each of them individually under caution. This, of course, was bluff – given the delicacy of the matter, I could not in fact have followed that course, because Diana had made it clear that she did not want to press charges even if the culprit were to be found. Still, none of her staff were to know that.

When I reached my office in the palace next morning, I found that an envelope had been left on my desk; in it were the missing earrings. The matter was dropped, with nothing more said either by me or Diana. I did, however, recommend to Richard Aylard, Prince Charles's senior aide at that time, that a new system for logging unsolicited gifts should be established. As a result a system of 'some sorts' was established, and from that moment everything had to be recorded. (I later found out who had taken the earrings. In due course this person left the staff.) Even so, the haphazard organization inside Kensington Palace makes it (and indeed other royal residences) a thief's paradise. At least Burrell should be thanked for highlighting that.

Just a few weeks after this book was published, Paul Burrell went on trial on charges of stealing 284 items belonging to the late Princess, 4 to Prince Charles and 22 to Prince William. The jury was told that Burrell had allegedly taken the items in the eight months before the Princess died in August 1997 and ten months afterwards. Confusion reigned when, famously, the trial collapsed, it having suddenly emerged that the Queen had had a conversation with Burrell in the course of a long audience at Buckingham Palace, during which he told Her Majesty that he had taken a few letters and other items of Diana's after her death for safe keeping. The Queen apparently offered no comment, but the fact that Burrell had told her was enough for the Crown's case to collapse in a blaze of publicity. Burrell wept in the arms of his QC, Lord Carlile, when he was told his ordeal was over. As he walked from court through a mob of reporters he remarked, 'She [the Queen] came through for me. The Lady came through for me.'

The embarrassing collapse of the Burrell trial led to one of the most uncomfortable periods in recent history for the British royal family, heralding a spiral of scandal that was to lead to senior Establishment figures calling for reform of the institution. Within days the press published allegations of a cover-up at St James's Palace of the rape of a former royal valet, George Smith, whom I knew personally, by a senior member of Prince Charles's staff. There were also claims that the Prince's valet and personal secretary, Michael Fawcett, had sold gifts given to Charles for cash and pocketed a percentage of the profits, giving the rest to the Prince as 'pocket money'. These were very serious claims indeed, and as a result Sir Michael Peat, the Queen's former director of finance and currently Prince Charles's private secretary, was called in to carry out an internal inquiry into the whole affair. In due course, on 13 March 2003, the Peat Report was published. Largely regarded by the press as a whitewash of the Prince and his household, it leveled a number of strictures against the handling of the rape allegation and the treatment of gifts to the Prince, but essentially left the status quo undisturbed.

Burrell sold his story to a tabloid newspaper – reputedly for £300,000 (US $450,000) – and, perhaps predictably, lashed out at the principal members of the Spencer family, whose evidence to police during the inquiry had contributed to his being brought to court. I am mystified as to why Frances Shand Kydd, for whom I have great deal of respect, and the Spencer family as a whole should have been unjustly criticized in the light of that trial. As executors of Diana's will, it was the duty of Lady Sarah McCorquodale and of Frances to cooperate fully with the police inquiry after it had been alleged that Burrell had taken property belonging to Diana's estate without their consent. Equally clearly, both the police and, crucially, the Crown Prosecution Service believed there was a case to answer, and it was as a result of the thorough police investigation, and in the ultimate judgment of senior lawyers of the CPS, that the case went for trial.

Burrell has said that, during a three-hour stand-up meeting with Her Majesty at Buckingham Palace in November 1997, he told her that he had possession of personal letters and other items belonging to the late Princess and that he intended to keep them safe, to protect the 'Princess's world'.

From my own experience, I seriously question whether the Queen, given her busy schedule, would entertain Burrell for three hours on a matter that at most would take fifteen minutes to discuss (in fact, Buckingham Palace later confirmed, on the record, that the private audience lasted ninety minutes). What was being discussed was, after all, not even the Queen's property, but belonged to Diana's estate. Yet if the Princess had wanted Burrell to take charge of her estate after her death then she would surely have made him an executor of her will. But she did not. Furthermore, if, as Burrell has stated, he was concerned about the safety of Diana's property and felt that he could not trust her immediate family, why did he not entrust them for safe keeping with the other executor, the Bishop of London (or at least tell the Bishop that he was keeping them)? Instead, he chose to tell the Queen. One can only speculate as to why this did not arise earlier.

Like the Spencers, Scotland Yard has also been heavily criticized in the aftermath of the collapse of the Burrell trial, which is said to have cost the taxpayer some £1.5 million (US $2.25 million). Some commentators have suggested that the case should never have been brought to trial. But what exactly have the police done wrong? During the course of their investigation they believed they had amassed evidence of a prima facie case of theft. They then tried to establish provenance of the possessions alleged to have been taken. They therefore, and properly, asked both Lady Sarah McCorquodale and Frances Shand Kydd if they knew the property to be Diana's and if they, as executors of her will, had given Burrell permission to remove it. On learning that no such authority had been given, the findings and recommendations of their inquiry were submitted to the CPS for judgment.

This was a sensational case that reached to the very heart of the British Establishment. Worse was to follow, however, for within weeks the case against Harold Brown – the 'second butler trial' – also collapsed. I like Brown personally, and from my experience believe him to be a good man who served the Windsors loyally for three decades. Like Burrell he was charged with stealing Diana's possessions. In his case he was accused of taking and trying to sell a solid-gold model of an Arab dhow and other items of her jewelry. (I remember the dhow well. It used to stand on a small table in the hall of the Waleses' apartments in Kensington Palace, where it was often treated rather disrespectfully by the boisterous young princes.) As with the aborted trial of Burrell, the prosecution abandoned the Brown case because, according to Crown counsel William Boyce, the prosecution's case had been based on the 'implausibility' of a servant being entrusted to dispose of royal property. Because of Burrell's conversation with the Queen, Boyce said, he felt there was no longer a reasonable chance of conviction.

The collapse of both cases was a humiliating shambles for the British justice system, caused further embarrassment to the royal family and, even worse, in my view, left Scotland Yard the scapegoat for the entire débâcle. As I have said, I believe there was a prima facie case to be investigated in both instances, and in my opinion, given that the CPS had decided to prosecute, it was the duty of the police to see both cases through to trial.

What I do know, from my own experience, is that valuable objects have disappeared from royal households before now, and that sometimes very little checking is done to establish where a piece is, or what has become of it if it has been moved. One day during the time when I was still with the Princess, I called in on some friends of mine who are dealers in antique clocks, based in St James's, that beautiful street with two great clubs, Brooks's and White's, at one end, and St James's Palace at the other. As we stood idly chatting, one of my friends asked me whether I knew the clockmaker at Buckingham Palace. When I said that I did, he went on to tell me that he had just bought a clock at auction, a piece by one of the great dynasty of clockmakers, the Vulliamys, which apparently had a provenance linking it to the royal family. Would I be able to confirm this with the clockmaker at Buckingham Palace, if they gave me the details of the piece, including its number?

Naturally I agreed, and not long afterwards, having to be at Buckingham Palace for some reason, I called on the clockmaker, Robert Ball, in his workshop. This was a kind of Aladdin's cave in the basement, from where he did his main work of cleaning, regulating and repairing the many clocks, some of them extremely old, that are to be found in the palace. He was a small man with a pepper-and-salt beard, and I found him with a jeweller's loupe screwed into his eye as he examined some delicate mechanism, in a room littered with clocks and parts of clocks and highly specialized tools. He heard me out, and then, taking the list of details from me, reached to a shelf and took down a dusty old ledger, which he began to leaf through. After a short while he suddenly started muttering in surprise, and then indicated an entry on the page he was examining. There was a brief description of the Vulliamy and its number, and beside that a note to the effect that the clock had been taken to Osborne House, the private house on the Isle of Wight to which Queen Victoria would periodically retire with her family and the Court, at some time in the late nineteenth century, and had never come back to Buckingham Palace when the Court returned. Clearly it had then been stolen from Osborne by someone with access to the house and sold; as it had been sold on several times since then, to people buying it in good faith, there was no question of its being returned to the royal family as stolen property, and in due course my clock-dealing friends found yet another buyer for it. So while the royal households do keep records of possessions, it is clear that these are not always used to advantage – perhaps not very surprisingly, given the royal family's vast collections. But if a rare and valuable clock can disappear, apparently without comment, and not resurface for nearly a hundred years, it is hardly surprising that other possessions or gifts, valuable or not, should continue to do so. (There was an interesting postscript to this incident. Quite recently I came across the following in a book called *The Royal Encyclopedia*, from an entry entitled 'Clocks and Watches': 'The clock which, we are told, Queen Victoria liked above all others because of the legibility of its dial was an eighteenth-century bracket clock of ebonized wood by Justin Vulliamy . . .' I hope the clock that disappeared from Osborne wasn't that one.)

In the summary of conclusions in his report, Sir Michael Peat wrote: 'In short, we have found no evidence of staff selling gifts or other items without authorization or of their taking commissions on sales. Gifts and discounts have been given to staff by suppliers; however, this was done with implicit authorization and we have found no evidence that it resulted in decisions being influenced. Policies and procedures in these areas have been deficient. They need to be, and are being, enhanced.'

As a final thought on disappearing royal possessions, 'gifting', as it has latterly been termed, was apparently common between members of the royal family and some of their personal staff. Burrell himself has written, with a sideswipe at police officers' probity, that 'it was not unusual for Prince Charles to return from a polo match at Smith's Lawn with a prize from one of the sponsors – Cartier, Rolex or Dunhill – and toss the unwanted gift in my direction (if a royal protection officer hadn't collared it first).'

The summer of 2002 saw the celebration of the Queen's Silver Jubilee, marking fifty years since her accession to the throne in February 1952. Amid the official festivities, which included a rock concert at Buckingham Palace and a huge and colorful parade that proceeded down the Mall and past the assembled royal family at the palace, it was soon clear that one royal person – or former royal person, to be accurate – was not going to be included: the late Diana, Princess of Wales. Few commentaries during television coverage of the celebrations made any mention of her, and official events seemed to be devoid of any trace of her, even though August marked the fifth anniversary of her death. In a television documentary about the Elizabeth II's fifty-year reign, Lady Kennard, a friend of the Queen, remarked that Diana had been 'damaged', a comment taken by some in the media as the Palace's official line on the dead princess. Then came the anniversary of the fatal car crash in Paris, the publication of this book, and the Burrell and Brown trials, by which time it had become clear that the Princess was still very much a part of this country's history, and still very much in people's minds; in the autumn of 2002, she was chosen, in a poll conducted for BBC television, as one of the ten greatest Britons of all time.

Looking back, it is curious to reflect upon so much that would never have happened had she not been killed, not least that this book would not have been written, and Burrell would not have been sent for trial. Those of us who knew her are left to reflect not only upon what might have been had she lived, but also upon everything that made this young woman so extraordinary. My closing memory of Diana, then, is not of her at an official function, dazzling with her looks and her clothes and the warmth of her manner, or even of her offering comfort among the sick and the poor and the dispossessed. What I remember best is a young women taking a walk in a beautiful place, unrecognized, carefree and happy.

As I have said earlier, Diana increasingly craved privacy, a chance 'to be normal', to have the opportunity to do what, in her words, 'ordinary people' do every day of their lives – go shopping, see friends, go on holiday, and so on – away from the formality and rituals of royal life. Her position and the continual public scrutiny made this impossible. She did not blame any one person for this 'restriction in her life,' as she once put it, but recognized that it was both necessary and inevitable; none the less, there were times when it irked her. As someone responsible for her security, yet understanding her frustration, I was sympathetic. So when, in the spring of the year in which she would finally be separated from her husband, she yet again raised the suggestion of her being able to take a walk by herself, I agreed that such a simple idea could be realized.

It came to a head during one of the regular Friday afternoon car journeys that she and I made from Kensington Palace to Highgrove. Much of my childhood had been spent on the Isle of Purbeck in Dorset, and as we discussed her taking a walk by herself, I remembered the wonderful sandy beaches of Studland Bay, on the approach to Poole Harbour.

The idea of walking alone on a couple of miles of almost deserted sandy beach was something Diana had not even dared dream about, but now she recognized that I was serious. At the time she was receiving full twenty-four-hour protection, and it was at my discretion as to how many officers should be assigned to her protection, whether in public or in private, and who they should be. 'How will you manage it, Ken? What about the backup?' she asked. I explained that it would require each other's trust, and she looked at me for a moment and nodded her agreement.

And so, early one morning less than a week later, we left Kensington Palace and drove to the Sandbanks ferry at Poole in an ordinary saloon car. As we gazed at the coastline from the shabby viewing deck of the vintage chain ferry, Diana's excitement was obvious, yet not one of the other passengers recognized her. But then, no one would have expected the most famous and most photographed woman in the world to be aboard the Studland chain ferry on a sunny spring morning in May.

As the ferry docked after its short journey, we climbed back into the car and then, once the ramp had been lowered, drove off in a line of cars and service trucks heading for Studland and Swanage. Diana was driving, and I asked her to stop in a sand-covered parking area about half a mile from the ferry landing point. We left the car and walked a short distance across a wooden bridge that spanned a reed bed to the deserted beach of Shell Bay. Her simple pleasure at being somewhere with no one, apart from me, knowing her whereabouts was touching to see. The ferry was now halfway across the entrance to the harbor on its return journey to pick up the small line of foot passengers and the cars parked neatly on the ramp by the water's edge.

Diana looked out towards the Isle of Wight, anxious by now to set off on her walk to the Old Harry Rocks at the western extremity of Studland Bay. Oystercatchers raced busily along the wet sand, and other birds stabbed at the sand or walked, in that rather self-important way that waders have, busily along the water's edge. I gave her a personal two-way radio and a sketch map of the shoreline she could expect to see, indicating a landmark near some beach huts at the far end of the bay, a pub called The Bankes Arms, where I would meet her.

She set off at once, a tall figure clad in a pair of blue denim jeans, a dark blue suede jacket and a soft scarf wrapped loosely around her face to protect her from the chilling, easterly spring wind. I stood and watched as she slowly dwindled into the distance, her head held high, alone apart from the busy oystercatchers that followed her along the water's edge.

It was a strange sensation watching her walking away by herself, with no protection officers following at a discreet distance. What were my responsibilities here? I kept thinking. Yet I knew this area well, and not once did I feel uneasy. I had made this decision – not one of my colleagues knew, and to this day still do not. Senior officers would have boycotted the idea had I been foolish enough to give them advance notice of what the Princess and I were up to.

Before Diana disappeared from sight I called her on the radio. Her voice was bright and lively, and I knew instinctively that she was happy, and safe. I walked back to the parked car and drove slowly along the only road that runs along the bay, with heathland and then the sea to my left and the waters of Poole Harbour running up towards Wareham to my right. Within a matter of minutes I was turning into the car park of The Bankes Arms, a fine old pub that overlooks Studland Bay, and from which, on a clear day, one can see the Isle of Wight. This was just such a day. Knowing that the walk would take Diana about forty minutes I left the car and strolled down to the beach, where I sat on an old wall in the bright sunshine. The beach huts were locked and there was no sign of life. To my right I could see the Old Harry Rocks – three tall pinnacles of chalk standing in the sea, all that remains, at the landward end, of a ridge that once ran due east to the Isle of Wight. Like the Princess, I too just wanted to carry on walking.

Suddenly my radio crackled into to life: 'Ken, it's me – can you hear me?' I fumbled in the large pockets of my old jacket, grabbed the handset, pressed the transmit button and said 'Yes. How is it going?'

'Ken – this is amazing. I can't believe it,' she said, sounding truly happy. Genuinely pleased for her, I hesitated before replying, but before I could speak she called again, this time with that characteristic mischievous giggle in her voice. 'You never told me about the nudist colony!' she yelled, and laughed raucously over the radio. I laughed too – although what I actually thought was, Oh shit! I had forgotten that a section of Studland Beach was a nudist reserve. Well, I thought, judging from her remarks whatever she had seen had made her laugh. It had simply not occurred to me that the nudists would venture out on such a cold day.

At this point I decided to walk towards her, after a few minutes seeing her distinctive figure walking along the sea's edge towards me. Two dogs had joined her and she was throwing sticks into the sea for them to retrieve. There were no crowd barriers, no servants, no policeman apart from me, no over-attentive officials. Not a single person had recognized her. For once, everything, for the Princess, was 'normal'. During the seven years I worked for her, this was an extraordinary moment, one I shall never forget.

Together we walked back towards the pub up a leafy lane and returned to our anonymous car. By now it was nearly two o'clock, and while Diana did not want this adventure to end, she knew that she would have to go back. In one last bid for freedom and anonymity, we decided to return to London via Corfe Castle, a ruined Norman fortification that once had dominated the Isle of Purbeck but which had been betrayed and partially destroyed during the Civil War. Parking the car near the village square, we walked to the base of the castle ruins, and then entered the National Trust shop where Diana bought cards and some small gifts. To my surprise, she paid for them in cash. Somewhat astonished – she rarely carried cash, and I was well used to paying for things she bought – I said, 'This is a first, ma'am,' to which she replied, 'It's being normal, isn't it?'

# Index